# Farming Around the Country

## An Organic Odyssey

A Year with WWOOF
(World Wide Opportunities on Organic Farms)

## Brian J. Bender

Copyright © 2010 by Brian J. Bender

NorLightsPress.com

All rights reserved. No part of this book may be reproduced or transmitted in any form or by any means, electronic or mechanical, including photocopying, recording, or by any information storage and retrieval system, without written permission from the author, except for the inclusion of brief quotations in a review.

Printed in the United States of America

ISBN: 978-1-935254-33-1

Cover Design by NorLightsPress Graphics Department
Book Design by Nadene Carter

First printing, 2010

To all my friends from Ohio,
wherever you may be now.

## With Gratitude

Thanks to every farmer, cow, and chicken that fed me during my journey. Thanks to Vipassana meditation for showing me how to access real peace and happiness. Thanks to Sammie, my editor, for nurturing a new author such as myself.

I send my love to Mom and Dad and all my beautiful nieces. Love to Andrea, Brent, and Brianne for sharing a bathtub with me. And love to Katherine G. Wood for sharing part of her life with me.

# Contents

*Introduction* ............................................. 1

*Chapter 1* - Hector's Farm (Vermont) ................ 3

*Chapter 2* - Applesauce Hill (Maine) ................ 17

*Chapter 3* - Peace and Plenty Farm (Maine) ........... 37

                Woodsong Farm (Massachusetts) .......... 45

*Chapter 4* - Clear Creek Homestead (North Carolina) .. 49

*Chapter 5* - Salamander Springs (Georgia) ............ 65

*Chapter 6* - Lucy's Farm (Florida) ................... 85

*Chapter 7* - Henry's Farm and Hostel (California) ..... 109

*Chapter 8* - Farm in the Canyon (California) ......... 129

*Chapter 9* - Chestnut Hill (California) .............. 149

*Chapter 10* - Rock n' Ridge Ranch (California) ....... 165

*Chapter 11* - Runnymede Farm (Oregon) ............... 185

*Chapter 12* - Going Home (Oregon, Washington, Ohio) ..211

*About the Author* ..................................... 229

*Route Map* ............................................ 230

# Introduction

My grandma always said I had wanderlust – and she was right.

At the age of 29, gainfully employed as a high school science teacher, I found myself hungering for adventure. In all honesty, I was eager to escape from the ornery teenagers who'd taken over my life. After only two years of teaching I felt a compelling urge to head into the country, looking for peace and quiet.

I chose to volunteer on small-scale organic farms through an organization called WWOOF, or World-Wide Opportunities on Organic Farms. Over three decades, WWOOF'ing has become the agrarian offshoot of eco-toursim, with nearly 400,000 volunteers helping on farms in over 90 countries. I could hardly wait to join their ranks.

In the cold middle part of the school year, as lockers slammed and the clamor of high school students spilled in from the hallway, I sat at my teacher's desk and flipped through a farm directory. I imagined working in the sun. As I turned the pages, the cinder block walls dissolved and the rows of desks became rows of plants.

The farm book contained descriptions like, "we raise Icelandic sheep" and "40+ miles from the nearest stoplight." Some of the farms mentioned I would "live in a tepee at the base of a mountain," or "pick avocados and tropical fruits." I felt as though I was shopping for a new life.

## Introduction

On one such day, as I circled farm choices during my lunch hour, a student pulled her friend in from the hallway and approached my desk. With a wide grin on her face, she said, "Tell Rushaun what you're doing this summer."

"I'm going to be a farmer," I said.

"No, tell her what *kind* of farmer."

I said I was going to be an organic farmer, and the two of them laughed. I wasn't sure what was so funny, but they kept repeating under their laughter, "Mr. Bender's gonna be an *organic* farmer."

Maybe this had something to do with the fact that I was the oddball teacher. I ate a vegetarian lunch and preached to my students about wholesome food and how they should watch less television. I wasn't exactly the classic figurehead for Lima, Ohio. Nor was I a natural teacher. I admit it. I never quite got over the fear of facing a room full of rambunctious teenagers, and I think my students sensed it.

I needed to move on. It was time to leave the windowless classroom and the life of books, grades, and discipline problems. I didn't have any plans to become a real farmer. I just wanted to get out of Ohio and see what it was like to work in the sun for a while. I wanted to produce something with unquestionable value: good, clean organic food. As things stood, I wasn't producing anything of clear value as a high school science teacher. I needed to put it all to rest and head outdoors.

I wanted to migrate from Maine to Florida as winter approached, and then skip over the middle states and farm up through California and Oregon. In no time at all, I'd selected eleven farms. School closed for the summer, and I kissed my blackboard and dress pants goodbye, bought a wide-brimmed straw hat, and took to the road. I was ready to begin a new life as a nomadic farmer.

# Chapter 1
## *Hector's Farm*

**Perfect Universe**

When the tractor tire fell on me, I thought, *maybe I shouldn't have left my teaching career after all.*

This was a freak accident. Hector, the head farmer, called me over to help take the tire off. The five-foot tractor tire was exactly like the ones I used to climb on at the school playground, using the deep tread like rungs of a ladder. I stood beside it, oblivious to the danger, and watched Hector loosen the bolts. The instant we lifted the tire from the last bolt, we lost control. The huge tire tipped over like a giant domino and pinned me to the ground. I felt like I'd been trapped under a sumo wrestler made of rubber and steel. I had no chance of wiggling my arms free. I was one with the tire.

I lay in the mud, immobilized for a moment of forced reflection. Why hadn't I realized the danger of standing beside this unleashed behemoth? Was the tractor tire another lesson, teaching me to be more mindful of my surroundings?

The most troubling part was that Hector and the other farmhands stood by and stared at me as the deep tread clamped my chest to the earth and squeezed air from my lungs. I had to ask for help.

"Could someone get this tire off me?" I squeaked. "Please!"

## Hector's Farm

When I first pulled up to Hector's Farm, nestled in the Green Mountains of Vermont, I noticed the colorful plaque hanging over the driveway: Universo Perfeito – Portuguese for Perfect Universe. Alongside the driveway, a flock of noisy hens in a coop welcomed me with a display of flapping wings and chaotic sprints. The vaguely sweet smell of chicken manure wafted through my car windows. It smelled like eating chocolate in the bathroom. After the chicken yard, I noticed several neat rows of salad greens a few steps from the farmhouse. As I parked, I glanced over at the old beat-up orange tractor. The tires were as tall as my car.

Now, don't get me wrong. I had good times on Hector's farm. I spent many hours with my hands in the sun-warmed soil. I cleared hiking trails and became part of a community centered on local food. But this was not a perfect universe.

For one thing, Hector worked us like animals. My first week on the farm, I put in over 50 hours. And the daily siesta he promised? It never materialized. Our lives were nonstop planting, watering, and weeding. "Grow, plants, grow!" was the mantra running through Hector's head every moment of the day.

I don't consider myself lazy. I worked 50-hour weeks as a teacher without giving it a second thought. But on Hector's farm, I felt like an unpaid migrant laborer. And the fact that work expectations were never clearly defined made me nervous. The only reference to work hours in Hector's farm description was a line that read, "not crazy hours or anything." I guess "crazy hours" meant planting by flashlight.

One evening, I stood behind his tractor out in the pepper fields, watching the sunset and wondering when the day would be over, when Hector turned the tractor off and took a call from his wife. She was obviously trying to find out when we'd be home. I heard Hector say, "I'm just thinking of what's best for the plants."

Well, that told me everything I needed to know. I was at the mercy of a dedicated farmer.

## Hector's Farm

Hector had good intentions. He placed a high value on the health of his farm, but not so much in his workers. I often felt my well being ranked below the tomato plants. Grow plants grow. Grow plants grow. Maybe it *was* a perfect universe. But not for people.

### Spotless White Eggs

Aside from the tractor tire incident, the ferocious little ticks I picked out from behind my knees and under my armpits, and the feeling that I was being exploited, I enjoyed my time in the Green Mountains of Vermont. I arrived in early summer, when the rolling mountains were covered with one continuous stretch of leafy green. From afar, driving along the highway, I stared at the peaks of the mountain range and knew that somewhere in that dense foliage, the Appalachian Trail followed the spine of the mountains.

As I drove into the Green Mountains, each bend in the road and rollercoaster drop gave way to small farms with grazing cows and vegetable crops. Stands of maple trees, called "sugar bush," dominated some properties. Along several of the old roads, remnants of stone walls stood as souvenirs of early settlers. The cozy, green farm country reminded me of shires inhabited by the hobbits of Middle-Earth.

I especially enjoyed the morning hours, when clouds formed a creamy froth over the rounded mountains tops. This was a different landscape from the countryside back in Ohio, where I rode my bike through a flat sea of corn and soybeans.

Having never worked on a farm before, everything was a novelty at Hector's place. I drank my first glass of raw milk. I took an egg right out from under a hen.

When Hector sent me on a milk-run one morning, I thought he meant the nearest grocery store for a gallon. That wasn't the case. He directed me to a neighboring farm with a handful of cash and instructions to knock on the woman's door and tell her where I was from. Apparently selling raw milk is a risky business, even in Vermont where it's legal to sell 25 quarts a day.

## Hector's Farm

After I found the place, I pulled the car up to a barn and walked to the main house, pausing to stare at the actual cows I'd be drinking from. These weren't the typical black and white cows pictured on milk cartons. They were smaller and golden brown, a breed called Jersey, known for the high butterfat content of their milk. Most of the herd went about their business, grazing on the pasture, but a few of the bigger ladies paused to stare at me as they chewed their cuds.

When I knocked on her door, the farmwife peered out suspiciously at me, not saying a word.

"Hi there. I'm from Hector's Farm. He sent me to get a gallon of milk." I smiled and held out the money.

Convinced I wasn't a government spy, she brightened a bit and directed me to the dairy barn. "Please mop up any milk you spill," she added.

Luckily, I didn't have to milk the cow myself. That work was already done. The barn was empty, as the entire herd was out in the sun enjoying a salad buffet. The farmwife directed me to a milk-room adjoining the dairy barn. The milk-room was separate from the main barn and received the Jersey milk through a pipe that ran overhead.

I expected the place to smell of cows. I thought there would be flies buzzing over fresh cow pies, but the milk-room was immaculate, the floor scrubbed clean and the walls white-washed.

A shiny metallic vat rested on the floor of the milk room—basically resembling a 50-gallon coke bottle tipped on its side. In place of a bottle cap, I found a hand-lever to turn on the milk.

When I turned the milk faucet, a stream of refrigerated raw milk poured into my glass jar. Naturally, I felt the urge to drink straight from the tap, but I didn't want to make a mess, so instead I took a big gulp from the jar and then topped it off with one last trickle from the milk vat.

This was the freshest, most unadulterated milk I'd ever tasted, yet it didn't seem much different than the 2% milk

# Hector's Farm

I'd drunk my entire life, only creamier. Still, the whole green pasture farm-setting added a touch of purity that made me feel I'd just tasted *real* milk – the kind of milk spoken of in the Bible, raw and flowing from the land of milk and honey.

On my way down the driveway, I couldn't resist giving the cows a little beep of the horn. They must've been desensitized by years of cars honking at them, because only the younger ones looked up at me as I drove off. The milk of the future.

* * * *

Collecting my first egg on Hector's Farm was a different experience than raw milk. This was another seminal moment in my life, in which I formed a closer connection with the source of my food. But the eggs seemed much less wholesome than the raw milk.

The hens' lifestyle turned me off. They certainly didn't live under inhumane conditions. Hector built two spacious chicken houses and fenced off a nice-sized yard for them. They appeared to be happy free-range hens, but they were filthy. I later realized they were just being chickens, but my first impression was, *these are some disgusting creatures.* They dropped white feces everywhere. In their food. In their water. In their beds.

Fetching a warm egg from under a hen wasn't the romantic experience I expected. Bits of feather and feces-encrusted straw clung to the egg. Inside the hen house, chicken manure fell as casually as rain. As I stared at the grimy egg in my gloved hand, a voice inside my head said, *don't eat that!*

After a lifetime of eating spotless white eggs, I thought eating this dirty egg would endanger my health. Besides that, Hector instructed me not to use soap on the eggs. He said the shells contained a protective layer that kept them fresh, and detergent or excessive scrubbing destroyed this natural protection.

That was all fine and dandy. I lived with minimal cleaning in all my college apartments, but when it came to cooking myself a couple of eggs, I turned into a serious germ-a-phobe.

### Hector's Farm

I meticulously scrubbed the eggs until they were spotless at the microscopic level, then I rinsed them one more time.

I behaved obsessively for only a couple of days. After I got over the initial fear, I graduated to eating minimally cleaned eggs, and when those didn't kill me, I began getting my two eggs-a-day straight from the laying boxes. Even when we had plenty of eggs in the fridge, I became fanatical about going to the chicken coop and retrieving the freshest eggs possible, preferably still warm from the hen's body.

Then, with the chorus of squawking chickens coming through the kitchen windows, I cracked my eggs into the cast-iron skillet and left my old sterile world behind.

## Rich, Fluffy Soil

Hector's farm provided food for 50 families in the local area. Each family was a CSA member (Community Supported Agriculture), which meant they paid an annual fee in exchange for a weekly delivery of fresh organic farm goods. Every family received weekly eggs and a box of produce harvested from the fields.

I was impressed that a five-acre farm like Hector's could feed so many people. Back in Ohio, the farmers planted giant squares of land in a single crop. I figured about twenty of Hector's farms could fit into each Ohio cornfield. But those mega-farms back home couldn't feed a single person. I tried once, and the corn was inedible. The beautiful sea of grain wasn't fit for human consumption – they grew it for corn syrup and the feedlot beef industry.

Diversity was the secret on Hector's farm. He grew tomatoes, squash, garlic, onion, broccoli, cucumbers, melons, herbs, flowers, salad greens, and peppers. And that only scratched the surface. Each crop had further variety. On the day we planted peppers I ran across the usual varieties, such as jalapeño, bell, cayenne, and paprika. Then I found types I'd never heard of: Thai peppers, jimmy peppers, chocolate peppers, turino, and ace.

## Hector's Farm

All of that diversity and organic farming meant hard work. No gas-guzzling machine can match the flexibility of the human hand. Human effort, rather than petroleum effort, is the most valuable resource on a small-scale organic farm.

Initially, I set off on my wwoofing tour with a romantic vision of how farming worked. I imagined planting a seed in the ground, gently patting the rich, fluffy soil around it, and then nurturing the plant with water and sunshine while I kicked back with a good book and a glass of lemonade. Real farming wasn't exactly like that.

I had the right idea, but it was a lot more labor intensive than I imagined. The seeds were first planted in starter trays inside Hector's greenhouse and allowed to sprout and grow a few inches. Then we transported the baby plants to the field, and the designated row that would be their new home. That's where the real work started. The job of transplanting.

To get an idea of five acres, imagine five football fields side-by-side. About one acre of Hector's farm was dedicated to tomatoes, salad greens, and garlic. Those plants were already in the ground before I arrived. As for the remaining four acres – each a football-field-sized garden – that's where the free labor came into play: wwoofers like me, who were willing to work in exchange for food and lodging.

Luckily, the other volunteers and I had the help of a tractor with bucket seats extended behind the giant rear tires. The tractor was equipped with rolling spikes that poked holes in the ground and simultaneously poured a stream of water into the freshly punctured earth. We perched in the bucket seats, hovering inches above the ground, and dropped plant after plant into the wet holes. Eggplant, eggplant, eggplant, a hundred times. Then squash, squash, squash, a hundred more times. It felt like we were feeding the land.

The poker machine was nice, but I preferred the times when it broke down and I could perform the whole process by hand. I thought it was great fun to poke a little hole in the earth and drop in a squash or pepper plant. I felt more connected to the

## Hector's Farm

land and the plant, and less like an extension of the tractor.

As for the rich, fluffy soil I romanticized about, it was there. Hector had it. I could thrust my arm elbow-deep into the black earth. But this soil didn't come as a gift from the Green Mountains. It was the result of compost – giving back to the earth what the plants took out. Compost is like gold to organic farmers, and probably what they dream about at night. An ordinary person might dream of sex or ice-cream sundaes, but I bet more than one organic farmer has dreamt of the sky raining buckets of compost on the land.

Compost can be made from any organic matter that will break down and turn into sweet smelling black soil. Manure, food scraps, grass clippings, leaves – anything that was once living can nourish the earth. The result of finished compost is a rich, fluffy soil that holds water and serves as a cozy home for worms, microbes, and plant roots.

I don't know exactly what Hector used on his land, but I dished out delicious raw compost to each of the baby plants I transplanted. According to Hector's recipe, I mixed up a slurry composed of chicken and cow manure, lime, peat moss, and green sand. As I crawled along the garden rows, I scooped out handfuls of the stuff and packed it into the newly punctured holes for the baby plants to dine on. I felt like a kid in a sandbox.

At first, I enjoyed working with the raw compost. I was convinced it smelled like chocolate. I must've been deranged by the clean mountain air, because by the third day, after about a thousand handfuls of the stuff, I had trouble picking up on that sweet scent. I was only aware of the fowl-smelling sludge (pun intended) that coated my hands like a pair of manure gloves. In moments like that, crouched on my hands and knees like a filthy medieval serf, I remembered my old student Rushaun's comment, "Mr. Bender's gonna be an *organic* farmer," followed by a burst of laughter.

*If only they could see me now,* I thought.

In complete sincerity, manure gloves aside, I thought I was exactly where most of my students *should* be. The vast majority them weren't happy about being trapped indoors all day. I thought they would benefit from seeing a farm like Hector's, to learn where their food came from, experience the joy of plucking salad greens straight from the garden, and watch raw milk get turned into cheese. They might enjoy reaching their hands under a hen to snatch fresh eggs for tomorrow's breakfast. I knew they'd love being outside in the fresh air and sunshine. That's what Hector's Farm was all about. Connections. Connecting people with their food and their natural environment.

## A Community Built on Food

Connecting with the people was my favorite part of Hector's farm. Back in Ohio, I liked going to the local U-pick strawberry and blueberry patches with friends. I chatted with the farmers while my berries were being weighed, usually about rain or lack of rain. As for the big farms, the ones that served as nice country scenery rather than something to eat from, I rarely saw a farmer in the fields. If I did, he was rolling over the land in an enormous tractor, leaving a cloud of dust in his wake.

The sense of community was alive and well on Hector's small farm, a beehive of activity. During my first weekend as a volunteer several CSA families came out to the farm for a potluck and helped build a storage shed for Hector.

Seeing people take an interest in their local investment made me think of the stock market, which I dabbled in during my years as a teacher. I made a few dollars playing the market but had no social connection with the companies I invested in. I didn't feel inclined to send the CEO a Christmas card or volunteer to help build a set of office dividers for the company. The relationship centered around cold-hard cash.

Investing in Hector's Farm was clearly a different model. Investors brought financial security for Hector, so he could buy seeds and equipment before the season started, and the investors received a wholesome and edible return. Instead of turning money into more money, they turned money into

## Hector's Farm

heirloom tomatoes and eggs and community. This was a community built on food. And on trust.

Hector encouraged his customers to visit the farm and help themselves to eggs whenever they needed a carton, or to grab a pair of scissors and harvest their own herbs and flowers. Imagine your local grocer giving you the keys to the store and saying, "just come in and get what you need anytime. We trust you."

One of my favorite parts of Hector's Farm was going to the Farmer's Market to sell the salad greens and garlic scapes I harvested that same morning. This was unlike any grocery experience I had ever had. No one hurried. A nearby fiddle and banjo player performed for the crowd. Smiling customers asked questions about the food. "Do you have any recipe ideas for these garlic scapes? How do you control pests?" This wasn't like the Kroger and Food Town of my youth. This was local food for local people.

### Ya Ya and Boo Boo

As I mentioned, an amazing amount of hard work lay behind all that great food and community. I was one of six volunteers, all wwoofers, each motivated by a different force. A young woman from Tennessee received college credits for a full season internship on Hector's Farm. A couple of potheads from California and Colorado had left college in pursuit of a more free-spirited life. We even had a wwoofing family – a couple who volunteered as a way of touring the country with their daughter, Ya Ya.

Ya Ya's father was into astrology, and when I told him my age and said I intended to live as a nomadic farmer for a year, he was convinced planetary forces were compelling me. He told me I was being "swept up in Saturn's return." Apparently, since Saturn takes a 29-year trip around the sun, I was ready for round two, a new revolution and period of personal growth in my life. This notion planted a new perspective in my mind.

After years of formal schooling and burying my head in a

## Hector's Farm

science textbook, I had no use for New Age ideas. I was a man of science. That's where we find the ultimate truth, right? Now I wasn't so sure. For what seemed the first time of my life, I was outside the classroom with my feet in the soil. I knew it was time to loosen up and open my mind to new possibilities.

Most of the wwoofers saw nothing strange about Hector planting crops according to the moon's phases. They considered it common sense. My first impression was: *This is absolute nonsense.*

Back in Ohio people saw me as an unorthodox teacher, but on Hector's Farm I felt like the only sober person at the party. Seeing how others approached life was a healthy eye-opener for me. Take Ya Ya's breastfeeding, for example.

Throughout my two week stay on Hector's Farm, Ya Ya never wore a scrap of clothing. She ran around stark naked while her parents strung up tomatoes or planted onions. She also continually asked for "boo boo."

I didn't know what she meant when I first heard it. "Boo boo?" I quickly learned the answer when Ya Ya's mother unbuttoned her shirt and openly breast-fed her daughter out in the fields.

I have to admit, the whole boo boo scene made me a bit uncomfortable. Mostly due to the fact that Ya Ya seemed rather big to be breastfeeding. I mean, she had a full set of teeth already. There was also the curious reference to boo boo as if it was a separate entity.

"Boo boo likes the sun," I heard Ya Ya say. And then another time her mom said, "Ouch! You're hurting boo boo."

I wasn't an expert on motherhood in *any* way, but it seemed to me if a child was strong enough to run at a full sprint and eat corn on the cob, then she might be ready for weaning. I wasn't sure. I took in the whole scene and accepted the fact that this worked for Ya Ya and her mom. And yet, sometimes it didn't work.

One night at dinner, Ya Ya had a panic attack when her mom refused to give her boo boo. Ya Ya fell off her chair in hysterics

Hector's Farm

and sobbed, "I want boo boo!" Her mom's response was, "You know Mommy doesn't give you boo boo at the table."

## Cucumber Beetles

One day, Hector assigned me the task of killing cucumber beetles. This was an easy job compared to the physical strain of transplanting and weeding, or the filth of dipping my hands into a bucket of compost manure, but at the same time I felt it carried bad karma. I mean, come on, all those beetles wanted to do was make love on a cucumber flower. And there I was with my jar of water, knocking them into their death.

After slapping the first few flowers over the jar, I noticed the beetles didn't drown easily, so I had to pour them out in batches and smash them under my shoe. I'll never forget the sight of that oblong yellow shell with longitudinal black stripes, especially since the memory is forever linked to the sound of shells crunching between my shoe and a piece of cardboard.

This certainly wasn't the most wholesome job. However, I did observe one interesting thing during my time as an insect executioner. I noticed when I knocked a pair of beetles into the jar, the male continued trying to have sex as they drowned, while the female frantically tried to operate her wet wings and escape. I wondered if that kind of behavior carried over to other species. Or was it just female cucumber beetles that had more sense?

When I shut my eyes for a nap that day, one of the rare days Hector actually gave us a siesta, I had an image burned into my retina of the beetles clustering together on the water's surface. They clustered so, one at a time, a beetle could launch from the backs of the others and fly away. The idea was clever and it appeared they were cooperating, but in all likelihood they were probably in a desperate state, clawing at the shells of their neighbors, selfishly looking for a way out.

In a way, I empathized with their plight. I felt kind of like one of those cucumber beetles when I set off on my trip. I felt

*Hector's Farm*

I was finally breaking out of the jar, out of Ohio. I would grab onto farming to see where it might take me – and cling to Saturn's rings for a new revolution.

## Chapter 2
### *Applesauce Hill*

Maine was the northernmost point of my journey. In a sense, I chose Applesauce Hill for the sheer remoteness of the place. I was attracted to its position on the map as much as I was to the prospect of working with sheep, chickens, and a goat.

Applesauce Hill bordered no cities or highways, only steep mountains and a cluster of lakes that looked like black ink had spilled over the landscape. Mooselookmeguntic and Rangeley were the two closest lakes.

After parking my car on the green hillside, I stretched and took deep breaths of pine-scented air. I was far from civilization. An aromatic blend of flowers and wet wool mingled with the cool forest air to give the farm a unique smell, like its own nametag. If I had ever gotten lost in the dense forest that pressed up against Applesauce Hill on all sides, I could've smelled my way home.

Fitting the rural landscape, where sheep and moose outnumbered the lake-side residents, I arrived to an empty house. I was greeted by the faraway sound of bleating sheep and a pair of hummingbirds that hovered near a birdfeeder and sucked on sugar water with their long, pointed beaks. A note on the farmhouse door said:

Applesauce Hill

*Welcome Brian~*
*I went to town. Will be back before dinner. Please make yourself comfortable.*
*~Joan*

While waiting for Joan to return, I put on a pair of boots and walked around the farm. I hopped over rivulets of fresh rainwater that had formed after a deluge of late-summer rain. A myriad of tiny rivers poured over the front face of Applesauce Hill and seeped into a field of chest-high perennial grasses and wildflowers.

From the top of the hill, I heard the steady rush of two engorged streams that flanked Applesauce Hill on both sides and emptied into Rangeley Lake. The lake was only a slingshot away, but hidden by a swath of dense evergreen forest. From where I stood, I could only see a few feet into the dim edge of the forest. Ferns and moss-covered rocks gave way to complete darkness.

Behind me, perched amid a rocky and lightly-forested sheep pasture, the main clearing on Applesauce Hill held Joan's house, garden, and the barn. The house was built in the old New England saltbox fashion, with spacious, south-facing windows to trap solar heat. On the green paneled roof of the unpainted wooden house, Joan added a touch of modern technology – an array of 27 solar panels. She did her best to harness every bit of the meager New England sun.

The house and matching two-story barn were separated by a large flower and vegetable garden that attracted songbirds, hummingbirds and an occasional escape-artist from the sheep herd.

Joan's cozy estate was worthy of the *Better Homes and Gardens* magazine, yet she wasn't dainty. The moment she returned home, I knew I was in the presence of a tough woman. Her appearance suited the cold Maine landscape – fair-skinned, with a rosy complexion. Even in the semi-warmth of late summer, her cheeks were flushed as though she'd just

## Applesauce Hill

stepped out of a cold wind. She maintained a strong build, one that seemed uncharacteristic of a retired teacher. Her lithe body was sculpted by years of wrangling bales of hay and walking the farm with a garden tool or lawn mower in hand.

Joan greeted me with a firm hug, and almost immediately we started talking about the animals.

"I spoil them," she said. "Unlike children, it's okay to spoil animals." Joan opened a can of cat food as she said this, while two cats paced alongside their bowls on the kitchen counter.

Joan was mother to every plant and animal on the farm. Each morning she cooked a pot of meaty stew for her dog, Meena. Then she dished out hay, grains, and garden scraps to the farm animals. Joan not only fed the animals, she spoke words of affection and sang little songs to them.

Each time Joan arrived home from town, she called out with high-pitched enthusiasm, "Meena, meena, meena! How's my little meena pooh doing?"

Later that afternoon, while Joan milked the goat, I stood outside the goat enclosure and listened to her sing a milking song to the goat-- "Jane! Janey, Janey, Jane! That's a good girl, Jane."

For the month of August, I was merely the latest addition to this diverse, multi-species family. As Joan prepared us a delicious dinner of lamb sausage lasagna that first night, she briefed me on her life history – thirty years as a high school science teacher, a daughter in Peru, and now the farm life. Her booming voice caused me to sit straighter in my chair, but her resonant laugh and the glass of wine in her hand reminded me school was out, for both of us.

The magnitude of Joan's solitary operation amazed me. She raised her own meat, eggs, milk, and vegetables. She knitted hats and sweaters from Icelandic fleece. In addition, her flower garden was the local Home & Garden tour's main attraction.

While many women Joan's age retired to a more comfortable life of book clubs and playing with their grandchildren, Joan opted to spend her golden years raising a flock of sheep, repairing miles of fence-line, milking a goat twice a day, and growing her own vegetables.

I liked to think Joan's rosy cheeks and snow-white hair were signs of her hard-working northern spirit. Even after I arrived and offered my inexperienced hand, Joan insisted on doing much of the work. "I think you've done your share for the day," was her usual refrain around 11:00 a.m. I never protested. I was happy with the role of part-time fence builder, feeder of the sheep, goat-milker, and garden digger.

## Icelandic Sheep

I only had applesauce one time on Applesauce Hill, and it didn't come from the slender apple trees Joan planted on the front slope of her property. Lamb sausage, goat's milk, and chicken eggs were the real gifts of Applesauce Hill, and Icelandic sheep were the main residents.

Joan and I were the ruling minority over a flock of 20 sheep. Molly, Helen, and Woolamina were the top-ranking ewes, and the rams consisted of two hefty males named Pumpkin and Spiderpig, plus a less-mature ram called Littleman.

Molly, a big-bellied mother, was the first Icelandic sheep I'd ever seen. While I leaned against the wire sheep-fence and waited for Joan to return from town on my first day, I saw Molly step out of the barn. She stopped and stared at me for a second and then called in the direction of the rocky pasture. Like the rest of her fully grown counterparts, Molly had a beautiful set of ribbed horns that curled back like nautilus shells from the crown of her head. When she bleated, I heard a "mah" sound rather than the typical "ba bah" depicted in storybooks about farm animals. Molly stood at the threshold of the barn and bleated in an impatient tone, as if calling for some lost sheep named "Matt." "Matt? Matt?"

In response, I heard a high-pitched, excited call and a chocolate-brown lamb ran in from the pasture, jumping over little streams and weaving between boulders. "Mah," the little lamb bleated. "I'm right here."

*Applesauce Hill*

Molly and her lamb were members of one of the oldest and purest lines of domesticated sheep, a breed introduced to Iceland by the Vikings nearly a thousand years ago. Icelandic sheep, although larger and more docile than their wild relatives, still carry many of their ancestor's traits – including color variations and horns on both sexes. The sheep of Applesauce Hill came in a variety of colors. Molly was chocolate brown, while Hilda, the senior citizen of the flock, was pure black. Some were blonde; others were charcoal gray with streaks of cream-colored wool. In addition, the sheep had a double layer of fleece, which made them cold-hardy and ideally suited for the long winters of Western Maine.

The sheep on Applesauce Hill were more a hobby than a business. Joan sold a few lambs and mail-order fleece, but when the sums were totaled up, she claimed to end up in the negative column every single year. She was in it for her own personal enjoyment.

Joan said when she came home to work with the flock after a stressful day of teaching, her tension instantly dissolved. The way I saw it, the sheep were there for Joan's physical and mental wellbeing. Satisfying the simple needs of the farm animals was a form of therapy.

Aside from a flock of chickens, Joan's other farm animal was a goat named Jane who roamed the lightly forested sheep pasture. Jane ate leaves and bark from the trees, and although she was only a quarter the size of the powerful sheep, every single ewe and ram was terrified of her. Jane's small nimble body and straight, devil-like horns made her an alien sight, and the sheep stayed out of her way. One day in the sheep barn, I saw another reason the sheep feared Jane. Helen, one of the larger ewes, stepped next to Jane to feed from the hay rack, and for no apparent reason other than having her comfort-zone violated, Jane thrust her chest out and cracked her horns against the sheep's head.

If the majority sheep could vote one individual off the farm, that unlucky animal would be, without doubt, Jane the goat.

But as far as Joan and I were concerned, Jane was wonderful. She gave us milk on a daily basis.

If I cast my vote for the number one problem child of the farm, the recipient would be the most cunning of all the sheep – Molly.

## Molly the Magician

After Joan retired from teaching, her only discipline problem was Molly, the sheep who loved to jump fences. Molly was an expert at finding her way out of the pasture and into Joan's vegetable garden. On occasion, Molly would flatten the wire cables of the fence so the chickens and part of the flock wandered off into the surrounding forest. I had to stand near the escape route and lure them back in by shaking grain in a plastic container.

One of my ongoing jobs on Applesauce Hill was to walk the fence line with a hammer and coil of wire, searching for Molly's possible escape routes.

Molly was clever. Like a burglar, she honed in on the slightest weakness in the fence and found her way over, under, or through it. As a result, she was fatter than the rest of the flock. On more than one occasion I spotted Molly on the wrong side of the fence, grazing on the dense green forage that only the moose had access to, while the rest of the flock looked on dumbly, as though Molly was a magician.

Molly didn't even look up when her two lambs called insistently through the fence, thirsty for mom's milk. Molly the magician was a bit selfish. But then again, after she was lured back to the barn with sweet grain, her lambs benefited from the milk, made nutritious after a feast of broccoli, cabbage, and fresh grass.

Like the rest of the flock, Molly was a fine specimen. Her chocolate brown coat seemed to belong on a wooly mammoth. Four black legs protruded like twigs from the mass of ropey wool, and hardly seemed capable of supporting her large, ruminant belly.

## Applesauce Hill

I was a bit early for shearing-season on Applesauce Hill, but I did work with some of Molly's fleece from a previous year. Joan took me back in time and taught me how to spin yarn from the wool. I felt like I was taking part in one of the oldest arts of human civilization, the art that allowed us to advance beyond wearing raw animals hides around our bodies.

First, Joan handed me the implements of hand-spinning – a drop spindle and a section of carded wool. The wool looked and felt like a loose scarf of fur that had been uniformly combed. The drop spindle was a simple wooden rod inserted through the center of a disc. Dangling from a piece of yarn, the drop spindle spun like a top in the air.

In order to make yarn, I gently pulled the wool apart, and just before it stretched too thin and threatened to break, I tied the wool to a notch on the wooden rod. Next, I held the drop spindle in the air, suspended from the thin rope of wool, and gave the bottom of the wooden rod a little spin with my fingers. The loose wool threaded together like strands of DNA.

Next, I wrapped the newly formed yarn around the wooden rod and pulled apart some more wool. Pull and spin, pull and spin. That's all there was to it. Spinning was satisfying work, and left me with a ball of yarn to show for my efforts.

Then came the knitting. Knitting, I discovered, was the hard part. The challenge of running knitting needles through loops of yarn for hours on end made me think wearing raw animal hides wasn't such a bad idea after all. I spent five days knitting and ended up with a wool blanket the size of a checkbook, perfect for a pet hamster. I called it quits on knitting and stuck with the simple art of spinning.

On the day Joan agreed to participate in the local Home & Garden tour, I decided to put my spinning skills on display for the guests, as I sat on a bale of hay in front of the sheep barn. The perfect place to spin, I thought.

So, after the friendly old ladies and summer vacationers wandered through the house, where they viewed the solar panel array on Joan's roof, a wood-fired furnace, and Joan's

*Applesauce Hill*

gorgeous flower garden, the guests walked cautiously over the muddy ground back to the sheep barn.

As soon as I saw a group coming my way, I set my drop spindle in motion. I was ready to pass on the invaluable knowledge of how to make yarn. However, I didn't see much enthusiasm. Only a couple of the guests wanted to know more about the drop spindle, and *no one* wanted to try it. Most of the guests were only interested in the sheep, and who could blame them. The sheep were the stars of the show.

The summer vacationers were easy to impress, as most of them were as new to the farm-setting as I was. I explained, "Both the boys and girls have horns." I discussed the sheep's diet of fresh grass and hay, and answered simple questions, like "What's the difference between a ram and a ewe?" This was sheep barn 101.

## Sheep Barn 101

The first lesson in the sheep barn was, "watch out for the fly paper." Strips of the sticky paper hung at eye-level from all the rafters. Each strip was studded with hundreds of flies that had met, or were in the middle of, a slow and torturous death. The strips were a lesson in mindfulness. On more than one occasion my head came in contact with one of the strips, and I ended up trading a good clump of my hair for a head full of sticky wings and legs and other fly parts.

Other than swarms of sheep-loving flies, the barn was home to two things—the sheep and their hay. The loft above the sheep stalls was piled with stacks of hay, and during the daily feedings, puffs of dust filled the air as I separated the compact bales of hay like pages of a giant book.

The dust never settled. It filled the barn with a translucent haze that gave the shafts of sunlight a physical quality. The barn air was sweet smelling, still reminiscent of the freshly cut alfalfa, oats, and barley. Grain dust mingled with the musty wool of the sheep, giving the barn a sweet and powerful animal aroma.

The smell was pleasant, and one I awakened to every morning, since it was my daily chore to feed the sheep. Every morning I followed the same ritual. I put on a pair of knee high rubber boots and trudged through the soggy flower garden that led to the barn. I threw the barn door open and stepped into the dusty interior, where I was greeted by a cacophony of sounds from hungry sheep. The noisy rams and ewes produced the same demanding sound I heard from Molly's lambs when they called for milk, only in the barn, it was amplified 20 times and carried the tenor-resonance of full grown animals.

The whole flock joined in on the chorus of "Matt" and "Mah." Regardless of what human letters they enunciated, their tone said: "Give us our breakfast already!" Breakfast was the craziest time of day, because along with their ration of hay, the sheep received a once-a-day serving of molasses-soaked grains. They went wild for this. Sweet grain was the drug of choice in the sheep barn. And the competition for the grains was never fair. The little sheep always got knocked off to the side by the uncivilized adults.

One enclosure housed the rams and the other, much larger pen, provided shelter for the ewes and lambs. The three rams were kept separate from the ladies until breeding season. Pumpkin, Spiderpig, and Littleman each had a full set of curling horns that were solid as rock. The rams were the first sheep I saw when Joan gave me a tour of the farm. And when I first saw them, I was a bit taken aback. Pumpkin and Spiderpig, both full grown rams, were equipped with the characteristic trait of their kind, an enormous set of testicles the size of tennis balls.

The size of the testicles was indecent. Absurd, really. The question, "Why?" ran through my head. And I thought of only two possible reasons why a ram would carry such a heavy sperm factory. Either the ewes were having sex with multiple partners and there was fierce competition *within* the uterus and fallopian tubes, with all of the various ram sperm butting their way to the egg. Or the ram sperm were altogether lazy and crippled, and it took billions in order to create a few good swimmers. Either way, I felt I now had insight into why those hyper-masculine institutions, like football teams and pick-up trucks, took pride in the name.

Upon first stepping into the rams' stall, I was a bit nervous. After all, Pumpkin or Spiderpig could shatter my leg with ease, if given a good reason and a few feet of charging room. Lucky for me, I had what they wanted—three bins of molasses-soaked grains. The rams were easy, since they each got their own bin of grains. Occasionally, Pumpkin knocked Littleman off his food, asserting his dominance over the ram half his size, but that only happened if Littleman ate slower than either of the two big guys.

The females gave me the hardest time. The roster included Molly, Hilda, Wooly, Woolimina, Helen, and the little lambs, who all went by the common name of "Earl," since they were typically eaten or sold off before the fall breeding season.

The craziness on the female side stemmed from the fact that 17 ewes and lambs competed for six bins of grain. It was madness. They swarmed around me the moment I stepped into their stall. I had to hold the sweet grain over my head and quickly break free to an open spot, which wasn't easy, because I had to maneuver over the bed of lumpy hay in my clumsy rubber boots. Once I found an opening, I dashed over to it and pretty much dropped the grains on the barn floor before the hungry ladies had a chance to charge in and knock me off my feet.

After the sheep were distracted with their grains, I went about filling their water buckets and stuffing books of hay into the hay racks mounted on the walls. My favorite part of the day was when the grain frenzy ended and the sheep settled into eating their hay. All the demanding cries ended and the cloud of dust swirled through the shafts of light and slowly settled onto the thick wooly coats of the sheep.

During this time, I usually filled my pockets with sweet grains and snuck a few handfuls to Molly's lambs. Then I just leaned against the fence, always mindful of the sticky strips of flypaper hovering around my head, and enjoyed the calming sound of the sheep munching their hay. The dining sheep sounded like someone walking through a field of dry grass, gently crunching the brittle stalks under their boots. Ruminants are so peaceful when all they're doing is ruminating.

## Jane the Goat

The daily sheep activities were basic. They roamed the rocky, forest-fringed hillside and ate grass. Pumpkin, Spiderpig, and Littleman grazed their own smaller strip of land, while the ewes ranged the greater part of Applesauce Hill, hopping over boulders and the little rivulets that flowed down toward the lake. The sheep searched out new growth, and oftentimes just stood around doing nothing. They didn't seem to mind the rain, especially since they were forever dressed in waterproof coats, the woolen fibers waxed over in lanolin.

Around sunset, the sheep ambled back to the barn to eat hay. Some of the sheep bleated, usually mothers calling their lambs in, or lambs calling their mothers in, and then the flock gathered around the hay racks and ruminated over that day's cud. The next morning it started all over again. They went mad for the grains and then settled into their daily routine and favorite foraging sites. They led such simple lives.

The sheep's only outside interaction was with me, Joan, and Jane the goat. Jane was on loan for the summer so Joan could have some goat's milk to make cheese. Jane had full access to the ewe's side of the pasture and when she walked into their barn, the sheep moved aside like she was an extraterrestrial being. None of them wanted to be anywhere near her. The sheep didn't even protest when Jane moved in on their sweet grains. Jane's unchallenged right to the sweet grains was a strong statement as to how much the sheep feared her.

Jane was another one of my chores. I fed her twice a day and occasionally milked her, but only when Joan already had enough milk for cheese and was willing to accept the drop in milk output. New milkers like myself always obtained less milk.

Milking Jane was my first experience with this event, one filled with many interesting dimensions. There was the strangeness of milking a goat by the same name as my mom, a goat even more stubborn than my mom. On top of that, I was instructed to sing to the goat or talk to her in a soothing way as I milked her.

The actual act of milking was downright difficult. In all the cartoons, movies, and books I'd seen of cows being milked, it looked easy. All I had to do was squeeze the teats back and forth and watch milk stream into the metal pail.

Extracting milk wasn't that simple. I got about a thimbleful before Jane kicked the bucket over on my first try. Jane's stall was basically a storage shed with a bed of hay and a long wooden box where Jane stood to eat from her grain bin. The wooden box made Jane's udders more accessible.

The milking started like this: I walked over to Jane's stall with a cup of grains, a metal bucket I'd sterilized with hot water, and a towel soaked in warm water. As soon as Jane saw me standing outside her house with a cup of grains, she went berserk and maneuvered over the rocky landscape to get back to her stall. Jane's voice was much harsher than the sheep's bleating. She sounded like a cross between a trumpet and a kazoo. I thought she had her foot caught in a bear trap when I first heard that ungodly noise. It was a voice I *slowly* got used to. It was just Jane being Jane.

So, after I got Jane into her stall and she was perched on her wooden box, I followed her in, always mindful of the fly paper dangling ominously overhead. After my first couple of milkings, I learned one important lesson: not to give Jane her grains until I was positioned and ready. Once I poured those grains in the bin, it was liking pressing the "start button." Jane only let me touch her udders while her face was buried in a bin of sweet-molasses grains, and even then it was a bumpy ride.

First, I took the warm towel and massaged Jane's udder to

stimulate milk-letdown. I also wiped her teats clean to prevent infecting the milk with any debris. Then I poured the grains into her bin and went at it. This was go-time, but it wasn't all about speed. The art of milking came first. During my first few squeezes nothing came out. Joan taught me I was basically squeezing the milk right back into Jane's udder, and in order to bring it *down* into the bucket, I needed to pinch the base of the teat to prevent backflow. I did this with the crook of my thumb and index finger, and then I used the rest of my hand to squeeze the milk out. I was exhilarated when I heard that first stream of milk hiss against the bottom of the metal pail. I was milking a goat!

So there I sat on the edge of the wooden box, as Jane ate her grains. And just as I reached a depth where the milk began to slosh around a bit, whack! Jane kicked the bucket over with her back hoof. That put a quick end to the session. Then on my next day, I'm milking, I'm milking, I'm milking, and out of nowhere, with the speed of a lightening bolt, Jane's dirty hoof is *in* the bucket. Another round of potential cheese gone to waste.

By the time I got to the fourth and fifth day of milking, I realized Joan was right. I would have to sing to this goat if I wanted to have any chance of a clean milking. I squeezed rhythmic streams of milk into the bucket and said soothing things like, "That's a good girl Jane, you're a good goat, it's okay, we're almost done, that's a good girl." In time, I got better and Jane mellowed a bit, but I never stopped watching her back leg, always ready to lunge for the bucket and slide it out of the way if her dirty hoof got the least bit twitchy.

After my first couple of clean milkings, Joan pointed out how little milk I had in my bucket. It was true, but I thought *come on, how about a little confidence boost here.* I figured Joan was probably just trying to challenge me to improve, and I took the challenge seriously. If I had a bad milking, I dwelled on it as I drifted off to sleep that night.

By the end of the second week, I had it down. I achieved the

## Applesauce Hill

ultimate goal. I emptied Jane's udder for the first time. I was in a good back and forth rhythm when I realized Jane was still eating, yet I wasn't getting any more milk. I had milked her out! This was a proud moment. I grabbed the milk pail from the wooded box before Jane could kick it over and spoil my triumph.

As on Hector's Farm, we drank the milk from Jane raw. I poured the bucket of fresh milk through a coffee filter and it was ready for consumption. The milk wasn't exactly flowing like a river. We got no more than a few cups a day. And with Joan's cheese operation, there was never enough milk to sit in the fridge for more than a few hours. Therefore, I always drank it slightly warm. Jane's milk tasted different from cow's milk, with a strong, grainy flavor some people describe as "barny." To me, it tasted Janey.

Cow's milk may be preferable in taste to some people, but from a purely nutritional stance, goat's milk is a superior product. Raw goat's milk is supposedly one of nature's only complete foods. A person can thrive solely on raw goat's milk for years at time. If that's not a testament to Jane's fine product, I don't know what is. Cheers to Jane the goat!

### Generous Joan

Goat's milk was the only scarce commodity on Applesauce Hill. Joan was one generous host. We had regular feasts with her sister and brother-in-law who lived on the lake a five-minute walk away. The meals usually contained sheep from previous years. We had lamb sausage and lamb lasagna from the sons and daughters of Pumpkin and Spiderpig. We had mutton chili and mousaka. I probably ate bits of Molly's brothers and sisters, and countless Earls. For dessert we had blueberry slump and steaming hot blueberry popovers slathered with butter. Maine was blueberry central in mid-August.

During one dinner, as I spread a pat of butter on my corn, Joan politely said, "There's more butter right there." I nodded at the full stick of butter sitting right in front of me and said,

## Applesauce Hill

"Thanks, Joan. I'm good." Then on my second piece of corn, as I rubbed the butter down to the wrapper, Joan reminded me. She said, "Help yourself to the butter. There's more right there."

Joan's home was an unlimited butter kind of house. Joan was constantly giving without expecting anything in return. She raised the sheep without any intent of profiting from then. She housed and fed me for a mere three hours of work a day. The mead and wine flowed freely. She took me into town to see plays and musical performances. And she patiently showed me how to spin and knit and care for the animals. The butter was certainly on the table.

### Thru-Hikers

With my ample free time, I swam and kayaked in the cold summer lake. I played croquet with Joan's brother-in-law. And I took a trip out to the blueberry fields with Joan's woofer from the previous summer, a guy from Ohio who'd decided to pick blueberries full-time. Often times, I did nothing and loved it. I just sat among the sheep and watched Jane chew bark from the trunk of a tree.

My most memorable time off the farm was when I hiked part of the Appalachian Trail, a 12-mile hike up Saddleback Mountain. From the trailhead parking lot, I felt as though I was stepping into a primordial rainforest with a day-pack full of water and chocolate bars. I felt like I was seeing the forest through the eyes of a farmer. I'd never noticed the soil in a forest, but after having come from Hector's farm, the first thing I did was hike off the trail onto the springy forest floor and scoop up a handful of earth. The soil felt spongy and smelled of sweet decay. Fine white hairs ran throughout it and when I crumbled some of the black soil to the ground, I saw nearly microscopic centipedes race back toward the darkness I held in my palm. The soil was alive.

The forest was alive too. Water dripped from above and landed on deep-green ferns that reached out from the

*Applesauce Hill*

forest floor like large feathers. Perfectly round orange and red mushrooms poked through the mats of bright green vegetation. The moisture that hung in the air gave the colorful mushroom caps a glistening appearance, despite the dimness of the forest understory.

The first hikers I saw trudged by with their eyes fixed on the path, giant packs sticking a foot above their head. All I received was a curt nod as they passed. They were thru-hikers, the term given to long-distance hikers of the Appalachian Trail. They were the most extreme hikers of the trail, an altogether different breed than day-hikers like me. In crossing paths with the many thru-hikers of Saddleback Mountain, some of them starting fresh on the southward voyage to Georgia, others looking like Green Berets on their way to Mt. Katahdin, I noticed they had a different look in their eye than the day-hikers I passed. With the day-hikers I usually paused for light conversation. We'd say, "Hey, how're you doing?" like we were long-lost friends, and exchange information about the mud and how far it was to the top.

Maybe the thru-hikers were warmer toward their own kind, but they passed me as though I was a stump on the trail. Me, with my cheerful greetings and little five-pound pack. In response to what I misinterpreted as rudeness, I became intentionally more light-footed, performing like an agile squirrel in front of the heavily burdened hikers.

I saw no enjoyment in the faces of the thru-hikers I passed, although I'm sure they experienced a dimension of pleasure and self-discovery I couldn't understand. Almost all of them were on a mission, striving for the next peak and the next great view, always enduring the shock on their knees and backs. But what was it all for if they didn't enjoy the immediate beauty, the ferns and mushrooms and orange salamanders they seemed to pass like a blur on the highway? I guess they were in it for the peaks, and the sense of conquering the trail. It didn't seem to be an experiment in living within nature. It was an experiment in traversing nature. The title "thru-hiker" was more accurate than I realized.

When I finally reached the peak, I did get a taste of the thrill the long-hikers must be addicted to. My heart raced and every cell of my body was saturated with oxygen and chocolate. The high-altitude euphoria was accompanied by an amazing view of the trees and lakes of Western Maine. The forest-filled valleys were touched with the first bit of fiery red from turning maple leaves.

I met a thru-hiker on the summit who spent our entire conversation swatting wildly at a fly. "It's been following me for three hours!" he exclaimed. The man was on his third attempt at hiking the trail. On his first try, he tore a ligament in his knee. Two years later he broke his ankle. Now he was on his third attempt, with a fractured toe and a serious limp. He embodied the kind of determination it takes to complete a continuous 2000 mile hike.

On my way down from the bald summit of Saddleback Mountain, I ran across a blue cooler nestled in the leaves near a stream. The cooler was loaded with oatmeal cream pies, pepperoni, string cheese, soda, beer, and candy bars. I felt like I'd stumbled upon a hidden treasure. The lid of the cooler had a note on it that said, "Thru-Hikers, Enjoy!" This was what long-hikers of the AT call "trail magic," a hidden stash of treats and pleasant surprises. I was tempted to grab an oatmeal cream pie, but I remembered the limping man from the summit, swatting at the fly that would probably follow him all the way to Georgia, and I considered all the other sweat-rimmed faces I'd seen earlier that day, half-bent under their heavy loads. The junk food was for them. I was only a day-hiker.

## Joan Gets Mad

My trail magic was raw goat's milk and sitting down in the sheep barn to bottle-feed Molly's adorable little lambs. The peaks and summits of my trip were learning how to milk a goat and stay upbeat through an endless day of planting peppers behind Hector's tractor.

## Applesauce Hill

The rewards far outweighed the challenges on Applesauce Hill. I enjoyed a sort of farm-version of summer vacation. However, the month didn't spin together in one smooth motion. There were a few knots along the way. In Vermont, aside from the grueling workload, the disease-carrying ticks unsettled me most of all. I never felt more violated than the first time I found one of the creatures burrowing head-first into my leg.

On Applesauce Hill, the no-see-ums plagued me – nearly invisible flies that flew right through the fine mesh of my bedroom window. By the third day on the farm I looked like a leper. My neck was lumpy with dime-sized welts.

The no-see-ums were a nuisance, but the pain they inflicted was only a physical one. I had a much harder time dealing with the time when Joan got mad at me.

On my last night on the farm, without checking with Joan, I gave my bedroom to a new pair of wwoofers and slept in the guest bed. The guest bed was piled with stacks of papers and a layer of dust, possibly indicating maybe it wasn't intended for sleeping. All of this went through my mind, but I thought, *oh, what the heck, Joan's generous,* and I relocated the stacks of paper to the ground.

Well, the next morning, I awakened to find Joan's typical rosy complexion transformed to angry red. The moment I stepped into the kitchen, I felt like a misbehaving student. It was as if I'd lost the entire flock of sheep. Joan proceeded to lecture me on my place as a guest, and then she tossed fresh linens on the floor and ordered me to change the sheets. I was stunned. All I could say was "I'm sorry, Joan." But I didn't know exactly why I was apologizing. Was it the guest-bed that evoked such a fiery response? Was it the two lawn-mower blades I bent during my failed attempts at mowing Joan's rocky hillside? Maybe Joan still carried some of the hot bloodedness of a veteran high school teacher. Or maybe she felt as if she'd spoiled me.

Whatever the case, I left the farm with fond memories. Joan

## Applesauce Hill

remains one of the strongest and most admirable women I've ever met. She showed me what one individual can achieve. Sheep, chickens, a goat, and a garden? No problem.

On my last visit to the sheep barn, I squatted down to say goodbye to one of Molly's lambs, one I bottle-fed during the morning feedings. Just as I thought the chocolate brown lamb was going to give me a kiss on the cheek, she started chewing on the brim of my straw hat.

I was enlivened by the good and simple energy of the sheep and ready to blaze my way south. The only kink in my itinerary was that I didn't have a next farm. The day before I left Applesauce Hill, my intended farm host from the Adirondacks called me with some bad news. "We won't be able to feed you for the *full* week," he said.

I didn't feel comfortable with this, especially after I'd just indulged in a month-long feast at Joan's place, so I ran my eraser over the entire month of September. I called up Joan's wwoofer from the previous summer, Travis the blueberry picker, and decided that while I searched for another farm, I would pick blueberries.

# Chapter 3
## *Peace and Plenty Farm*

### Blueberry Fields Forever

No one greeted me upon my arrival at Peace & Plenty Farm. A solitary blue barn was the only sign I'd come to the right place. Beside the barn, a perfect rectangle of forest had been replaced by a field blanketed with ankle-high blueberry bushes. The berries were fully ripe and there wasn't a soul in sight to eat them. At first, I stood next to my car in awe. *Where am I?* I wondered.

I was in the middle of nowhere, Maine. Joan's old wwoofer, Travis, had directed me to Peace & Plenty farm, using old sawmills and bridges as landmarks, since most of the warped roads were unmarked. I received instructions from the owner of Peace & Plenty farm to pick for as long as I wanted, or until the chest freezer in the blue barn was full.

After reality set in, and I accepted the fact that for the first in my life I could eat as many blueberries as I wanted, free of charge, I broke out of my state of wonderment and walked past a sign that read "Organic & Native Blueberries." I dropped to my hands and knees like a hungry bear to sample fruit from the low-lying plants. My first handful of the pale-blue fruit filled my mouth with cool sweetness that seemed to carry the refreshing night air in its juice. *Now this is a piece of trail magic,*

## Peace and Plenty Farm

I thought--- something far better than a blue cooler packed full of junk food. I had found a farm that offered exactly what it advertised—peace and plenty.

For three days, I picked and ate blueberries until my fingertips and tongue were stained blue. I was the lone-picker. An occasional family showed up for the U-pick side of the business, but I was the only paid worker. Travis was with a crew of Brazilians picking the southern parts of Maine.

Before Peace & Plenty Farm, the only blueberry bushes I'd ever seen were tall ones that could be picked standing up. The ankle-high plants in Maine were a low-bush variety. Peace and Plenty Farm grew a variety called Canadian sour-top blueberries, a name that couldn't have been more misleading.

Each morning, I sat down in a dense patch and had myself a mono-meal of blueberries. After eating my fill, I started picking. I discovered after the first day I didn't need to bring water out into the field with me. If I got thirsty under the summer sun, I ate a handful of plump, juicy berries and spit out the skins.

When Travis told me he "raked" blueberries, I imagined him scraping the bushes with a garden rake. Well, it wasn't quite like that. The rake for harvesting blueberries resembled an oversized dustpan with metal teeth. I raked each plant from the ground upward, and the blueberries spilled off their stems and rolled into the reservoir of the pan. After a few rakings, I poured the berries into a wooden box. The cascade of blueberries pouring into the box produced a soft pelting sound, like fat raindrops hitting a wooden roof. For me, it was the sound of money.

I stripped the full bushes quickly, so I was constantly on the lookout for the next dense cluster and the next handful of dollars. The repetitive motion and direct sunshine made for hard physical labor. I squatted. I hunched over. I lunged. I tried every possible raking pose to take the strain off my back, but in the end, I discovered it was just a matter of staying flexible with daily stretches and yoga. As is the case with most farm work, the key requirements for raking blueberries were flexibility and stamina.

After I filled a few boxes out in the field, the job was only half done. The next step was running the berries through a winnowing machine to weed out debris and irregular fruit that got mixed up with the Grade A blueberries--the well-rounded deep blue ones.

The winnowing machine was an upward moving conveyor belt attached to a fan. The black rubber belt and a steady rush of wind carried all the misshapen berries and bits of grass and twigs over the top and dumped them into a trash bin. At the same time, the nice ball-shaped berries rolled downhill faster than the belt could carry them up. The fast-rollers ended up in the Grade A bucket. The winnowing machine was a clever invention, and a big time-saver over having to pick out all of the "field trash" by hand.

After separating all the field trash, I inspected the Grade A bucket for any green or red berries, commonly called "chokeberries," then I weighed out 5-pound bags and stashed them in the giant chest freezer. That was it. The bags were ready to be sold at the farmer's market.

Raking blueberries was good money. I took in about $150 each day, but the work was hard on my body. I got out of bed each morning feeling as though I'd lost a wrestling match. Plus, I discovered that it *is* possible to eat too many blueberries. By the end of my three-day career as a blueberry raker, I found myself spending a lot of time on the toilet. Unlike raw goat's milk, I don't think it's possible to live entirely off of blueberries.

During one of my many blueberry feasts out in the field, I thought of the old Beatle's tune, *Strawberry Fields Forever*. Only, instead of strawberries, the chorus that played through my head was *Blueberry Fields Forever*. As I lunged, hunched, and squatted on aching knees to pick the ripe berries, the song took on new meaning. I thought how a migrant laborer might interpret the chorus to that song. To them, "Strawberry Fields Forever" might sound like a nightmare of endless fields of strawberries and blueberries that had to be picked and winnowed.

I know one thing for certain—you can't *eat* blueberries forever. For me, three days was the perfect taste. I left Peace & Plenty Farm with a blue tongue and a new farm lined up in Shelburne Falls, Massachusetts. I loaded my cooler with a few zip lock bags of blueberries and started my southern migration.

## Ten Days of Silence

Before I started in Massachusetts, the owner of the farm recommended I check out a meditation center down the road from her farm. She said I was arriving just in time for the start of a ten-day meditation, and if I wanted, I could "sit the course."

I'd never meditated in my life, at least not in a formal setting. After work, I sometimes sat cross-legged in my basement and tried to concentrate on my breath or get absorbed in the *Ommm* mantra. As far as relieving stress after a day of teaching, it was no more effective than a glass of beer.

The meditation course in Massachusetts was different. The purpose of the 10-day course was to learn Vipassana meditation, the same technique the Buddha, Gautama Siddhartha, used to reach enlightenment. This meditation wasn't a casual retreat with hot springs and massages.

The course involved ten days of pure silence. Complete celibacy. No books or music. I couldn't even bring a pen and paper with me. The schedule sounded grueling. I was to wake up at 4:30 in the morning and spend most of the day engaged in deep meditation. *Was Hector running this place?* I wondered.

Despite the unappealing schedule, it didn't take me long to decide I was going to sit the course. After all, I'd set off from Ohio to broaden my horizons. And if the path to enlightenment was being served to me on a silver platter, free of charge and free of any religious affiliation, of course I would take it.

Reality quickly settled in. I contemplated leaving on the

second day. Then again on the third and fourth day. Not until day ten, when I walked out of the meditation hall glowing and feeling like a vacuum cleaner had sucked all of the cobwebs from my mind, did I realize what a gem I'd stumbled upon. Vipassana meditation was the ultimate trail magic—a direct route to peace and happiness. But the rewards didn't come easily.

## Distraction

The silence was difficult. Several people packed up and left on the second day. One guy was gone within the first few hours. The challenge wasn't so much boredom as the difficulty of learning how to concentrate. I had spent my entire life concentrating on the outside world – plates of sushi, stimulating books, a beautiful woman. Even when I closed my eyes, the outside world played on the big screen of my mind, looping all my desires and preoccupations. Never once had I turned my concentration inward for an extended period of time. And when I did, I felt uneasy. I wanted out!

At first, I distracted myself with people watching. I watched an actor from New York run gel through his hair and adjust the collar on his glittery nightclub shirt before entering the meditation hall. I watched the curious habits of an obsessive-compulsive man. He brushed his teeth five times a day and wore extra long sleeved shirts so he didn't have to touch anything with his bare hands. On the walking path, a well-dressed businessman looked at me with desperation. The silence appeared to be driving him crazy.

Just when I settled into a nice stroll and got absorbed in the insect life of the forest bordering the meditation center, I heard the gong ring. The buzzing ring hung in the air and signaled it was time to sit and meditate. After breakfast, after break, after lunch, the gong rang. The heavy brass gong summoned us back to our pillows. Fifty or so silent men made their way to the meditation hall. The same ringing resonated through the trees and tents and residence halls for the sixty or so women

## Peace and Plenty Farm

on the other side of the meditation center. I stepped indoors, took off my sandals, and sat.

Each meditator had a personal nest of pillows or a chair for those with back problems. I sat cross-legged on my stack of pillows and closed my eyes. Everyone settled into a favorite sitting posture and awaited the baritone voice of the teacher—a Buddha-like man named S.N. Goenka. First, Goenka chanted a piece of sweet-sounding ancient wisdom delivered in the Buddha's own language, which was translated later in the day. Then Goenka said with coach-like encouragement, "Start again, start with a calm and quiet mind." He stretched his adjectives so it sounded as though he said, "start with a caaaaaalm and quiiiiiiiet mind, an alert and attentive mind. Be very vigilant. Very vigilant." Then he gave specific instructions.

There was no question about what I was *supposed* to do. The first three days were dedicated to concentration. I was to follow my breath. No mantras or controlled breathing. Just pure, natural breath. Following my breath for a prolonged period of time was much harder than I expected. I stayed with my in-breath and out-breath as it caressed my nostrils, and not until day three could I achieve even a minute of pure concentration. Even when I tried to shut off the distractions, all sorts of mind-movies visited me. Just as I slipped into the deep peaceful concentration of my own breath, Jane the goat would appear. She stood on a rock and ate leaves from a branch. I pulled myself back to my breath, and then I was transported to a couch, eating a never-ending pint of Chubby Hubby ice cream. My mind was forever seeking distraction.

My concentration improved as the days went by, but there was still plenty of fuel for distraction, especially outside the meditation hall. The meditators and I didn't have books, music or TV, but we did have pinecones. I mostly watched the chipmunks as they scurried about the high branches and knocked pinecones loose. The heavy cones pelted the canvas tents below, and several meditators went to work creating art with the fallen pinecones.

I enjoyed the distraction of watching art evolve during breaks and meal periods. The pinecone art started with a simple design. Someone arranged the scattered pinecones into triangles. Then someone else arranged the triangles into a larger triangle – a pinecone triforce. From that point, it took off. By day four, someone had constructed a labyrinth below the triforce, adorned with yellow flower petals, red berries, and colorful rocks gathered from the woods. The simple pinecone triangles blossomed into a beautiful mandala – a meditators mecca of distraction.

When the course manager saw the magnitude of distraction the artwork was taking on, he dutifully destroyed it. He ran a stick through the triforce and colorful mandala of pinecones and reduced it to a scattering of its parts. Impermanence! The course manager taught us a lesson in what we were all there to learn.

## Vipassana Meditation

Day four marked the beginning of what is called Vipassana meditation. The breathing meditation was just training. On day four, I listened as Goenka gave new instructions. Starting from a point on the very top of my head, I was to observe every square inch of my body with a balanced mind. If a sharp pain arose in my back or an itch cropped up on my head, I was not supposed to react, not even to scratch.

Try that for an hour. I probably went through five different pillow variations. I tried forming a chair of pillows. I used a stool. I thought I would find the perfect seat, where all of the pain would melt away. My attempts were futile, of course. The frustrating part was that most of the pain I observed arose because I had to sit there and observe it. *What's the point?* I wondered.

I was never kept wondering for long, for Goenka delivered an evening video discourse explaining everything with the precision of a scientist. He likened the meditation technique to a "surgical operation of the mind." Blind faith was not part

*Peace and Plenty Farm*

of Vipassana Meditation. Every stage of the technique was explained with perfect clarity. Yet, the pain and frustration were still there.

A balanced mind was essential for getting good results from the meditation. Apparently the Buddha made an important discovery when he achieved enlightenment. The discovery was this: When a person generates craving or hatred, they give birth to a mental impurity. Throughout a normal human lifetime, these impurities pile up in thick layers around one's mind. More impurities equal more suffering.

The cool thing about Vipassana meditation was that I was given a tool to rake away the old mental debris. Every time I observed a pain in my back or an itch on my forehead without reacting, I zapped an impurity. Every time I observed a rush of pleasant vibrations without clinging to it or wanting more, I zapped another impurity. The elimination of impurities was like playing a spiritual video game. With a balanced mind, I could zap the old mental layers, and with each impurity gone, I was rewarded with a small degree of peace.

I certainly didn't achieve enlightenment in those ten days, but I did come out of the meditation center with a pleasant, glowing sensation. I had a calm and quiet mind. I felt peaceful. I suppose it was the result of ten days of hard chipping, clearing away the old mental plaque.

## The Physicist and The Buddha

Other than becoming equipped with a life-long tool for reducing my suffering, my favorite part of the meditation was the concept of "anicca" (ah-knee-chuh), an old Indian word that means impermanence. Anicca is the idea that everything is constantly in a state of flux, ever-changing, trillions of subatomic particles arising and passing away every second. Anicca. Change. Anicca. Change.

During an evening discourse, Goenka told the story of how the Buddha reached the understanding of anicca. Evidently, the Buddha had a much sharper mind than I did. He wasn't distracted by goats and ice cream. He was able to observe far subtler sensations than a mere itch on the forehead or pain in his back. He was able to get to the point where he observed vibrating wavelets of matter, which he called "kalapas." He described these kalapas as arising and passing away trillions of times every second. Trillions of subatomic births and deaths taking place at every point in his body. Anicca! The Buddha realized he was being reborn as a new person every second.

The interesting thing about this was that back in the 1960s a physicist from Berkeley won the Nobel Prize in Physics for discovering the same thing. Both the physicist and the Buddha came to the exact same conclusion, yet they clearly received two different rewards. One got a Nobel Prize and the other received infinite wisdom.

From a teacher's perspective, I knew the reason for this discrepancy. It's called experiential learning. When you learn something on an intellectual level, using tools and books, you acquire an intellectual understanding. But when you learn something on an experiential level, using your own mind as the only tool, it leads to a much deeper and lasting understanding.

I learned more about the nature of my mind and body in ten days of meditation than during ten *years* of college and teaching. I was ready to resume my farming tour with the understanding that I was a changed person. Anicca!

## Woodsong Farm

The transition back into farm life was easy. I wasn't thrust into the noise and speed of Boston and New York City, as was the fate of many meditators. I walked twenty minutes through a colorful autumn forest to Woodsong Farm, which shared a property line with the meditation center.

A deciduous forest, home to deer and a healthy mosquito population, wasn't all Woodsong Farm shared with the Vipassana Meditation Center. The farm also shared the peaceful atmosphere. After my first two farms, working under Hector and Joan, I'd begun to think farmers were generally

## Peace and Plenty Farm

hardened and somewhat unpleasant people.

David and Amanda, of Woodsong Farm, were Vipassana meditators of 20 years, and it showed. The pleasant, glowing sensation I experienced on my way out of the meditation center showed on their faces. They radiated good health and clear minds. Before I experienced my own meditation and shared the floor of the meditation hall with actors, musicians, mothers, and businessmen, I pictured serious meditators as hermits and subdued human beings, or robed monks at the very least. David and Amanda were neither. Aside from raising their son, playing the stock market, and teaching yoga classes, they also found time to keep a nice-sized garden, from which I would harvest pears.

I graduated from the ground-level work of raking blueberries to leaning against a ladder with my head in a pear tree. The pear trees were so laden with fruit, that when I jostled a branch the pears rained down, thudding against the earth like billiard balls. I was half-tempted to get them out of the tree by shaking the branches, but I saw that the fruit incurred little bruises and nicks after slamming against the ground. *If only I could build some kind of net*, I thought. Oh, well. I stuck with the old fashioned method. One pear at a time.

The short week and a half I spent on Woodsong Farm was filled with a measure of freedom. Part of the freedom came from getting rid of so much mental debris. But I was also granted smaller freedoms. I could read again. And talk. I didn't have to obey the gong. In a sense, this was comparable to the bliss I felt when I closed my classroom door for the last time. I knew I would never have to hear another bell ring, ever again.

While picking pears one day, I remembered what one of my fellow teachers said to me the week before school let out: "I wonder how you'll feel next fall when school is back in session. I wonder if you'll miss it at all."

I looked around at the September foliage. "Next Fall" was here. I imagined facing a classroom full of nursing students, dressed in their green scrubs and pouring gossip into each other's ears before the bell rang. I imagined patting my shirt pocket to make sure the PowerPoint clicker was there.

Then I looked at where I actually was, standing on a ladder with my head in a pear tree. Birds chirped and the colorful trees surrounding the farm steadily dropped their leaves. I snapped a pear from the branch and stuffed it into my cargo pocket. I knew I was in the right place.

\* \* \* \*

I did a variety of jobs on Woodsong Farm. I prepared meals for the family. I chopped wood and picked tomatoes. Mostly, I made apple and pear sauce. By the time I left the farm, David and Amanda had nearly 40 jars of apple-pear sauce in their pantry. The abundance of preserved food made David happy. He told me it was better than gold, having a stockpile of food and wood to last through the winter.

The recipe for the pear sauce was simple. I cut the pears into quarters, leaving the skin on, but removing the seeds and stem. In a large pot, I added a splash of apple juice or maple syrup water to prevent scorching, then added the fruit, cinnamon, ginger, and a pinch of salt. No sugar was necessary. The ginger brought out the sweetness.

For myself, I made seven jars of blueberry-pear sauce for the road. The small stockpile gave me a dose of food security, a fuzzy feeling knowing I had something good to eat on my way to the next farm. Like David, I felt I had something of real value.

I didn't spend long on Woodsong Farm, but I left the place in high spirits. I had mason jars of Maine blueberries and Massachusetts pears tucked away in my trunk. I had a meditation technique that could bring me peace of mind anywhere, at any time. My body and soul were well-nourished. I kissed New England goodbye and aimed my car south.

## Chapter 4
*Clear Creek Homestead*

**Blue Ridge Mountains**

The road to Clear Creek Homestead circled upward like a spiral staircase leading into the Blue Ridge Mountains of North Carolina. As I drove, I envisioned the primitive living arrangements that awaited me. "You'll be staying in the tepee," Whitney told me in a brief e-mail correspondence, "and you're our only wwoofer. George and I would love to have some help with the garden."

Almost everything I knew about Clear Creek Homestead came from a description posted in the WWOOF-USA Farm Directory. George, Whitney, and their daughter, Adalaya sustained themselves on chickens, ducks, apple trees, berry patches, and a large garden. "We do eat meat," Whitney said. "George gets a deer on occasion." By "get" I knew she didn't mean "go to the grocery store for a leg of venison."

I imagined a family of homesteaders, chopping wood and frying duck eggs in a cast iron skillet. In between thoughts of the homestead I focused on hairpin turns in the road as I steadily gained elevation, catching glimpses of an enormous mountain that dwarfed the one I was on. The base of the mountain was blanketed in light green, transitioning into a patchwork of orange, yellow, and red foliage higher up, and

## Clear Creek Homestead

then back into dark alpine green before giving way to a rocky summit.

One of the things that attracted me to George and Whitney's place was the piece in their farm description that read, "We live next to Mt. Mitchell, the tallest mountain east of the Mississippi." Clear Creek Homestead was perched on the mountain next door, so to speak.

Fall colors enveloped both sides of the well-paved mountain road. Instead of a patchwork of colors as I'd seen on the distant slopes of Mt. Mitchell, I drove through moments of pure red, then a stretch of beeswax-orange leaves, followed by a burst of lemon. The trees were like fireworks, beckoning me to take my eyes off the road. A dogwood explosion; then maple, oak, sassafras, and hickory. As my ears popped with the higher elevation, a soothing green returned to the scenery in the form of white pine, spruce, and other evergreens.

Periodically, I rolled my car windows down, listened to the rush of a river winding alongside the road, and let the cool mountain air blow against my face.

After eight hours on the highway, I felt greasy and sedentary inside the car. The mountain air caressed my face like a cool washcloth. In order to keep my hands warm and agile for the steering wheel, I took turns sitting on them, refusing to roll up the windows and deprive myself of the invigorating mountain air.

Motorcyclists, families, and retired couples drove down the mountain, sometimes in a string of 10-20 motorcycles, sometimes as a lone mini-van or sedan with a car-top carrier, usually with a license plate from New York, Ohio, or other points north. Vacationers parked along the road to snap photos of the river and eat sandwiches. Despite the cool weather, little kids ran around the roadside picnic tables in shorts and T-shirts, clearly delighted to be released from the cars for a few minutes.

Through holes in the colorful foliage, I saw what the tourists captured with their cameras: fallen leaves rafted swiftly along the river's current beneath a tunnel of flamboyant orange, yellow, and red leaves.

The first locals I saw were huddled around pick-up trucks in the parking lots of rundown gas stations. These were the hunters of the Blue Ridge Mountains, dressed in bright orange camouflage from head to toe. Many of the gas stations sold no gas and appeared to serve only as a meeting point for the men.

All the hunters were chewing on something – whether tobacco, fresh jerky from one of their kills, or a stick of gum, I couldn't say. As I drove past, the chewing slowed and they stared at me with expressionless eyes. I was another Yankee coming to view their scenic mountains. Little did they know, my real intention was to shovel manure, pull weeds, and dig potatoes out of the ground. Clear Creek Homestead, a mountainside farm, was my destination for October.

## Clear Creek Homestead

Moments after I took the last turn shown on my map, I drove slowly alongside a large garden neatly organized into quadrants: three for crops and one for the chickens. No address was posted, but this had to be the right place. A peace sign was nailed to the chicken coop, and a threesome of ducks waddled across the dead-end road. The sight of a tepee standing next to the garden erased all doubt that I'd found my destination.

I parked my car on a grassy landing by the creek and immediately got out to examine my new home. Inside the tepee, I found two pieces of furniture – a flat bedrock about two feet thick, and a wooden sleeping platform raised a few inches off the earthen floor. Later in the month, I learned that George, with the help of a previous wwoofer, dragged the several hundred pound bedrock into place and built the canvas tepee around it. Initially, there was no wooden platform. George thought his wwoofers would *prefer* to sleep on the slab of rock. "It's nice and cool on hot summer nights," he said. During the month I was on Clear Creek Homestead, the bedrock felt more like a slab of ice, especially during the two nights when snow

## Clear Creek Homestead

blew around the tepee and accumulated on the wooden poles that joined to form the tepee's open-air crown.

    Given the cold mountain conditions, I opted for the wooden platform. I spread out a large quilt and unrolled an Army sleeping bag stuffed with down feathers. I'd inherited the sleeping bag from my uncle in Colorado, who'd spent cold nights working search and rescue in the Rocky Mountains. As for the bedrock, I used it as my dresser, spreading out my clothes and books atop the smooth surface. On one end of the bedrock, I positioned my only piece of decoration--a piece of red bark shaped like the state of Tennessee. I found it on a hike back in Maine.

    After unpacking, I strolled up to George and Whitney's house. The grassy path meandered in switch-back fashion, gaining elevation slowly rather than in one steep shot. The path was wide enough for a truck, as evidenced by faint tire tracks worn into the grass, but it was primarily used for foot-traffic. Much as people leave their shoes at the front door, George and Whitney left their truck and small Volkswagen car down by the road, near the garden and chicken coop.

    About halfway along the ten minute hike, I passed a blueberry patch containing nearly 100 chest-high blueberry plants. Clear Creek Homestead wasn't a for-profit enterprise, so initially I wondered: *Why so many blueberries? Surely a small family could get by on 20-30 plants.* Whitney later admitted she and George got a bit carried away with the patch and were in the process selling some of the blueberry plants to their friends. "We've been making *a lot* of blueberry jam," she told me.

    Uphill from the blueberry patch, I passed six beehives, each painted white like a chest of drawers. A cloud of bees hovered around the entry of each hive. Apparently the honeybees were still scoring nectar from autumn flowers hidden away in the forest, for I didn't see any blooms out in the open, nor in the garden, which was down to a few heads of cabbage, some kale, and several rows of potatoes. The blueberry plants remained full of leaves, but were long past bearing fruit.

The final stretch of the walking path led through a section of forest. After dodging poison ivy on both sides of the trail, I soon came upon a perfectly round house surrounded by many signs of life. A chopping block outside the woodshed sat amid several inches of wood-splinters, bark, and sawdust. The blade of an axe was sunk into a tree-stump. Next to the house stood a massive apple tree with a long grabber pole, used for retrieving apples. Two men stood near an array of solar panels, chatting about voltage and battery capacity.

I expected an older couple when I imagined the homesteaders George and Whitney – perhaps a bearded man with a sturdy wife. Instead, I was greeted by a slender, clean-shaven man who had a strong South Carolina accent. George and Whitney were no more than a few years older than me, both in their mid 30s. Adalaya, their lovely and well-mannered daughter, was nine years old.

My arrival at Clear Creek homestead coincided with a solar-home tour George and Whitney were part of. Aside from a nearby intentional community called Celo, they were the only people in the neighborhood with solar panels. George and Whitney's nearest neighbor, a few hundred yards down the creek, had a white horse grazing in the front yard – essentially a solar-powered lawnmower, but with the exception of the horse, that neighbor's house was similar to all of the others in the area – square and connected to the power grid.

George stood next to the solar panels with Whitney's father, who was visiting from across the state. George immediately recognized me as the new wwoofer and greeted me with a big smile. Whitney's father gave me a firm handshake and nodded toward George. "Watch out for him. He's an ornery one."

Apparently George had a wild past. During his Siddhartha Phase, as he called it, he reduced his personal belongings to a backpack and traveled around the country. Then he went through a rock and roll phase, growing his hair down to his waist and playing as a drummer in a local rock band. George

> Clear Creek Homestead

still played gigs with the band, but since Whitney and Adalaya entered his life, he'd shifted gears yet again. He was now a family man and fulltime homesteader.

He was also a talented carpenter, as my first tour of the roundhouse showed. George and Whitney had gone through a progression of accommodations since they moved onto Clear Creek Homestead, which was originally nothing but trees. First they lived in tents, then graduated to a simple yurt. Their most recent upgrade a few years earlier was the roundhouse, which George had constructed, using clay and straw for cement and wooden boards for the frame of the house.

When George led me into the roundhouse, I was stunned by its beauty. A circle of windows wrapped around the dome shaped ceiling gave me the feeling I'd stepped into a cozy spaceship. The kitchen, living room, and bedroom were all one room. Although completely open, each space seemed to have invisible walls. When I sat at the ground-level kitchen table and had dinner with the family, I wasn't aware of the king-sized bed just a few feet away. When I sat on the couch and played mancala with Adalaya or George, I was only aware of the kitchen when the aroma of sautéed onion and garlic wafted my way.

A wood-fired Amish stove heated the entire house quickly and efficiently, and the space never seemed cramped. A hammock was strung up next to bay windows looking out onto the woodshed and apple tree. A ladder led downstairs to Adalaya's bedroom, a bathroom, and a root cellar where George and Whitney stored cabbage, potatoes, carrots, beets, blueberry jam, canned tomatoes, honey, and a chest freezer full of venison.

Solar panels, wood, and underground water pipes that picked up geo-thermal heat, provided all of the electric and hot-water needs for George, Whitney, and Adalaya.

The three of them had carved an oasis of sustainable living in the Blue Ridge Mountains. The forest behind their roundhouse, which grew on the face of an east-facing ridge, supplied all the wood they would ever need, and a well pumped an ample supply of clean water from the ground.

I was a bit dreamy-eyed by the self-sufficiency George and Whitney crafted for their family. They had the ultimate security – food, plus energy independence. One evening as I shared a meal with the family, consisting of mashed butternut squash, sautéed kale and garlic, and deer burgers, while logs crackled in the wood-fired stove and the solar-powered lamp lit up the spacious one-room house George had built by hand, I said, "George, you're in good shape if we have another Great Depression."

He nodded, but with some reservation. Apparently I'd missed one thing. George said if a doomsday scenario ever did unfold, he would need a small army to protect his land. In fact, George's brother had already volunteered to help defend the place. Clear Creek Homestead was far from civilization, but the local mountain was teeming with skilled hunters. The gun-toting men I'd seen hanging out in front of rundown gas stations were presently hunting deer, but who could say what they'd do with their guns if things fell apart.

## Deer

Deer hunting was a popular sport in the mountains of North Carolina. My arrival at Clear Creak Homestead coincided with black-powder season, the time when nostalgic hunters get out their one-shot muzzleloader guns and take to the woods like old-time confederates. If I'd arrived one week earlier, I would have been in the truly old-fashioned bow and arrow season. Two weeks later it would be anything-goes-season: rifles, cannons, poison-tipped darts.

The mountain folk ate their way through the ample deer population. Even George, the self-described "hippie" and peaceful man, was a hunter and filled his chest freezer with meat from the local fauna. To George, this was a responsible choice. If he was going to eat meat, he wanted to participate in the whole cycle, from slaughter to butchering, to cooking.

> Clear Creek Homestead

Even the tepee I slept in was connected to the hunting culture. George received the 20-foot tall Plains Indian home in exchange for a flintlock muzzleloader. Many nights while I slept in the white canvas tepee, I awoke to the thump of deer hooves as the gentle animals congregated around a nearby apple tree. At first I was scared, thinking this nocturnal visitation was the black coyote George claimed was eating his ducks. I glanced at the flap of canvas that served as my door and slid a baseball-sized rock close to my sleeping bag for protection. My fear dissolved when I discovered a family of deer snacking on apples.

The deer had every reason to be afraid, because for them, the local forest was home to a serious predator named Randy – George's friend and a welcome hunting guest on Clear Creek Homestead.

## Slippery Red Flesh

I didn't kill the animal, I just helped turn it into hamburger. One night after dinner in the roundhouse, Randy showed up with a present. For the privilege of hunting on George and Whitney's property, Randy brought us part of his kill in a heavy-duty black garbage bag that contained a leg, shoulder, and part of the deer's spinal column. George looked at me with a grin and said, "It's time you learned how to make hamburger."

"That's alright," I told him. "I'm just going to head down to the tepee and do some reading."

After George prodded and insisted this was an "essential wwoofer experience," I gave in and tried my hand as a butcher.

The deer flesh wasn't dirty. In fact, it was probably the cleanest meat I'd ever handled, but it was off-putting in the kind of way that one fears sticking their hand into a bucket of worms or writhing eels for the first time.

From the black garbage bag, I grabbed a piece of slippery red flesh, still warm from the deer's body. I half-expected the leg muscle to twitch and run off as I cut strips of the slick membrane-encased flesh from the bone. *I'm becoming closer to my food, just like I wanted,* I reminded myself as I suppressed my gag reflex.

After George and I filled a large ceramic bowl with strips of raw meat, we ground it in the hamburger machine – a hand-cranked device from Germany called the *fleisch hacker.* Underneath the German name was an English alternative--the *porkerator.* Regardless of the name, the fleisch hacker served one purpose: turning raw animal flesh into hamburger.

I turned the hand-crank and fed deer strips into a metallic whirlpool that pulled the flesh in like a meaty screw. The meat was forced through several small holes and oozed out with a slurping sound. The deer exited the fleisch hacker as several undulating worms of flesh. And there it was: hamburger.

I was amazed at how quickly we transformed the deer. Earlier that evening, the gentle creature had padded around the forest, eating apples and leaves. A few hours later, it was being fed into a hamburger machine. The following night, George served the skillet-fried deer with a side of mashed potatoes. I ate the meal with much respect, having a stronger awareness of the transfer of life involved, and also the determination to never make hamburger again.

## Sweet Potato Row

Whitney schooled me on a much nicer food preparation involving cabbage rather than raw animal flesh. She taught me how to make sauerkraut. We cut the cabbage up, pounded it with salt until the cabbage cells ruptured their juice, and then packed the kraut tightly into a glass mason jar to ferment for a few days. The result was the best tasting sauerkraut I'd ever eaten. The cabbage still retained some of its vegetable crispness and lacked the puckering sourness of commercial varieties.

Whitney also taught me how to make granola and eggrolls. She and George were the nicest, most patient farm hosts I had encountered. Clear Creek Homestead was a middle ground between the long days on Hector's Farm and the vacation-like schedule on Applesauce Hill. I worked 25 hours a week at a variety of chores. The thing I enjoyed most about George and Whitney was their grateful attitude after I did something as simple as pull weeds or clean their chicken coop. When it came time to do a more skill-oriented job, one of them always worked alongside me until I had the hang of it. When I pruned raspberry canes, George showed me how to fan the canes out like slender fingers to improve air circulation.

When we chopped firewood, George showed me how to root my feet to the ground and avoid knots in the wood. Strenuous chores, ones that turned my calories into clear results, gave me the most satisfaction. I enjoyed leaning on the shovel after I turned a flattened piece of chicken yard into neat rows of raised garden beds. Oddly enough, shoveling manure gave me the most satisfaction. The day George pulled up to the homestead with a pick-up truck full of horse manure, I felt I was engaged in *real* farm work.

I shoveled the steaming pile of horse manure on a cool October morning, and the powerful scent of composted hay and oats hit my face with a warmth and eye-opening sharpness that felt almost refreshing. In terms of waking me up, the fresh manure was far better than a cup of coffee. *Now I'm farming!* I thought. I shoveled scoops of it into a wheelbarrow and spread it over the entire garden, with George's help.

I had the same *now I'm farming!* sensation when I cast handfuls of seeds over the garden to plant a cover crop of winter wheat and Austrian peas. Never had I literally sown the seeds of new plant-life.

I knew I was farming when I developed deposits of dirt in my fingerprint grooves. My soiled fingertips and the dirt caked beneath my fingernails were a constant source of attention in the shower.

Of course I received great rewards for all of the hard, dirty work. The biggest reward was living a slow, peaceful life; one where I could work, meditate, and hike at my leisure. I also enjoyed edible rewards, as I frequently visited the five apple trees and snapped off a snack.

I picked fresh tomatoes, potatoes, and kale, and had raspberry, strawberry, and blueberry jam for breakfast. For lunch, I usually fried a couple of duck or chicken eggs to go along with mashed sweet potatoes and kale sautéed in garlic and butter. For dessert, if I didn't feel like an apple, I foraged for red raspberries and wild grapes. With the exception of butter, oats, and salt, most of the food I ate came from the land I slept on.

Other rewards on Clear Creek Homestead were chance encounters with furry animals that inhabited the garden. One day, while digging sweet potatoes out of the ground with George, we uncovered a family of voles. The first vole must've thought her home was collapsing. I grabbed the end of a large sweet potato and pried it from the earth. Simultaneously, a furry black animal the size of my thumb, jumped out from underneath a bed of leaves and took off at a full sprint. A runaway vole! George and I decided it was the mother vole, because a little farther down the row, we uncovered five unattended babies, wriggling and blind, with squinted eyes. The marble-sized babies squeaked high-pitched cries, but Mom didn't come to their rescue. She had abandoned ship.

I thought the voles were wonderful little creatures, but I had the feeling George felt differently. I didn't have to read his mind to know how he felt about the gnaw-marks on nearly every single sweet potato. To George, the voles rendered a portion of his family's winter food unfit for storage, turned into compost material. I saw the way George looked at the little nest of babies without a hint of affection. To him, the squirming babies were next year's bandits.

Lucky for those voles, I was there to express my joy and urge George to take the peaceful route. George scooped them up, all five easily fitting into the palm of his hand, and relocated them in the direction their mom had fled.

The voles' lives were spared, yet I knew tough times had come upon the sweet potato row. The voles' *entire* food store had been dug up. Their home destroyed. Families dislocated. Talk about a Great Depression.

## Pulling the Oxcart

Farmers always seem to be moving dirt around, and George was no exception. One day he recruited me to help him move a large pile of dirt to the top of a hill. The job sounded easy enough, but the hill was steep. George, always the handyman, had a special piece of equipment for the job – an oxcart. And since no oxen lived on the homestead, George had designed the yoke especially for the shoulders of a human. More specifically *my* shoulders.

I felt a sense of humility as I wrapped my arms over the wooden frame of the yoke. I couldn't help thinking I'd taken a serious step backward in my personal evolution. First I was a student, then a teacher, and now I would perform the duties of an ox.

With George pushing the cart, I ran up the hill at full speed. George, always with a sense of humor, hollered at me from behind, "Yah mule! Yah!" The wheels of the oxcart squealed during the initial burst of speed, but as I approached the top, my neck strained forward and my legs slowed to a steady, shoe-bending climb. I felt like a true beast of burden. The pile of dirt doubled in weight until, right before the ground leveled out, I felt like the load was going to drag me and the yoke back down the hill and steamroll George.

Pulling the oxcart was a chore that made me feel I'd put my energy to good use. I was an egg and mashed potato powered machine, moving dirt from one place to another like a true farmhand.

## Sugar Water for the Bees

Beekeeping was another new job for me on Clear Creek Homestead. The bees didn't require much care, since they had all the resources they needed with the plentiful Blue Ridge Mountain wildflowers. Bees were probably the only animals on the farm that could completely feed themselves. They didn't depend on humans like chickens did. We depended on them. Most of George and Whitney's bees involuntarily donated their mountain honey. Therefore, in order to get the bees through the winter, George and I had to stock the hives with a supply of sugar water.

For this, I dressed in a beekeeper's suit, complete with a screened helmet, arm-length gloves, and a baggy white jumpsuit that sealed off every entry to my body. George walked next to me in a t-shirt and jeans, wearing nothing more than a helmet. "Getting stung is part of the fun," he said.

George told me he'd been stung countless times. He was used to it, and I guess a sting was a small price to pay for robbing the bees after all their hard work. I still had a healthy amount of fear, going back to childhood and the time I had stuffed a half-dead yellow jacket into my pocket to show my mom. The memory was twenty years old, but the sensation of being stung repeatedly in the leg stayed with me. Besides, we were invading the bees' home.

Before we opened the five box-shaped hives, which were nothing more than stacks of 6-inch chambers housing individual frames of honeycomb, George dropped smoldering pine needles into his smoker. The smoker resembled an oilcan connected to a cloth-encased gas pedal. George pressed on the pedal with his hand and a stream of smoke poured from the spout and filled the hive. The smoke was intended to calm the bees so they'd be less inclined to sting us. From one of the hives, a mouse ran out. Apparently, he'd taken up residence in the honey den.

Each of the hives had a divider, called the excluder, to keep the queen separate from the honeycomb frames. The excluder's purpose was to keep the honeycomb frames, which only the workers had access to, in pure honey, so when George and Whitney harvested the honey, the honey jars would be free of bee larvae.

Giving the bees their winter supply of sugar water didn't

take long. With George's help, I disassembled the hives and slowly lowered a jar of sugar water into each one. Even though I was completely sealed off, sweating within my biohazard suit, I felt if I moved with exaggerated slowness the bees would be okay with me invading their space.

Neither George nor I got stung, thankfully. However, the bees clearly got the lousy end of the deal. Clear Creek Homestead provided nectar in the form of apple blossoms and the entire array of flowering berries and vegetables that George and Whitney planted, but the bees were royally screwed with the winter tradeoff. They got refined sugar dissolved in a jar of well water in exchange for the tremendous feat of retrieving nectar from millions of flowers and turning it into pools of viscous honey. Thanks, bees!

## Home Sweet Home

Gusts of wind blew the trees bare of red and yellow leaves. Each gust picked up another swirling ball of color and erased it from the landscape, and by the end of the month the ridge-side forest overlooking Clear Creek Homestead was stripped down to drab grey and brown branches. I left only one dash of new color in my wake. The cover crop I sowed earlier in the month had sprouted and covered the garden in a blanket of vibrant green.

The purpose of the cover crop, I discovered, *wasn't* to harvest peas and wheat the following spring. Peas and wheat were only chosen because they were winter hardy, and the wheat would serve as a green ladder for the peas to climb upon and pump nitrogen into the soil. In addition, cover crops held the soil in place so it didn't wash away in the winter rains. Weeds were outcompeted, and during the following spring, the winter wheat and peas died back and acted as a kind of green manure, nourishing the soil with fresh organic matter.

Cover cropping had a lot of benefits, but for me, it was all about aesthetics. The fresh shoots of green plant-life raised my morale and seemed to say *job well done* as I drove away and looked back at Clear Creek Homestead one last time.

George, Whitney, and Adalaya generated such a warm family atmosphere that I felt I was saying goodbye to my own relatives. From my car window, I saw the top of my tepee standing behind the peace sign adorned chicken coop.

Over the course of the month I'd come to think of the tepee as *my* tepee, my own home. After a day of work or hiking in the mountains I crawled back into my sleeping bag and switched on my battery-powered reading light. *Home Sweet Home*. On clear nights I built a fire outside my tepee and enjoyed the cool mountain air. I concentrated on the swirl of steam rising from my cup of tea and the splash of stars overhead, which appeared wavy through the fire heat. Ohio seemed distant in those moments. My roots had settled into new places.

Then, at the end of the month, it was time to uproot, go to seed, and disperse myself down the highway again. I hugged the family of homesteaders goodbye, packed my car with a pillowcase full of apples, and drove down from the mountains. I entered the forests of central Georgia, where autumn was starting all over again.

# Chapter 5
## *Salamander Springs*

**Spring Water**

The homestead Salamander Springs was named after a crystal clear pool of water that percolated up from the forest floor. Thumb-sized salamanders swam and lounged alongside the shaded pool. Whenever I crouched next to the spring to refill my water bottle, the tiny amphibians froze in their revelry and became invisible to the untrained eye.

I don't know the water's journey, but I imagined it filtered through hundreds of feet of porous rock in the earth's crust, becoming mineral water along the way.

I drank the naturally cool water as if it was on tap and infinitely available. The level never dropped in the spring. I ladled out 20 gallons of water and almost instantly a fresh upwelling took its place and continued to spill over into a tributary that fed the stream. I soaked my oats in the spring water and used it to prepare giant pots of sweet potato stew when it was my turn to cook for the other wwoofers of Salamander Springs.

Each day I made the ritual one-mile hike into the woods to refill empty water containers. Sometimes I carried only my own water bottle. At other times, when the group-supply ran low, I pushed a wheelbarrow over the bumpy trail as a

## Salamander Springs

large plastic jug and screw-top thermos knocked against one another.

The dense clay earth of central Georgia was dry and hard underfoot. Even underneath the low canopy of second-growth trees where a thin sprinkling of leaves covered the flat red terrain, I felt like I was walking on pavement. The 50-acre forest of Salamander Springs was still young. Many of the trees were no thicker than a telephone pole, each entwined by a tangle of vines that snaked around the slender trunks and hung from the topmost branches.

I knew the trail to the spring intimately, so by the end of the month I could maneuver the wheelbarrow with ease, even in the dim afternoon light. I knew where to duck under a low-hanging vine. I anticipated a major dip in the trail. And when I saw two particular trees hugging the trail closely on either side, like sentries guarding the pathway, I knew to watch for the exposed root that blocked the trail. I gripped the wooden handles and took the wheelbarrow on a detour around one of the trees.

Shortly after dodging the exposed root, I heard the rush of a stream, a soothing sound that grew softer as the November days passed without rain. This stream marked the deepest and oldest section of forest. The nearby forest floor was cushioned by a thick layer of leafy duff that masked the hardness of the earth and gave it some bounce. By the time I reached the stream my eyes had adjusted to the permanent shade in this part of the forest.

I crossed the wooden footbridge that spanned the stream and entered a green tunnel comprised of leafy vines trained overhead to form an arch. The green tunnel acted as a front door to the spring. And as soon as I left the tunnel I expected the spring to be waiting with a radiant glow, like a pot of gold. But usually it was invisible until I spotted the brass dipper hanging from a branch directly over the pool.

Below the dipper was the prize I'd come for-- a depression in the earth no bigger than a bathtub. Out of ritual, I took my first gulp of spring water straight from the brass dipper. Then I carefully went about ladling water into the containers.

My favorite part of retrieving spring water was the slowness of the process--- the hike into the woods and the mindfulness of pouring water into small-mouthed jugs. I always felt a sense of accomplishment after I made it back to the outdoor kitchen without spilling too much. I lifted the jugs onto the countertop and admired the 20 gallons of fresh spring water that would hydrate and give life to the crew of wwoofers.

During my first few days on the farm I saw the mineral-rich spring water as a luxury item, but after awhile I came to see it was as essential as the air we breathed. The only other source of drinking water on the homestead was well water, which had to be raised to the surface by a noisy gas-powered motor; not quite the romantic hike into the woods to the salamander's hangout.

Salamander Springs was completely off-grid. No water, electric, or telephone lines fed the homestead: only spring water, sunshine, and wwoofers of varying degrees of work ethic.

## Pre-Atlanta State

My arrival at Salamander Springs was a day of stark contrast – city versus country. I descended from the Blue Ridge Mountains and stopped in Atlanta to visit my brother's family.

The sudden change of scenery left me feeling out of place, especially after having lived in a tepee for a month. Colorful leaves were replaced by the green, yellow, and red of stoplights. Mountains turned into skyscrapers. In the Chicago-style pizzeria where I met my brother's family, we could hardly hold a conversation over the screaming television near our table.

After a month of living outdoors and tuning into the subtle sounds of deer hooves and the wind rustling against leaves, the manic soundtrack of commercials and sports commentators was truly abrasive. My two-year old niece, Bella, was clearly

## Salamander Springs

desensitized to the noise. I watched as she picked cheese off her pizza as though the TV wasn't even there.

I felt out of place with my bag of organic apples I'd picked from George and Whitney's tree that very day and brought along as a gift. Even the ice cubes floating in my water seemed wrong somehow. I enjoyed the few hours with my family, but I was ready to head back into the country.

Though only a few hours' drive from Atlanta, Salamander Springs seemed centuries apart. The homestead was in a pre-Atlanta state – slow-paced, unpaved, and disconnected, with not a single ice-cube anywhere on the property, except on cold mornings when a thin sheet of ice formed on the water bowls in the chicken coop.

The bumpy dirt driveway to Salamander Springs told me I was leaving modern civilization. After each bend in the driveway I expected to see the homestead, not realizing it lay all around me. The forest that walled in the driveway on both sides was Salamander Springs. Every few hundred yards I noticed signs that humans did in fact inhabit this place – a cabin set back in the woods, a fenced off garden, or a trailhead sign painted with a colorful salamander.

Twenty minutes after I drove past the mailbox, I arrived at the core meeting area of Salamander Springs – an outdoor kitchen and a fire pit. Beside the kitchen stood a one-room library filled with thousands of books, a bed, and a pot-bellied stove. This would be my new home for the month.

In all honesty, I felt a bit intimidated driving into the woods in the middle of the night. With previous farms, I stepped up to the front door, knocked, and introduced myself. At Salamander Springs, I came upon a roaring fire encircled by six strangers. I felt like an outsider, looking to gain acceptance with an established tribe.

Luckily, I had one trick in my bag – two gallons of cookie dough ice cream. I shook hands with the new wwoofers and got a hug from my new and incredibly sweet farm host, Debbie.

I didn't offer the ice cream so much as force it on them.

There was no freezer anywhere on the property, so when I saw someone scrape the bottom of their bowl I said, "Here, I think you need a little more," and passed the ice cream their way. I was instantly accepted.

"Initially, I thought this might be some kind of cult," I said, "especially after that long driveway."

Debbie, a youthful woman in her 50s, said, "The Parisian woman last summer thought the same thing." Apparently, the meaning of the phrase "off-grid homestead" got lost in translation. "The woman was petrified," Debbie said. "She didn't know what to make of the outdoor kitchen, the fire pit, and the outhouse." When the woman from Paris realized she'd be living without electricity and running water, she had Debbie drive her back to the airport the following morning.

I knew my fate would be different. I approached Salamander Springs with a good idea of what I was getting into: a personal experiment of living off-grid, without the normal comforts of electricity and running water. I knew I would find other comforts in such a lifestyle – peace, quiet, and a new appreciation for the conveniences I'd once taken for granted.

As everyone contentedly shoveled spoonfuls of the quickly melting ice cream into their mouths, our faces reddened with warmth from the fire, I sized up my new wwoofing companions.

A strongly built man from Texas traveled with a squirrel-sized dog named Junebug. Tired of his nine-to-five as a masseuse, the Texan left his career to travel around the country for awhile. Debbie enthusiastically described all the carpentry projects he'd completed for her, including a footbridge, a new door for the chicken coop, and a deer fence.

A young couple from Pennsylvania wanted to learn the ways of homesteading. They were in the process of building a dome-shaped cob oven that could be used to bake bread and pizza. A hitchhiker from Austin didn't know what he wanted. He told me he planned on writing poetry and selling his poems for a dollar apiece on the street. If that didn't pan out, he wanted

Salamander Springs

to be a full-time street-musician. The clear theme for him was *life on the street*. Sitting next to the drifter was a young hippie chick who just wanted a place to enjoy the outdoors with her grungy dog.

After we polished off the ice cream, the hippie chick dropped the flame of a lighter into her glass bowl and drew in some smoke. One of the Pennsylvania homesteaders handed me a glass of water and said, "Here you go; this is the good stuff."

I took my first drink of the famous Salamander Spring Water. The water didn't taste all that special, just free of chlorine and any off-flavors. Free of everything but clean liquid water. Later in the month, after I made the trek into the woods and used the brass dipper to ladle water directly from the spring, I came to the same conclusion. This was the best water I'd ever had.

## Debbie's Dream

During my month on Salamander Springs, I witnessed a continual rotation of wwoofers. A young man from Israel arrived during my last week on the homestead, fleeing the turmoil of his home country. He would end up staying long-term, eventually purchasing forestland for his own homestead, which merged with Salamander Springs.

I worked alongside a young woman from England, a dropout college student on his way to work at Disney World, and a pair of 19-year old lovebirds who couldn't keep their hands off each other.

Each unique personality at Salamander Springs found a matching job. The Pennsylvania homesteaders built the cob oven, using bricks and a natural cement material made from a paste of straw, mud and sand. The Texan spent most of his work-time sawing and nailing boards together for doors, bridges, and shelves. The young lovebirds painted murals in the bedrooms. I cleared hiking trails and worked in the garden. And the aspiring street-musician drank beer and quoted Bob Dylan.

We were an eclectic crew engaged in a wide variety of

jobs, yet we all had a common goal: to move Debbie's dream forward.

Debbie was one of the rare flower children who came out of the 1960's with her dreams and her mind still intact. After the drugs wore off, she still wanted to live on the land, and she set about doing just that, with money saved from teaching high school English for 20 years.

In the mid 90's, Debbie bought a 50-acre piece of deforested land – the blank canvas for the Salamander Springs of today. She dreamed of turning the land into a sustainable-living learning center, a place for people to experience growing their own food and living off-grid: a place for people to live sustainable, fulfilling, happy lives.

With help from hundreds of wwoofers and many years of redirecting her teacher's salary into resources for the homestead, Debbie's dream quickly turned into reality. By the time I arrived at Salamander Springs, the place was already a hotspot for eager young homesteaders, and a popular destination for environmental and sustainability students from the Georgia College in Milledgeville.

In addition, Salamander Springs was re-inhabited by its original residents – plants and creatures of the forest. The trees had regrown to a point where one could easily get lost hiking the spider web of trails that criss-crossed the property. Well-beaten trails led from the spring and garden to the central meeting area with an outdoor kitchen and fire pit. Less-defined, narrower trails led deep into the old growth forest that lined the stream, and snaked through gently rolling forest. On one occasion, I got lost hiking on the perimeter trail and I came out in some native Georgian's backyard, which contained ten junkyard cars, a fully grown pig tied to a stake, and five chickens running wild. After several hours of backtracking, I finally followed the rooster's call back to the outdoor kitchen.

Ironically, much of the work I engaged in at Salamander Springs involved taking *back* acreage from the forest to create a larger garden, since a sustainable food source was essential for a homestead.

In Debbie's own words, her dream is "to educate as many young people as possible about living on the land, living sustainably, living in community, living meaningfully, living aware of nature, growing your food, developing meaningful relationships, enjoying life, inspiring others and being inspired by others, living, living, living, making every moment count, teaching and learning and being real with no B.S."

Debbie was as real as they come. She walked what she talked. She didn't just dream. She acted on her dream. She lived by the words of Gandhi engraved on a plaque hanging in the outdoor kitchen. "Be the change you wish to see in the World."

## Boot-Sucking Muck

Debbie's dream was noble, but it would take many hours of grunt work to transform Salamander Springs into a fertile and sustainable homestead. Most of my work on Salamander Springs involved breaking new ground for the garden and filling buckets of muck from a creek bed. A pickaxe and a shovel were my two primary tools for advancing Debbie's dream.

Mucking was the first major task for which all the wwoofers put aside their individual projects. Those who were painting, building a cob-oven, clearing trails, making love, or drinking joined together to shovel hundreds of pounds of leafy sludge from the bottom of the creek. Our mission was to transport the muck to the garden and infuse the hard Georgia clay with a good helping of organic matter. But before we could harvest the muck, we had to empty the creek.

During the muggy summertime heat, the creek was a natural swimming pool behind the concrete dam Debbie erected. So, in order to get to the precious muck, we first had to open the dam and drain the swimming pool. To achieve this, one of the homesteaders-in-training from Pennsylvania fearlessly peeled off his shirt and dove head first into the cold, murky water to find the plug. He came to the surface with the plug in hand, but apparently leaves had clogged the pipe, so he swam back down with a bamboo pole and jabbed the clump of leaves through to the other side.

Within minutes, the 15-foot deep swimming pool eddied its way downstream, leaving behind a knee-deep layer of muck. The muck, essentially decayed fish, crawdads, and copepods mixed in a sludge of fermented plant matter, released a foul smell of rotten-eggs when my boots slurped into the goo and liberated pockets of gas.

Of the many varieties of muck on this planet – manure, factory sludge, and lake sediment – the muck of Salamander Springs is best described as boot-sucking muck. On more than one occasion, as I tried to lift my foot against the quick-sand strength smoothie of decaying matter, it sucked the rubber boot right off my foot. Then I performed a delicate balancing act while carefully lowering my bare foot back into the boot.

The system of moving muck went like this: Someone stood on the concrete dam spanning the creek and used a rope to lower an empty bucket down to the muck-shovelers below. The shovelers filled the bucket and waited for the next round.

At first everyone wanted to be a bucket-operator, because this meant they didn't have to stand in the black goo. But after a few strenuous rounds of gripping the rope hand under hand while the heavy bucket swung like a pendulum, scraping against the concrete dam, everyone wanted to join the hard-working Texan down in the mud-pit.

As a bucket-operator I had the first major accident I'd experienced since being trapped under a tractor tire back at Hector's Farm.

Lifting the heavy, muck-filled bucket was like raising a bucket of molten lead. Even when the 5-gallon bucket was half-full I felt the muscles in my neck and face contract. The rope bit into my palms.

The fatigue came not just from raising the buckets, but from carrying them from the dam to a clearing in the woods. The

## Salamander Springs

wet muck was too heavy to haul directly to the garden, so we up-ended the buckets in a sunny clearing where it would dry for a few days. The hundreds of emptied loads looked like black, half-melted sandcastles along the creek bank.

The accident happened just after my bucket was filled by one of the shirtless muck-shovelers, fifteen feet below. The Texan reached for his beer and said, "You're all set," meaning I could raise it.

Just as I gripped the rope and put my body into the initial heave-ho, flexing every muscle in my back and chest at full force, the rope snapped. The instant the bucket broke free, I fell straight back, toward the rocky creek bed on the other side, which ran with no more than a trickle of water.

I'm still not sure exactly how I came out unscratched. All I remember is the slow-motion sensation people describe in life or death situations. With both feet in the air and my body parallel to the ground, like I was reclining in a lawn chair, I watched the tread of my boot scrape down the vertical wall. I twisted by body around and somehow managed to push off of a jagged rock and land shoulder first with a small splash. After such a long fall, the incredibly small splash seemed almost like a joke.

The muck-shovelers ran around the dam to see if I survived. The Texan was shocked that I wasn't injured, and for the rest of the day, he told everyone how "Brian almost died today," chalking it up to some kind of miracle.

I don't think it was a miracle, but I did get lucky. The fish that swam upstream from the dam, however, weren't as lucky as I. After the muck was shoveled clear of all the dam's drainage pipes, the upstream part of the creek ran dry for a hundred feet or so, and in it's wake hundreds of fish flopped around on the creek-bed.

My first reaction was, *what a tragedy*. We had unintentionally pulled the life support out from under the fish. They flopped around, suffocating, with nowhere to swim. With help from Debbie's daughter, the two of us cleaned out some mucking buckets and relocated as many fish as we could to deeper waters. The big fish we kept for dinner, making it the easiest fishing any of us had ever done.

That night we had a fish fry over the open the fire, and the man from Texas made sure everyone knew: "Brian almost died today."

In a way, I think I needed to hear that. His words reminded me of how fragile life is, how quickly things can change. I think it was a sign to be more careful, more alert, and more in the moment.

## The Wheelbarrow Machine

After the muck dried, we reached phase two of the operation – spreading it on the garden. During one of my 60 or 70 round trips with a hundred pound load of muck in my wheelbarrow, it hit me that farm work is far superior to the exercise routines people pay for at gyms.

With the wooden handles of the wheelbarrow in my hands, I was walking on a treadmill with a set of dumbbells. My mind stayed active, alert for bumps in the path. Sunshine soaked into my skin, generating Vitamin D and a good tan. And most of all, I knew that the exercise produced valuable results other than sculpting my body.

Instead of watching a series of electronic red dots travel around the loop on the treadmill screen, I watched the garden fill up with hundreds of pounds of organic matter, good quality muck I almost died extracting from the creek bed. I knew the rich soil would feed Debbie and future wwoofers, students of sustainability. Instead of paying for a monthly pass to a television-filled gym, I improved my physical health, all the while investing in the sweet potatoes and okra and watermelon that would one day grow from that muck-enriched soil.

## Breaking New Ground

The garden of Salamander Springs was in its infancy. If I tossed a handful of seeds onto the ground, none of them would germinate. The seeds would lie on a hardpan of red clay and bake in the sun.

A team of wwoofers created the one-acre garden plot the previous year when they came through with chainsaws, cleared away a tract of second-growth forest, and erected an eight-foot high deer fence around the whole area.

We now faced the task of removing roots and stumps that remained from the forest-clearing. Unlike the pesky roots of weeds, the trees had spent fifteen years growing like pythons through the hardened clay earth, traveling deep in search of water. In order to remove such a root, I had to dig around the root to expose it, and then chop it out with an axe. Sometimes I bear-hugged the root and physically wrestled it out of the ground.

The process of removing tree roots gave new meaning to the terms "breaking new ground" and "getting to the root of the problem."

Rich fluffy soil had to be transformed from the concrete-like earth, much like a pepper mill turns peppercorn into ground pepper. After the wwoofers and I removed stumps, we turned our attention to the soil itself. We dug deep into the clay, turned it over, and broke up clods of earth with our hoes and the backs of shovels. We pulverized the compacted soil into a pile of crumbs, so when seeds did germinate, their roots had a loose medium for growth.

After several days of extracting roots and turning the hard earth into well-defined garden beds, the next step was to amend the soil. Amendments are anything that improve the soil, ranging from high-powered fertilizer like bat guano and fish emulsions, to expensive additives like worm compost and mycorrhizal fungus. At Salamander Springs the key word was *sustainable*. In other words "local and renewable." We didn't have a farmer's market or CSA revenue source. Every bit of food and shelter on the property was for the people of Salamander Springs. By the people and for the people. Therefore, we used soil amendments we had on hand – chicken manure direct from the lovely chickens next door to the outdoor kitchen, plus all of the muck we could move from the creek.

Chicken manure, muck, and bedding from the chicken coop added a good deal of nitrogen and coarse material to improve the structural quality of the soil, so the garden wouldn't revert right back to a crust of hardened clay after a summer of baking in the Georgia sun.

Through the combined efforts of me and the other wwoofers, I watched with satisfaction as we transformed the garden from a piece of stumpy, weed-covered land into rows of mounded garden beds, enriched with all of the organic goodness the creek and chickens could offer.

I wouldn't be around to enjoy the watermelon, tomatoes, and okra that would soon grow from the garden space, but the joy on Debbie's face when she stepped into the garden after a day of teaching and saw a layer of muck spread over the whole thing was my reward.

Besides, every sweet potato, pickle and spoonful of jam I ate on Salamander Springs resulted from someone else's hard work. With each root I wrestled from the ground and each wheelbarrow of muck I hauled to the garden, I improved the homestead for next year's wwoofers, and benefited from those who came through before me. Food was our link. Through food, I forged a positive relationship with people I would never meet. I ate from the past and grew for the future.

## Quail Eggs

Chickens were the only food source I had a direct relationship with on the homestead. Sometimes I ate my fried eggs directly in front of the chicken coop and tuned into what was essentially *Chicken TV.*

I enjoyed watching the interplay between roosters and hens, which basically went like this: the roosters obsessed over the hens and the hens completely ignored the roosters. As I bit into my egg sandwich, I watched the alpha rooster crow. Immediately, another smaller rooster tilted his head, as if to

## Salamander Springs

say in a quizzical way, "Are you talking to me?" The smaller rooster thrust out his chest and gave a less impressive crow.

This game of one-upmanship went back and forth as I ate my sandwich. All the while, the hens pecked and scratched for food as though the roosters didn't exist. Only when a rooster forced himself on a hen and pinned her to the ground in the typical display of rough chicken sex, did a hen give any notice. She got back on her feet, ruffled her feathers a bit, and then went right back to foraging for grubs and snipping off greens from the weed pile. Another good episode of *Chicken TV*.

Each morning I fed the chickens and gave them fresh water and weeds I picked from the garden. As soon as I tossed a clump of weeds in the coop, the chickens flocked to the pile, clucking with excitement.

In exchange for the minimal work of caring for the chickens, the other wwoofers and I had access to a supply of fresh eggs with golden yolks from the free-range diet of greens, grains, and grubs.

Chickens weren't the only egg-laying birds on the homestead. I also sampled quail eggs for the first time. About halfway through the month, a wwoofer picked up a litter of live quail from a University research lab in Macon, Georgia.

At first, I tried the eggs over easy. I carefully cracked the brown-speckled shell against the rim of a skillet and tried to flip the nickel-sized egg with the corner of the flipper. When I discovered it took ten or so of the eggs to cover a slice of toast, I realized how silly this was, and I resorted to cracking the eggs straight into my bowl of hot oatmeal, adding a touch of quail creaminess to my breakfast.

Like their eggs, the quail were tiny birds, no bigger than a common songbird and just as ill-equipped to handle the cool winter nights in Georgia. Sadly, the quail-population crashed and burned. Within a week, we found every last quail dead in their outdoor enclosure.

I'm not so sure if the cool nights killed the quail, or it was the sudden shift of environment. I think the birds endured an unhealthy shock when taken from the cozy climate-controlled environment of a university laboratory and thrust into an off-grid situation, with fluctuating weather and no heat lamp to keep them warm.

## Four Elements

To a small degree, I empathized with the quail. I didn't face a life or death situation like those poor little birds, but I did experience a sudden shift in my own environment. The absence of electricity and running water was the biggest change.

For the first time of my life, the four elements of earth, water, fire, and air became part of my daily survival. No longer could I rely on flipping a switch or turning a knob to transform electricity into heat and light. I couldn't turn the faucet to draw a warm shower or fill cooking pots from the seemingly bottomless reservoir outside my hometown. In civilization, even the earth was hidden with pavement and sidewalks, lost under carpet and wooden floors.

At Salamander Springs, I experienced the four elements in their raw form. Air was air, untainted by the smell of cars and tire factories. Earth was earth, naked except for a thin veil of leaves and sticks. Fire danced on burning logs every morning and night, as I cooked food and warmed my hands over the flames. Water came the spring or creek, and if it rained we caught the raindrops in 50 gallon catchment barrels.

Fire and water were the two elements I had to work for. They were not given. They had to be earned. A plaque hanging from the entrance of the outdoor kitchen described the essential work on Salamander Springs: "Before enlightenment, chop wood, carry water. After enlightenment, chop wood, carry water."

I was constantly on the lookout for sticks. En route from the garden or spring or while on a hike to the stream, I combed the forest floor for twigs and dry branches. Firewood was a commodity far more valuable than paper currency. Fire was the center of my life on Salamander Springs, not only for

# Salamander Springs

cooking but also for the comfort it offered.

Instead of watching television at night, I watched a fire. The red-hot dance of wind and flames lulled me into a peaceful trance as the other wwoofers drank beer, smoked pipes, and played their guitars.

I became so intimate with the fire-centered life, that during my second week on the homestead I began thinking about my food in terms of how many sticks it would take to heat up. A big pot of rice needed several medium sized logs. If I wanted a bowl of hot oatmeal in the morning, I only needed a handful of twigs. I discovered I could save a few sticks if I squatted upwind of the little fire and positioned my pot just right, so the flames licked the bottom.

Cooking over a fire was far more rewarding than my old method of punching buttons on a microwave. As the steam curled from my spoonful of oatmeal, I knew I'd earned that warmth.

## Water Conservation

A finite water supply was another new concept for me. At the corner of every sloping roof on the property stood a 50-gallon rain catchment barrel, positioned to catch rainwater streaming from the gutters. Water conservation was a big issue on Salamander Springs, because central Georgia stayed dry for long stretches of the year.

Therefore, we stretched our water supply. We used water from the rain barrels to wash our dishes. Usually, I ended up washing my dishes in cold, brownish water, since it was a hassle to start a fire solely to heat dishwater. The dish sink contained no drainage pipe. The dirty dishwater emptied straight into yet another catchment bucket and became grey water, used to water plants. We didn't waste a drop.

In the garden, we dug swales next to the garden beds so when the dry summer arrived we'd have low-lying wet trenches to plant in.

Of course, without electricity and modern plumbing,

## Salamander Springs

going to the bathroom was a matter of sitting over a hole in the earth and tossing a scoop of sawdust over each deposit of human manure or "humanure" as it's called. Luckily, previous wwoofers had made the experience more comfortable by building enclosed outhouses, basically freestanding wooden closets we could move from site to site. When one hole filled, we simply dug a new hole for the next bathroom.

Digging in the hard Georgia soil was difficult. I shoveled about a foot deep before I struck hard red clay. After reaching the hardpan, I assumed the slow and steady work of scraping scoop after scoop of compacted earth with a post-hole digger, until I finally reached a depth of four feet. After finishing the new hole, another wwoofer and I picked up the colorfully painted bathroom and positioned it so the toilet seat aimed directly over the site.

The humanure-filled hole of the previous site became a planter for fruit trees. A bit of soil was combined with the human waste and sawdust matrix, and in the wake of hundreds of wwoofers and visitors who'd made deposits in the Salamander Spring earth, out grew peach and apple trees.

I never got to sample any of the human-fertilized fruits growing from the old bathroom sites, but I reckon the peaches were every bit as sweet and nutritious as fruit grown from a compost of chicken and cow manure.

Going without flushing toilets wasn't a big deal for me, but I did miss having a warm shower. To bathe, our two options involved fetching water from the creek. For option one, we built a fire under an oil drum connected by pipe to an old fashioned claw-footed bathtub. Located in the middle of woods with the stream running alongside, the bathtub had a romantic feel. But what a pain in the ass to fill up the oil drum – fetching one bucket at a time from the creek, and another two hours just to heat the water.

Option two was to fill up a five-gallon solar shower bag, essentially an oversized juice pouch, and then lay the bag in the sun to bake all day. By 5 o'clock p.m. the heat of a cloud-free day produced enough solar heat for a lukewarm five-gallon drizzle. The main problem was finding a good tree to wedge the bag into, so the hose was higher than my head and I didn't have to squat under the shower. Plus, I had to watch for hikers while standing naked out in the open.

Given those two options, the oil drum and the solar shower bag, I made an important discovery. I realized I didn't need to shower every day. I found the longer I went without a shower, the shinier and silkier my hair got, and my skin took on a healthy sheen, as though rubbed with mink oil. As a bonus for not showering, my body odor acted as a natural insect repellent. What can you do but look at the positive side in these situations?

## Living Off-Grid

Life at Salamander Springs was uncomfortable at times. I admit, by the end of the month, I craved a heated room and a warm shower. The fire was a pleasure, but at times the smoke got to me. With each change in wind current I had to squint and hold my breath. For most of the month, my clothes and hair were coated with ash. In time, I came to see all the little discomforts as appreciation-builders for the *on*-grid lifestyle.

I think some people have a romantic view of what it's like to live off-grid. When they actually set about doing it, they feel the cold slap in the face of being left without easy energy, water, and easy food for the first time of their lives.

Some of the wwoofers who came to Salamander Springs did everything in their power to remove themselves from the challenge of living off-grid. The lovebirds from Atlanta, for example, made daily excursions to town for snacks and movies. They came back to the farm with cappuccinos in Styrofoam cups, and spent their nights watching movies on their laptop. In a way, I thought what they did was sacrilegious. They had access to the pure water of Salamander Springs, yet drank sweetened coffee. They liked the idea of living off-grid, but not the reality of it.

*Salamander Springs*

Most of the wwoofers embraced the lifestyle with open arms. They drank the good water and heated their hands over the fire. They allowed themselves to change. Annica!

Throughout my month on Salamander Springs, the only distinct reminder that the outside world was still going about its business was during the night that we received news of the presidential election. While we sat around the fire, staring at the flames like primitive humans, Debbie relayed the simple message: "Obama won." The world seemed distant.

In the end, the pleasures of living off-grid far outweighed the challenges. I worked at my own pace. I lived at my own pace. I took daily hikes in the woods and found pockets of stillness in which I meditated and did yoga to the gentle soundtrack of a forest stream.

After a strenuous round of hauling muck or uprooting stumps, I often found a soft, springy bed of leaves in the middle of the woods. I pulled my hooded sweatshirt securely around my face and took a nap under the trees.

When I awakened from my nap, I followed the stream down to the spring, walked through the green tunnel of vines, and spotted the big brass dipper hanging from the branch. I ladled water from the spring and drank until my heart was content and my cells swelled with Salamander Springs. I knew this was the best water I'd ever had.

# Chapter 6
## *Lucy's Farm*

As I traveled south, I watched autumn repeat itself. Starting in Maine, fiery red maple leaves led the way, signaling a change in the green canopy that covered mountains and filled in the space around lakes, farms, and cities like a great leafy sea. Tree by tree, New England exploded with color. Millions of leaves blew free from the branches and sprinkled to the ground like a piñata spilling confetti over the landscape.

Southward, I traveled into the mountains of North Carolina where I watched a whole new episode of autumn. I hiked on the crunching leaves and watched piles of them skitter down the street in whirlwinds of orange, yellow, and red.

My car felt like a time machine, with winter nipping at my heels but unable to catch me. By the time I left Salamander Springs, after watching my final and least colorful version of autumn in mild-weathered Georgia, I pulled away from winter completely. I arrived on the southern tip of Florida, to a place where winter and autumn didn't exist. Lucy's farm occupied a sub-tropical zone: a place of coconuts and bananas, where tomatoes ripened in January.

### Vultures

Initially, I had a bad impression of Florida. Alongside the highway, instead of autumn leaves swirling in the wind, I saw

## Lucy's Farm

a gyre of vultures. Soaring above a massive landfill, the birds circled and dove into Miami's trash pile.

The vultures flew in a formation so dense it resembled a black tornado spinning over the landfill. *Is this a bad omen?* I wondered. The image of the vulture tornado came back to me three weeks after I arrived on Lucy's Farm, when Lucy's uncle disappeared and I participated in a search party that eventually uncovered his body. *Were the vultures harbingers of death?* I wondered.

After giving the bad omen concept more thought, I came to the conclusion that it was only a coincidence. Any event prefacing a death – a black cat, a crow, a bat – can be imbued with meaning and predictive powers when viewed in hindsight.

The vultures were fixtures over the landfill, flying in their dark formation and diving for trash 365 days a year, common as ants on a honey jar. Lucy's farm, on the other hand, was an anomaly: a lush organic farm in an otherwise not so organic part of the country.

### Delicious Monster

The miles of countryside between Lucy's Farm and the Everglades were covered with monoculture farms. First, I passed five city blocks of nothing but palm trees, bunched together in tight rows. Then I saw a neatly organized farm of star fruit trees, growing in the same straight-line fashion.

An abundance of avocado farms covered the flat landscape, each and every one protected by barbed wire fencing. As I later discovered on bicycle rides into the country, the farms were also patrolled by guard dogs. I saw indicators of the avocado's success in the names given to local establishments, such as Avocado Elementary School and Avocado Lane. A new subdivision of two story houses neared completion just down the road from Lucy's Farm. It's name? Avocado Estates.

A farmer can grow almost anything in the frost-free climate of southern Florida. In the middle of December, I drove past

*Lucy's Farm*

a crop of nearly mature yellow summer squash. The squash grew in what looked like gravel, and I couldn't see a single weed in the pathways.

Ever since I learned how to spot an organic farm – by looking for weeds and grass in between crops – I enjoyed studying farms I drove past. The farms I viewed from my car window had no weeds or grass anywhere. Most likely, the squash farm, the star fruit, avocado, and palm tree farms grew on pesticide-laden earth. The gravel served only as a medium to hold their roots in place, so the root hairs could be doused with chemical fertilizers.

Lucy's Farm was the only one in the neighborhood without tractor pathways. Weeds grew freely between Lucy's avocado trees, but not out of control, for she employed an ancient method of weed control known as human labor: notably, a crew of six wwoofers.

Lucy's farm, fenced in like her neighbor's farms, contained five acres of lush avocado forest interspersed with trees of papaya, pomegranate, banana, fig, coconut, star fruit, and exotic fruits like cotton candy, longan, and monstera deliciosa. Twenty different kinds of salad greens, sprouts, and common vegetables made Lucy's Farm the most diverse of my wwoofing tour.

When Gus, the head wwoofer, took me on a tour of the farm my first day, I spotted a strange fruit sheathed in green scales. The fruit looked like a piece of corn on the cob, growing from a broad-leafed ground plant, much like a pineapple. "What's that?" I asked Gus.

"Monstera deliciosa," he said. "Delicious Monster."

When we returned to the outdoor kitchen, Gus pulled what looked like a rotten banana out of a brown paper bag. "This is it," he said. Then he proceeded to give me some advice on eating the strange fruit. "You never want to eat Monstera before it's completely ripe. It feels like fiberglass going down your throat."

Gus handed me the fruit and I grabbed the end still encased

Farming Around the Country | 87

in a sheath of green scales. A small cloud of fruit flies hovered around me, waiting for a moment of stillness to land on the gooey brown flesh. I nudged a few of the scales with my fingertip and they easily separated from the fruit and fell to the ground.

"That means it's ripe," Gus said. He nodded his approval and handed me a spoon. "Go ahead."

I scooped off some of the rotten looking flesh and introduced my tongue to a tropical flavor like nothing I'd ever experienced. My taste buds lit up with an intensely sweet combination of pineapple, mango, and banana, riding on a soft custard-like flesh. The delicious monster had me.

## Lucy's Farm

Much like monstera deliciosa, Lucy's Farm tickled my senses from the moment I stepped out of my car.

Edible flowers adorned trellises along the pathways and bees buzzed from flower to flower collecting nectar to fill the hives, from which Lucy filled mason jars for the wwoofer's kitchen.

We planted gardens in clearings of avocado trees, providing a winter and spring harvest of tomatoes, cucumbers, eggplant, melons, broccoli, squash, peas, beets, carrots, parsley, and basil. In place of grass, wild mint grew. After a large meal I gathered a handful of mint and brewed myself a nice digestive tea.

Initially, I thought avocados were Lucy's cash crop, but I soon learned that sprouts and baby salad greens took that title. The center of the farm contained a pie-shaped garden with baby spinach growing in one slice, baby kale in another. In alternating slices, baby arugula, baby mizuno, and baby mustard grew for only a few weeks before they were harvested with scissors. Fancy restaurants in Miami purchased bags of the tender baby greens for their high-priced organic salads.

For lunch and dinner every day, I complimented my meals with a baby green and avocado salad topped with cilantro sprouts and edible flowers, such as nasturtium, sun hemp, papaya petals, and squash blossoms.

Throughout the day, I sampled exotic fruits like cotton candy fruit, a tiny red berry that tasted almost identical to cotton candy, with the texture of a seedless grape.

To satisfy my strong sweet tooth, I snacked on longans, a tree fruit that grew in clusters and contained a milky white fruit surrounding a large inedible pit. Unopened, the longans looked like shrunken coconuts, the size of eyeballs. I opened the fruit by pinching it between my fingers. The outer skin of a fuzzy brown shell split open and revealed a rubbery white ball of flesh. I felt like I was eating a sugarcoated eyeball when I bit into my first longan. The small fruit met my taste buds like a spoonful of pure sugar, and for that reason I could only eat a few at a time without getting a stomach ache.

I ate papayas the size of footballs and short chubby bananas. Star fruit, also called carambola, lay in piles on the kitchen counter. We could only eat so much star fruit, so we pitched the overly ripe fruit into the compost heap.

For a couple of weeks, another wwoofer named Austin and I fell into a coconut-craze, I think mostly because we enjoyed the challenge of hacking open the nut with a machete. Opening the thick-shelled nuts required a precision chop. Oftentimes, Austin and I riddled the coconut shell with 15-20 cuts before either of us got it open, but the reward was worthwhile. First, we drank the coconut water, a mildly sweet and powerfully thirst-quenching beverage, perfect after a day of working under the Florida sun. Then we scraped out the flesh, blended it, and pressed the liquid through cheesecloth to use as coconut milk for smoothies and curry dishes.

On a couple of occasions, Austin and I tried climbing the coconut trees to get to the extra young coconuts, which have flesh so soft one can spoon it out like butter. We put on bike helmets to protect against falling coconuts. I only made it a quarter of the way up with nothing but scraped thighs to show for it. Austin made it nearly to the top, with a machete

## Lucy's Farm

slung over his shoulder, but couldn't quite get a good chop on the stem, so he monkeyed his way down and we resorted to collecting the fallen coconuts again.

Every part of Lucy's Farm reminded me I was in a foreign land, despite wwoofing within the borders of my own country. The coconuts, exotic fruit, and tropical December weather were enough, but even the insects were like creatures from a different world. A spider called the spiny-orb weaver spun webs between the avocado trees. Every morning the webs became visible with a necklace of dew, like sparkling water jewels hanging from the spider's silken strands. The spider itself was truly bizarre. A crab-like shell armored with six red spikes plated the spider's back, and in between the spikes a symmetrical display of white and black spots formed what looked like a sinister smile. I never knew such a strange creature existed.

When I walked back to my tent at night, I made sure to walk the well-beaten path that was clear of spider webs. The spiny orb weaver wasn't poisonous, but I certainly didn't like the idea of walking face first into that smiling exoskeleton.

The accommodations on Lucy's Farm blended seamlessly with the natural landscape. My campsite nestled into a stand of shiny black bamboo. Two avocado trees shaded both sides of my tent, and a thick carpet of wild mint grew up to my front flap, where the mint gave way to beach sand. A winding path led from my campsite to a gazebo, and along the way avocados in all stages of ripeness littered the ground.

A massive gazebo, equipped with all the luxuries of a modern kitchen plus couches and papasan chairs, served as the central eating and hangout place for the wwoofers. A 15-foot tall trellis covered with nasturtiums formed a flowery tunnel leading into the gazebo. Avocado trees surrounded the open-air structure on all sides.

I ate, slept, and lounged in the company of avocado trees. I never sealed myself off from the warm air and high-pitched chirping sounds of insects and giant toads that inhabited the farm. Openness dominated. However, the place was far from primitive. Electricity, Internet, and hot water fed the farm. Not only did Lucy's farm spoil me with perfect weather, 70-80s during the day and 50-60s at night under clear skies, but for the first time in a couple of months I enjoyed the ultimate luxury – a hot shower whenever I felt like it.

## Hugo's Question

Once the work actually started, my dreamy tropical mood changed a bit and I discovered the farm was highly profit-driven, because Lucille marketed her organic goods to high-end chefs in Miami. In order to profit from five acres of baby greens, avocados, and produce, she depended on volunteer labor. The deal worked like this: In exchange for 30 hours of work per week, I ate a spectacular vegetarian diet, which included an unlimited buffet of exotic fruits, avocados, salads, and sprouts. Plus, I slept in the comfort of dry tropical weather while the rest of the country was gripped by an unusually cold December.

I soon discovered the actual situation didn't match the deal Lucille offered. She'd convinced the other wwoofers to work a 35-hour week. This was only a five hour difference, but upon hearing the news, I feared another Hector situation, where the farm host tried to squeeze extra hours out of eager young volunteers.

Lucille didn't work alongside us in the fields and get her hands in the dirt. Instead, she acted more as a farm-manager. She struck me as an intelligent and open-minded woman, but I often wondered if she was too absorbed in the business side of the farm, for I rarely saw her in a relaxed state as she rushed around the avocado trees discussing work.

During my first day on the farm, I decided to take action against the longer-than-expected work schedule. Over lunch, I mentioned the discrepancy to the other wwoofers, and there was an immediate outpouring of comments. Apparently, Lucille had designated Fridays as "creative project day," but

## Lucy's Farm

none of the wwoofers had seen any project-time other than general farm labor. Therefore, we took the matter into our own hands and shortened the workday by an hour.

However, when we worked, we worked hard. Lucy's Farm, during December of '08, hosted the most productive group of wwoofers I had ever met. Gus, a young farmer from Illinois, displayed unmatched intelligence and physical stamina. Not only did Gus have an encyclopedic knowledge of every aspect of farming – able to begin a new task without any prior instruction – he was also in peak physical condition. He weeded, planted, shoveled, and harvested at the pace of three men, yet never showed fatigue. One day, when a man brought a sample of his compost to the farm, I watched Gus take a pinch of the dirt and put it in his mouth. "Slightly acidic," he said, "but good stuff."

Lucille entrusted every operation of her farm with Gus. When it came time to irrigate or prune or harvest, she passed the message onto Gus, and he showed us how it was done. Gus aimed to start his own CSA farm outside of St. Louis one day, so he approached Lucy's farm as a kind of trial run, giving it all the love and attention he'd give his own farm.

In addition to Gus and the other wwoofers, Lucille had a full-time crew of Mexican women who seeded, harvested, and packaged the baby greens. These friendly and loquacious women, who spent most of their time in the two greenhouses, fulfilled Lucille's mantra: "Always be planting."

Two groundsmen, Hugo and Juan, rounded out the work crew. Hugo lived on the farm in one of the storage buildings converted into a living area. Hugo was a young Guatemalan who spoke maybe 50 words of English. And although I spoke probably half as many words of Spanish, he and I cultivated a friendship based on smiles and nods.

When we crossed paths on the farm, both of us wearing our wide-brimmed straw hats, we sometimes made eye contact and burst into laughter for no apparent reason. Hugo had an eye for the more subtle creatures of Lucy's Farm, and sometimes he waved me over and secretly pointed out wildlife no one else seemed to notice—a snake coiled on an avocado branch, a chameleon, or a giant toad in the spinach beds.

Hugo had two main conversation pieces when he talked to me. He said, "Hi, Brian," and "Are you happy, Brian?"

Maybe he asked everyone if they were happy. The greeting might have been the Guatemalan version of "What's up?" or "How's it going?" But I took the question literally. Usually, I just responded with a casual, "Yes, I'm very happy, Hugo," but then after Hugo smiled and walked away, I gave the question more thought.

I think Hugo missed his family and homeland back in Guatemala, and he saw a piece of himself in me. We were both in an unfamiliar land, living among strangers.

*Am I happy?* I thought. Maybe I gave Hugo's question too much thought, because I began to look at my whole life through the scope of that single question. *Was I happy with my family?* Yes, very much so. *Was I happy with myself?* Yes, indeed.

*But was I happy?* When I forced myself to answer Hugo's question in the broadest possible sense, I couldn't give an honest and unwavering yes. I could say, *yeah, sure I'm happy.* But I knew something was still missing. I hoped one day I could answer Hugo's question with an honest yes every moment of the day, not just in a casual sense, but from the bottom of my soul.

## Avocados

After the 35 hours per week issue was straightened out, I was sincerely happy with the work on Lucy's farm. I participated in a variety of farm work, guided by Gus. I thinned beets and carrots, so each root would mature to maximize size. I weeded. I planted squash and broccoli. Perhaps the easiest work was picking flowers. I leisurely walked around the farm with a wicker basket and filled containers with nasturtiums, roses, wild petunia, marigold, papaya, clitoria, sun hemp, squash

## Lucy's Farm

blossoms, and basil tops. The edible flowers found their way into the mouths of wealthy restaurant guests and tourists of Miami.

Of all the produce items on the farm, the avocado was most central to my meals, work, and the scenery. Every day, the other wwoofers and I made guacamole in giant punch bowls and had it for lunch and dinner. Occasionally I even made guacamole under my boots, as I walked the pathways at night and stepped on an old soft one that squirted out of its split black skin like brown toothpaste. A few times an hour, while I meditated in my tent or lounged in the gazebo, I heard the pleasant thud of an avocado hit the ground.

The avocados on Lucy's Farm were not small hass avocados, typically carried in grocery stores. They were big, glossy green Monroe avocados, about four times the size of a hass, with a lower fat content.

Much of my life on Lucy's Farm revolved around collecting, eating, and admiring these beautiful fruits. I also dodged them on harvest days, when Juan and I jostled a tree branch and the rock-solid fruits detached and fell like cannon balls.

A local grocery store bought most of Lucille's avocados and we picked 35 boxes for them each week. Before the transaction could be made, Gus and I drove over to the USDA inspection office, where the fruit was checked for disease.

The USDA inspection procedure was quite an eye-opener for me. Here's how it worked: Gus pulled the avocado van into the parking lot of an unmarked brick building. A handwritten sign in the front window read "Florida Department of Agriculture."

Next, an old man dressed in plain clothes came out and looked at the two boxes we had selected from the back of the van. He didn't even lift a piece of fruit to examine it. Gus knew how it worked, so back at the farm we placed all of the nicest looking avocados in what we called the "perfect boxes."

All the USDA man said was, "looks like more of the scab." He was referring to a hardened black substance that marked some of the avocados. I assumed the "scab" was completely natural and harmless, but I was curious, so I asked the inspector if he knew what the "scab" was. "Is it a fungus? Can it spread to other plants?"

His response—"We just call it the scab."

Okay.

For the next step, the inspector gave us a roll of "USDA Approved" tape, a stamp and ink pad, and left us to certify our own boxes. For all he knew, those other 33 boxes could've been diseased, caked with pesticides, or an altogether different food.

The USDA inspection process was certainly a good look at what goes on behind the scenes, or rather what doesn't go on. The procedure was yet another affirmation that in order to know the quality of my food, I needed to know the source of my food, either by buying directly from a farmer or through a farmer's market.

## Dinner on the Farm

Aside from oats, beans, and rice, most of the food I ate on Lucy's Farm grew from the land around my tent. All the meals were vegetarian, heavy with avocados, salad greens, and sprouts. A sign at the entrance of Lucy's Farm announced the two things that were not allowed. "Welcome!" the sign said. "Please, No Meat or Cigarettes."

However, once a month, Lucille bent her vegetarian policy and allowed fish, lobster, and shrimp onto the farm for an event called *Dinner on the Farm*.

Chefs from Miami came out to the farm and prepared fancy meals for anyone who wanted to fork over $150 a plate and eat in the gazebo. The dinner guests received fine linens and dishes, of course, but with the exception of things like calabaza flowers filled with almond mousse, cotton candy fruit with mango sorbet, passion fruit champagne, and lobster sauce reductions poured over grilled wahoo, the Miami elite ate the same stuff we consumed every day. The main difference was

## Lucy's Farm

in the artful presentation and the fact that the meal was spread over six courses, rather than served buffet style in large bowls, as the wwoofers and I were accustomed to.

During *Dinner on the Farm*, me and the other volunteers refilled water glasses and cleared tables. The big perk came after each of the six courses, when we bussed a few plates of food some picky eater left completely untouched.

During those in-between-course moments when we were gifted with delectable creations from the finest chefs in Miami, the dietary resolve of my fellow wwoofers surfaced. For example, if extra servings of avocado-shrimp puffs or lobster bisque came back to the dishwashing station, somebody announced its contents, and although I saw a few of the wwoofers look longingly at the food, nobody touched it. I thought they were crazy, but I didn't complain. Austin and I, the least fundamental of the group, as far as diet went, gave each other a knowing smile and swooped in to eat the delicious food.

Although I'm an opportunivore, choosing to eat whatever tasty foods come my way, regardless of animal content, I like to think I have some dietary standards. I avoid factory-farmed meats, conventional produce, and most items that come in a colorfully wrapped, shiny package. I ate an almost entirely vegan diet on Lucy's Farm, one that excluded *all* animal products, including dairy and eggs. But when the Miami chefs came out to the farm and made extra portions of truffle and bleu cheese stuffed potatoes, I certainly didn't stand by idly with the vegans. It's as important for me to eat cheese as it is for the vegans to not eat it.

To someone with loose dietary standards like myself, veganism appears to be a limited diet, bordering on the extreme, but as I discovered on Lucy's Farm, there are diets even more extreme than veganism. One of the wwoofers who visited Lucy's Farm, a man by the name of Malcolm, practiced a truly bizarre diet called the 80-10-10 diet.

*Lucy's Farm*

## Malcolm

Lucille asked Malcolm to leave the farm after only two days. She said it was because he never smiled. This was true. But I think it also had something to do with the way Malcolm crept up on people and began evangelizing about raw food.

On more than one occasion, as I chopped vegetables in preparation for dinner, I received a jolt of surprise when I discovered Malcolm, a 50 year old man with short blond hair, standing directly behind me and peering over my shoulder.

"Are you cooking those?" Malcolm asked. "I don't want any. I'm just curious."

Malcolm had a way of appearing out of nowhere. My first meeting with him happened in typical surprise fashion. Without any prior notice from Lucille, Malcolm simply appeared on the farm.

On a sunny December day, as I walked the path between my tent and the gazebo, studying the banana trees along the way to see if the green bananas were big enough to cut a bunch from the tree, a strange man stepped out from behind an avocado tree and stood on the path in front of me. He looked nervous and his face blushed bright red.

The first two things he said to me were, "Hi, my name's Malcolm," and then "I'm doing the 80-10-10 diet."

*An odd way to introduce oneself*, I thought. Malcolm defined himself not by his occupation or family or hobbies, but by his diet. The 80-10-10 diet, I soon learned, meant that Malcolm got 80% of his calories from carbohydrates, 10% from fat, and 10% from protein, each and every bit of it from raw fruits and vegetables.

Malcolm subsisted almost entirely on bananas. He pureed 8 or 9 bananas in a bit of water and that's all he ate for breakfast, lunch, and sometimes dinner. A pound of greens, also blended, rounded out his diet. He practiced what's called the mono-meal: a meal consisting entirely of one fruit, and lots of it.

"The bananas leave no residue in your intestines," Malcolm told me. "It's a very clean burning fuel."

## Lucy's Farm

Admittedly, I thought Malcolm was a bit eccentric, not only with his unusual diet, but also with his behavioral traits. Most notably, he photographed everything I ate.

As I chopped vegetables for a soup one night, Malcolm pulled out his camera and snapped several shots of the carrots and onions on the cutting board.

After I put a large bowl of guacamole on the table, everyone reached for a chip. Malcolm reached for his camera.

One morning, as I ran some sprouted wheat berries through the food processor, Malcolm startled me from behind. Without any greeting he asked, "What're you making there? I don't want any, I'm just curious." Any time Malcolm inquired about my food, he always reminded me, "I don't want any. I'm just curious."

Then he asked, "Are you going to bake that?" He accompanied this question with a grave expression that indicated I was about to make a big mistake.

I responded, "I'm only putting it in the food dehydrator,"

"But it will be above 115 degrees, won't it?" he said, clearly unimpressed.

Malcolm instructed me that cooking destroys important enzymes in the food, and without those enzymes, people's digestive systems are over-taxed, drawing energy away from the immune system and opening the doors to disease. "Aging is the result of a lack of food enzymes," Malcolm told me.

He also emphasized that all raw-food diets are not the same. He said that some raw foodists had lost their way by loading up on fatty foods such as nuts and avocados. In the rare moments when Malcolm did talk, he sounded like an evangelist for raw food, as if he'd found the holy grail of diets. Eighty-Ten-Ten. All Raw. With Lots of Bananas. Everything was about enzymes, enzymes, enzymes!

Malcolm claimed he'd interviewed nearly every major raw food expert in the world while writing a book on the 80-10-10 diet. He said the book was yet to be published. For all I knew, his authority on the subject might have been genuine.

However, he also claimed to have written a 300-page book titled *UFOs and the Government Cover-up*, and another one simply titled *Jokes*. Oddly enough, me and the other wwoofers never heard Malcolm tell a joke, let along laugh or crack a smile during his brief stay on Lucy's Farm.

Malcolm was a serious man. And who knows, maybe his book *Jokes* was his way of saying the joke was on us. Everything we thought we knew about eating healthy was wrong. All I knew for certain was that Malcolm truly did live on bananas, and he appeared physically healthy.

Despite his eccentricities, or maybe because of them, Malcolm made a lasting impression on me. I sympathized with his plight. He lived as an outsider in a world of omnivores and enzyme-deficient food. He held fast to his personal belief that diet is a vital key to physical health. And on that note, I agreed with Malcolm. I don't think I could live entirely on bananas or raw food, but Malcolm raised my awareness about the importance of food enzymes and finding the right diet. Then, just as suddenly and mysteriously as Malcolm arrived, he was gone.

## Biodynamic Bread

Fats, protein, and carbohydrates, along with vitamins and minerals, used to be the only important factors in a diet. Now, as Malcolm educated me, enzymes and micro-nutrients are the latest craze in determining what's healthy. *What's next?* I often wonder. Will food quality be measured by its molecular vibration?

Already, organic farming has proven to yield more nutritious crops than conventional agriculture, but I wonder, as our understanding of food and the natural world advances, will organic farming advance as well? Will today's organic farms appear primitive and unenlightened compared to the farms of the 22nd century?

During my stay on the farm, Lucille introduced me to a form of agriculture called biodynamic farming, which appeared

## Lucy's Farm

strange and nonsensical at first glance. When she invited me and the wwoofers to participate in a water vortex, one of the techniques employed by biodynamic farming, I thought, *This is weird.* However, I also remained open minded. After all, a 19th century farmer would've never believed invisible creatures lived in the soil and provided food for the roots of plants.

I witnessed some interesting farming practices coming down the east coast, especially on Clear Creek Homestead where George and I harvested certain vegetables based on whether the moon was waxing or waning.

However, biodynamic farming took the prize for the form of agriculture most removed from the world of modern science.

Biodynamic farming is often touted as a higher form of organics, for it adheres to all the organic principles and then adds a touch of the spiritual. According to Rudolph Steiner, the pioneer of biodynamic farming, certain biodynamic preparations, such as the water vortex, harness cosmic energies that result in vegetables and fruits of a higher vibrational frequency. Supposedly, biodynamic food resonates with your very soul and enhances physical health. Thus, my recurring thought: *This is weird.*

The water vortex I participated in began with cow manure, as all good farming does. However, the other wwoofers and I didn't spread the manure onto the fields in typical fashion. We sprayed it on.

Lucille ordered special manure that had been packed into a cow horn and buried underground for six months, then unearthed on the spring equinox. The cow horn manure supposedly contained bacterial goodness that enlivened the soil. However, before we sprayed the dung onto Lucy's Farm, we mixed it in a vortex of water to energize the solution.

For a full hour, the other wwoofers and I took ten-minute shifts, stirring a 10 gallon pot of water. I used my arm like a paddle to create a whirlpool. The idea was to create a vortex that cosmic energy could be funneled into. In addition, Lucille encouraged us to put our good intentions into the water.

After we charged the solution with cosmic energy and completely dissolved the cow horn manure, we split the water up into spray bottles and fanned out to deliver the precious solution. I can't lie, I felt silly walking around the farm with a spray bottle, spritzing fruit trees and tomato patches. I reminded myself, *I'm helping to enliven the soil.* I thought of the delicious spiritual guacamole I would make that night, and how *maybe I'm taking part in a highly advanced, yet to be proven, form of agriculture.* I thought these things in order to counter the one overwhelming thought: *This is weird.*

As if the biodynamic preparation wasn't strange enough, later that same day a group of people dressed in white robes came to the farm and helped us spread a second round of cosmic water, this time using palm leaves instead of spray bottles.

The visitors, members of a Shanti Yoga group the wwoofers and I called The Spiritual Food People, were guests of Lucille's who had come to perform a winter solstice ritual. My first impression of the Spiritual Food People was that they were some kind of cult.

I struck up a conversation with one of the women dressed in white, as we walked around the farm and dipped our palm leaves in the cosmic water. She seemed friendly and interested in my farming trip, but in the middle of our conversation, an old Indian man glanced back at her, and her face immediately turned serious as she sped away from me. I worried she was part of some oppressive society.

Regardless, I grew to enjoy the guests. After the biodynamic application, the Spiritual Food People invited me to sit in on their winter solstice ritual. The ceremony began with prayers and blessings in ten different religions. Then a woman from the group stood up and began reading passages about a new era of human evolution. She read, "Beginning in the year 2012 there will be a spiritual awakening. A common memory of all the past wisdom will be shared by all, and humanity will shift away from a materialistic existence into a simpler yet more advanced form of society, similar to the economy and agriculture that existed 5500 years ago..." I could hardly believe my ears. I'd heard interesting predictions for the future, but the Spiritual Food People delivered the most fascinating one.

The woman went on to explain the importance of the winter solstice of 2012. Supposedly, on that date the Earth and the Sun will line up with the center of the galaxy, and a jet of consciousness expanding energy will be directed right at yours truly – planet Earth. Who knows if there's any validity to it. But the idea sounded nice.

After the solstice ceremony, the Spiritual Food People shared their food with us – raw milk and biodynamic bread. I cut myself an extra thick slice of the biodynamic bread, knowing that if "a new era of human evolution" was around the corner, I needed all of the spiritual nourishment I could get.

## Sweat Lodge

Lucy's Farm had two faces: the Profit Farm and the Spiritual Farm, both feeding off one another. Although Gus, me, and the other wwoofers worked hard toward completing Lucille's weekly farm agenda, we also enjoyed projects that had nothing to do with food or money. A few days after the Spiritual Food People left, we built a sweat lodge, using bamboo freshly cut from the farm. We bent and tied the bamboo poles into a dome structure, and then covered the whole thing with a heavy duty army tarp.

After constructing the lodge, we built a roaring fire outside the dome. For two hours we fed the fire hundreds of dry avocado branches and watched as five smooth and rounded rocks glowed in the center of the fire. The rocks would be brought into the sweat lodge one at time as the ceremony progressed.

At sunset, we all crawled into the small dome and gave ourselves over to the guidance of Miguel, a Cuban immigrant who served as Lucille's beekeeper and had led sweat lodge rituals several times before. As I crawled through the entrance I summoned the spirits, according to Miguel, and said "all my ancestors." The greeting supposedly attracted past ancestors who would act as spirit-guides and impart wisdom during the ritual.

After all eight of us snugly sat in a circle inside the pitch black dome, Miguel retrieved the first rock. The soft-ball sized rock glowed red hot, as if Miguel had just fished it from a river of magma.

We all said, "Welcome, Grandfather," as Miguel instructed. At first, the heat wasn't so bad and felt like a stovetop I could warm my hands over. Then Miguel poured water on the rock. The instant I heard the water sizzle, a blast of moist heat hit me in the face. I felt a burning sensation in my lungs when I tried to breathe, and for a moment I thought I was going to panic and claw my way out of the tent, but I withstood the initial furnace blast, and the heat slowly let up.

After a few minutes, Miguel brought in the second rock, and we all said "Welcome, Grandfather." I heard the young woman next to me say, "Welcome *Grandmother*," obviously offended that the wise old women weren't being greeted.

When Miguel tossed water on the second and third rocks, the heat became suffocating. Sweat poured from every pore of my body. I felt like I'd descended into the depths of a volcano.

Two of the wwoofers bailed out, and as they exited I stretched my head toward the door flap and breathed in the cool, sweet air. The refreshing breath was just enough to keep me going, enduring the most extreme sauna I'd ever experienced.

In addition to the oppressing heat, I sat next to a muscular Cuban man who consistently disrupted the spiritual mood. I had no idea who he was or where he came from – a guest of Miguel's I presumed. Whenever the heat turned up, the man started humming and repeatedly slapped his chest in a violent manner. At random times throughout the sweat-lodge ceremony, the muscular Cuban man let out baritone evil-sounding laughs and said, "May everybody find peace."

After I made it through the "warrior round," the name given to the third round, I stayed strong through the fourth and final heat-wave. I didn't notice any newfound wisdom afterward, but I did feel totally refreshed. When I emerged into the clear starry night, I felt as though I'd crawled from a steamy womb. I poked my head out of the tent flap, pouring sweat, and drank in my first breath of cool air. The sweat lodge had been preceded by a one-day fast. After a moment of standing shirtless under the clear sky, letting the light breeze caress my body, cooling me like one of the red-hot glowing rocks dropped into a pool of water, I set to work devouring some of the juicy tropical fruits hanging on the trees all around me. I felt rejuvenated, if not reborn.

## That Turtle is Stupid

With the exception of an occasional trip to Miami to deliver Lucille's goods, I only made two off-farm excursions – to the Everglades and the Keys.

The Everglades were full of the expected sights: birds and alligators and beautiful mangrove swamps that seemed to conceal whole other worlds. I discovered that in order to properly explore the Everglades, a canoe and mosquito net would've been more appropriate. Me and the other wwoofers were literally chased out of one of the mangroves by mosquitoes. As I jogged along the path, I stopped at gaps in the trees and sacrificed a couple of bites in the neck for a glimpse into the mysterious swampy world, with its gas bubbles and hidden birds and mangrove trees that stood propped above the water on spindly roots.

We only found mosquito-relief in open areas, where boardwalks spanned the waterways. However, in those places we encountered much larger pests—obnoxious tourists. I'm not sure what the open-container policy was in the Everglades, but from the looks of things, we guessed alcohol was definitely encouraged.

While Austin, myself, and two other wwoofers quietly observed the wildlife, we came across a group of rowdy young Latinos clutching cans of beer and walkie-talkies. The group enjoyed the Everglades more as a television show, one to be critiqued and laughed at, rather than admiring its natural beauty.

One of the young men saw a turtle basking on a rock and reported this news at full volume over his walkie-talkie. "We found a fucking turtle!" After he and his buddies watched the turtle remain motionless for a few seconds, the guy next to the walkie-talkie operator said, "That turtle is stupid, man." His comment brought sounds of agreement and laughter from the rest of the gang as they tilted their beers back. "Yeah," said one of them, "That turtle *is* stupid."

## We Were Put Here to Eat Meat

I took my second adventure to Key Largo, where I arranged to go out to the coral reef with a couple of locals I met online. Initially I sent them an e-mail asking where I might find some good snorkeling, but they responded by saying, "Come on down and we'll take you out on our boat!"

Not only did I get to hover over the coral reef with my snorkeling gear, but Tom, the owner of the boat, strapped a scuba tank on my back and let me go in for a dive. I was certified in scuba diving about 5-years earlier, after which I'd been on one dive, helping a friend collect zebra mussels at the bottom of Lake Erie. The crystal clear blue water off of Key Largo hardly compared to the cold, murky waters of Lake Erie.

Within minutes after I jumped in the water, a six-foot nurse shark swam beneath me. My heart raced. The incredible array of color amazed me most of all. The metallic green scales of a parrotfish flashed in front of my mask and an occasional rainbow colored school of small tropical fish swam in unison over the sandy bottom. Everything moved in unison. The sea fans and sea anemones swayed in rhythm with the current. The subtle colors of the coral reef served as a backdrop to the whole scene, like a child's paint canvas, streaked and dotted with every possible color.

In the midst of the beauty and weightlessness of hovering underwater, I also stayed conscious of what swam above me. The little voice in my head reminded me that Tom was snorkeling overhead with a 5-foot long harpoon gun. I wasn't scared, so much as aware of the fact that he and I saw the underwater world through a whole different set of goggles. He as a hunter, and I as an explorer.

Later that night, after we finished diving and sat around a fire in Tom's front yard, we got onto the topic of food, and Tom the hunter came out with *his* dietary beliefs. He said, "We were put here to eat meat."

I told him about the vegetarian diet on Lucy's Farm and how I felt healthy on it. Tom responded less to me, I think, than to vegetarians in general. He didn't back up his statement with any religious belief or health reasons. He simply declared his opinion as if stating a universal truth. "We were put here to eat meat."

I smiled and nodded, not wanting to go into the many points of interest his statement inspired in me. Were we *put* here, in this body on this planet? Or did we choose to come here? Did humans evolve as meat eaters? Or could one thrive on a meatless diet? I didn't raise any of these questions. In that moment, I decided to be a gracious guest and enjoy the warmth of the fire.

## Sylvester

My month on Lucy's Farm ended with the disappearance of Albert, Lucille's 89-year uncle. Hugo found Albert's body lying face down in the tall grass beside a road. I shared a very short relationship with Albert. On two occasions I served the old German man his beans and greens and he tried talking in German with me.

Albert spoke fluent English, but Lucille said that in the last months of his life, he'd reverted back to his native tongue.

## Lucy's Farm

He also adopted a child-like mind. After I served Albert his dinner, he pointed excitedly at the flowers and colors on his dinner plate. Albert no longer recognized Lucille as his niece. He simply referred to her as "that woman" when he wanted something.

Toward the end of his life, Albert became preoccupied with going to the bank. He was convinced the American dollars in his wallet were worthless, and he wanted to trade them in for Deutsche Marks.

So when Albert disappeared one day, during an informal meeting with Lucille, we discussed that maybe he'd set off to find a bank. However, after three long days dragged by without any sign of Albert, we knew he probably wouldn't be found alive. He walked without a cane, but mentally he'd deteriorated to a point where he couldn't take care of himself.

For three straight days we put aside farm work and gave top priority to finding Albert. Lucille deployed blood hounds, search parties, and flyovers. She sent Albert's photo to the local news agency to be posted on television. She even called a psychic who told us his body would be found "near the water where Mexicans live." The psychic's information was worthless, since Lucy's Farm was located in an area where Spanish dominated, and we were basically in the Everglades.

On the third day, Lucille sent all the wwoofers and employees out to the neighboring orchards and farms to comb the area. When Hugo spotted him, Lucille seemed more relieved than anything. She said that he'd gone out like a true German—"stubbornly and on his own terms."

A few days after Albert's death, New Year's Eve was upon us. Albert was onto something new and so were we. For the occasion, Lucille led us all through a German New Year's ritual called Sylvster. The ritual worked like this: Each person melted a coil of soldering lead by holding a spoon over a candle fire, and then as soon as the coil melted, we poured the liquid metal into a bowl of water. The liquid metal solidified into that person's fortune for the coming year.

## Lucy's Farm

One of the wwoofers fished out a piece of lead that looked like a turtle. We interpreted this as yet another year of living in his VW van, since a turtle carries its home on its back. Some of the fortunes took the shape of birds, flames, or sperm. When I pulled mine out of the water, it looked like a snake hatching from an egg.

The baby snake worried me at first, but Lucille assured me the snake represented wisdom. Phew! What a relief.

Coincidentally, on that very morning, Hugo, ever with the keen eye, signaled for me to look at something in the trees. When I stepped closer, I saw a snake coiled atop of an avocado, the first and only snake I saw in Florida. I thought back to the vultures I'd seen spinning in tornado fashion over the landfill, and then Albert's death. I wondered once again if I was playing connect the dots, trying to tie seemingly unrelated events together, or if omens and signposts for the future truly did exist.

As I loaded my trunk with avocados a few days later, preparing for my cross-country trek, the Sylvester ritual burned bright in my mind. I hoped Lucille was right and that wisdom would hatch from that egg.

# Chapter 7
## *Henry's Farm and Hostel*

My car turned into a second home during the cross-country trip between Lucy's Farm at the southern tip of Florida and Henry's Farm, located just north of Santa Barbara, California. I slept in the backseat when an oil leak left me stranded in a remote Texas town on a Sunday night. Banana peels, cracker boxes, and empty jars of peanut butter filled the plastic grocery bag that doubled as my car's trashcan.

The trunk served as a pantry for all the goodies I accumulated along the way: avocados, oranges, applesauce, pearsauce, and strawberry and blueberry jam. If I grew tired of supermarket food, I popped the top on one of the mason jars and enjoyed cinnamon ginger apples from Clear Creek Homestead or a sampling of the pears and blueberries I harvested back in New England.

I covered the cross-country trip in a leisurely month and a half, enjoying cities and scenery along the way.

For entertainment on the road, I listened to local radio stations. I tuned into jazz as I passed through the cypress-filled swamps of southern Louisiana. From my car windows, I saw hundreds of small woody pyramids stand a foot or so above the green algae-covered water. These so called cypress "knees" were above-ground extensions of the root system.

*Henry's Farm and Hostel*

The knobby stumps encircled a thick-trunked mother tree like a group of worshipers rising from the swamp to pay homage to their creator.

After crossing Louisiana, I entered the Lone Star State, where bad country music and static dominated the airwaves. The drab, dusty landscape of western Texas seemed to synchronize with the poor radio signals. Tumbleweeds rolled across the highway and thousands of wind turbines appeared to spin in slow motion off in the distance. During such long stretches of flatland driving, I stepped on the gas pedal a little harder, fast-forwarding through the changeless scenery.

As I passed through El Paso and New Mexico, upbeat Mexican music took over the airwaves. However, the steady dance beat and Spanish lyrics failed to stir the motionless desert. Saguaro cactuses punctuated the rocky red, almost Martian, landscape of southern Arizona. The long-lived cactuses stood as silent sentries, their enormous needle-covered fingers pointing toward the clear blue desert sky.

For hours at a time, I shut the radio off and listened to the soft howl of wind as my car raced through the desert, moving ever-closer to the Pacific Ocean.

In retrospect, I probably could've made the cross-country trip in four or five days, pausing briefly to walk on the beach and admire the cypress-filled swamps and wide-open desert. I could've gone on a diet of caffeine and classical music and made good time.

However, if I made "good time" I would've bypassed so many interesting people. I would've missed the people and food of Louisiana and meditative hikes into the mountains of Arizona. For me, *making good time* meant taking things slow and easy.

## Couchsurfing

I took mini-vacations as I traveled across the country. In New Orleans and Lafayette I spent a week listening to live music and sampling spicy Cajun dishes. In Austin, Texas I hiked

*Henry's Farm and Hostel*

through urban parks and swam in Barton Springs. I bicycled through Tucson, Arizona and hiked to the top of Finger Rock Trail overlooking the entire city.

The long stretches of driving, sometimes ten hours in a day, became more bearable after a prolonged rest stop. I felt rejuvenated after a few days of riding the streetcars of New Orleans and sitting as a passenger in the busses of Austin. The simple act of walking around on my own two feet refreshed me.

In many cases, the people I stayed with along the way were more a destination than the actual city or natural wonders of the region.

I thoroughly enjoyed the white sandy beaches of Sarasota, Florida, but my most vivid memory of Sarasota is the ex-helicopter pilot who let me stay in his spare bedroom for the night.

I connected with the ex-civilian helicopter pilot through an online network called Couchsurfing, whereby he offered a spare bedroom to thrifty travelers such as myself. I e-mailed him a week in advance and he responded, "you've got a place here," followed by his address and phone number.

The clean-cut young man greeted me at his front door with a slapping hand shake and showed me in. He occupied a two bedroom house large enough for a small family, yet not a single pet or houseplant lived with him.

My couchsurfing host furnished his place in typical bachelor pad fashion. A leather couch faced a flat-screen television and two video game controllers rested on a glass table top. Posters of the Chicago Bears football players covered his wall space. When I grabbed a drink from his fridge, I saw it was mostly empty, except for beer, milk, ketchup, and leftovers. "Help yourself to anything you want," he told me, pointing to six different kinds of cereal on his countertop.

My host appeared like an ordinary bachelor in his early thirties, but as the evening unraveled, I questioned his sanity. I spent a better part of the night listening to the ex-helicopter

## Henry's Farm and Hostel

pilot spout off conspiracy theories while Fox News blared at full volume from his big screen TV. He believed elected officials were working to undermine public health. After a diatribe on the government's hidden agenda, he took me out to pick up dinner from 7/11, rounding the street corners in his pick-up truck at dangerous speeds.

After we returned to my host's house and he polished off a dinner of 7/11 chili dogs, I watched him unscrew several prescription bottles and tilt back a bottle of Mountain Dew to wash down a handful of pills. As he played video games, he told me he'd lost his helicopter license after being deemed "unfit to fly." I assumed he wasn't referring to anything of a physical nature.

I departed Sarasota the following morning, relieved to be on my way. At the same time, I felt grateful to the ex-helicopter pilot who generously took me into his home. Although I didn't share his taste in food and entertainment, I recognized generosity when I saw it. I turned down his offer to "smoke some ganja" several times, and on my way out the door the following morning, he insisted I fill up my bag with as many oranges as I could pick from the tree in his backyard. "I don't eat fruit," he said.

Couchsurfing fulfilled all my lodging needs as I traveled across the country. Initially, I chose couchsurfing as a way to bypass the cost of hotels and campgrounds, since my only cost was a gift of avocados or a jar of homemade applesauce. However, I soon discovered my hosts offered more than just a free place to stay. They offered a unique experience, which sometimes involved a home cooked meal or a tour of the local area. In each and every case, I caught a glimpse into the life of my couchsurfing host.

The night after I stayed with the ex-helicopter pilot in Sarasota, I couchsurfed in Destin, Florida with an active helicopter pilot from the United States Air Force. My host, a combat pilot, took me out for sushi with his Air Force buddy who was being deployed to Afghanistan the following morning. After dinner, I watched as my host gave his friend a farewell hug. I shared a sense of adventure with the two Air Force pilots, but they were clearly on a different trip than the one I'd embarked on.

## New Orleans

In Louisiana I took my first set of mini-vacations, first in New Orleans and then in Lafayette. My couchsurfing host in New Orleans drove me all over town, showing me historical sites, such as the above ground tombs of 18th century cemeteries. Even the earliest settlers of New Orleans contended with a notoriously high water table.

When I set off on jaunts of my own, riding the streetcar around town, I saw artsy new houses sprouting amid post-Katrina wreckage. I chatted with locals who still harbored anger toward the government's handling of the post-Katrina recovery. Four years after the event, Katrina still weighed heavily on peoples' minds. However, the hurricane didn't dampen the spicy food or friendly spirit that characterized the Big Easy. Live music still poured from wide-open doors seven nights a week. Within the space of three hours on Frenchmen Street, I watched a live show of gypsy swing jazz followed by a twelve piece brass band, and then an improvisational guitarist who plucked the strings of his electric guitar with his toes. One night, my couchsurfing host directed me to a local bar that hosted Tuesday free red beans and rice night, accompanied by amateur banjo and fiddle players.

During daylight hours, the spontaneity of street performers and loquacious strangers kept me on my toes. On one occasion, an old black man with smoky white hair and a thin gold necklace sat down beside me on a park bench. At first I didn't think anything of it. Then I felt the sleeve of the man's denim jacket brush against the back of my neck, and I realized he'd put his arm around me. He did this as naturally as possible, as if the two of us were good buddies and had known each other our entire lives. The park bench was long enough for a large

## Henry's Farm and Hostel

family, and suddenly there were the two of us – a white boy from Ohio and an old black man from New Orleans, pressed shoulder to shoulder and thigh to thigh, with nothing but space on either side.

I had a paper plate of red beans and rice raised to my mouth, and on the street in front of us, a five-piece brass band played "When the Saints Go Marching In." The old man tapped his foot to the music.

"Don't worry, I'm not gay," the old man assured me. I considered walking away. Why would a complete stranger sit down and put his arm around me? Out of curiosity, and in the friendly spirit of New Orleans, I continued eating my red beans and rice and listened to him talk for awhile. He engaged me in conversation with a few unexpected questions. He said, "My brother, you look like an intelligent individual. I bet you've been to college. Tell me, how do you find the area of a circle?" He asked me a few other geometry questions, as if he'd come to tutor me. Then his mind bounced off like a ping pong ball and he simply asked questions to preface some random story he was about to tell. He said, "Why are white girls so easy?" followed by a story about how he offered a woman $100 for her panties while waiting in line for food at McDonalds.

He asked me what I knew about Vietnam. Then he flashed his disabled veteran's card and told me how he'd been exposed to agent orange during the war. As he spoke, he continued tapping his foot, and the brass band kept playing. Tourists dropped dollars in a hat and photographed themselves with the band in the background.

When I told the old man I had to leave, he offered me a pair of leather gloves. "Here, you'll need these," he said. I politely refused. He insisted I take the gloves, but I felt like something fishy was involved, so I gave him a warm handshake, which ended with him pulling me in for a brotherly hug. Looking back on the event, I think he was just a lonely guy who wanted someone to talk to. The gloves were probably his way of saying *thanks for listening*.

*Henry's Farm and Hostel*

## Lafayette

After New Orleans, I surfed through Lafayette, where I stayed with a charming, heavyset fellow named Gene. Everything about Gene seemed well-rounded, including his belly and smiling face. He spent most of his adult life as a lawyer, yet retained a free-spirited side, serving as a couchsurfing host and keeping his hands in the dirt with a lush backyard garden.

"Follow me, I want to show you something," Gene said while giving me a tour of his spacious property. He led me into a greenhouse and pointed to what looked like a rainforest exhibit. Underneath a set of heat lamps and vegetation, three tortoises munched a pile of mangos and collard greens. "I let them roam around the backyard when it's warm out," Gene said.

During my stay with Gene, he treated me to zydeco music and Cajun food. For three straight days, I ate from the Creole cookbook. Gene whipped up shrimp etouffe, a gravy-like seafood stew we poured over rice. I ate jambalaya, gumbo, and red beans and rice. On my last day, Gene took me out for boudin-- a sausage made from ground up pork livers and hearts combined with rice and Cajun seasonings. By the time I left Gene's home, any vegetarian purity I'd attained while living on Lucy's Farm was gone. The good food of Louisiana turned me back into a carnivore and left me a few pounds heavier.

Gene was the perfect host. Generous and authentic, he was as much a part of the swamp as the cypress knees that emerged around their mother tree. During my stay, he referred to me as "you old Yankee," despite the fact that I was half his age. As I ate my breakfast in his backyard one 60 degree morning, he said in a slow southern drawl, "What're you doing out here in the cold, you old Yankee?" With the spicy food, long dinner conversations, and unrushed manner of doing just about everything, Gene embodied southern hospitality and the couchsurfing spirit, which seemed to be one in the same thing.

*Henry's Farm and Hostel*

## Ten Days of Silence, Again

In the truest sense of the word "vacation," I took a serious vacation with another round of Vipassana meditation, this time in a center located just outside of Dallas, Texas. For ten days, after my feast in Louisiana and a week in Austin, I vacated my mind of all distraction and scraped away another layer of mental plaque that separated me from infinite peace and bliss.

As in Massachusetts, my mind ran wild during the first few days of silence. Between meals and meditations I strolled through the windy hill country of Texas and watched cattle from a nearby ranch amble about the pasture, eating patches of yellow grass from the dry land. I grew absorbed with watching other meditators, most notably a man with Lou Gehrig's disease who managed to get through the entire ten days without any assistance other than a walker and someone to hold the door open for him.

I experienced hour-long sits with painful knees and stabbing sensations in my back, without budging an inch. Finally, on day ten, I felt smoothed over and glowing, as if all the knots in my mind had been untied. A few pinholes of light and peace shone through the plaque.

I left the meditation center with a renewed sense of anicca, ah-knee-chuh---the changing nature of reality. The scenery changed as I drove from state to state. My bed changed from night to night. Every day I met new people. Every day I became a slightly new person.

## Bulgarians

From Texas, I drove through the deserts of New Mexico and Arizona, stopping along the way to hike in the Organ Mountains outside of Las Cruces and the Catalina Mountains of Tucson. I ate the best fish tacos of my life, couchsurfed with a puppeteer, and then made my way into southern California, where I ended my cross-country trip with a five star couchsurfing stop.

After driving through several days of desert, I exited the

> Henry's Farm and Hostel

highway into Palm Springs, California, where miles of palm tree covered golf courses displaced any authentic nature.

I pulled up to a large house in an upscale neighborhood. My Palm Spring couchsurfing hosts were clearly well-to-do. Grape vines snaked around a wooden arbor framing a patio on the side of the house. Olive and lemon trees grew in the front yard, giving the place a Mediterranean feel.

My hosts, a good looking couple in their 50s, each with dark brown hair and a Bulgarian accent, greeted me with wide open arms. "Come on in," they said enthusiastically. "Sorry our English isn't so good." In my opinion, they spoke perfect English.

The couple had an empty nest since their two daughters had gone off to college, so I slept in an intensely pink bedroom, still decorated with artwork and high school photos from their daughter's adolescent years.

For dinner, my hosts served a home-cooked meal of Bulgarian influence. The father and I sat at a long polished oak table as his wife brought out dishes.

First, we had a salad topped with olives and feta cheese with olive oil drizzled over the top. The main course consisted of wild mushroom gravy poured over roasted potatoes infused with rosemary, thyme, and oregano. For dessert we had homemade baklava--crispy layers of buttery paper thin dough with crushed pistachios and honey sandwiched in between. I had excellent meals in Louisiana, but my meal with the Bulgarians surpassed them all.

Over the course of dinner, the Bulgarians told me about fleeing from their home country fifteen years earlier. "We escaped an oppressive government," the father said.

"Yes," his wife said, "And we earned a new one."

The couple had fled their home country for political reasons, yet they spoke of their homeland as if it remained the best country on the planet.

I mentioned that my next farm was just a few miles from the beach and they said, "Yes, Bulgaria has fine beaches too.

# Henry's Farm and Hostel

Some of the best." When I mentioned my interest in traveling to Bulgaria someday, they said, "You will quickly fall in love. Bulgarian women are the most beautiful." They said the food, the beer, and the countryside were the best of the Balkans. "Bulgaria has everything," the husband said, not in a joking manner, but in a matter-of-fact tone.

By the time we finished dinner, as I nibbled on my third piece of baklava, the mother was saying, "Yes, you will go to Bulgaria and stay with my brother. He lives in the countryside." She wasn't joking either. She left it as an open offer. "Call us when you're ready to go," she said.

The following morning, I gave the couple a hug goodbye as if we were family. I felt eternally grateful. After many long hours of traveling alone on the road, their companionship gave me a renewed sense of belonging. In Shakespeare's words, I felt invigorated by the "milk of human kindness."

Like every other couchsurfing host, the Bulgarian couple had overcome the fear of letting a complete stranger into their home. They ignored the constant drumming of news channels and newspapers that say, *the world is a scary place, be afraid*. Anyone who's ever couchsurfed knows that isn't true.

After I pulled out of Palm Springs and continued westward, I witnessed one final change in scenery. The dry clear skies and rocky terrain of the desert gave way to greenery. Cool, moist air filled my lungs. The humidity rose as I approached the ocean, then just ten miles from the coast, rain poured down as I drove into the lush green hills north of Santa Barbara.

A month and a half after leaving my winter refuge in southern Florida, I arrived to spring wild flowers in California, in the middle of February. Just as I prolonged autumn by chasing it down the East Coast, I geared up for an extended spring season, ready to wwoof my way up the Pacific Coast.

## Henry's Farm & Hostel

I thought I'd taken a wrong turn as I neared Henry's Farm & Hostel, because the map led me through a residential

*Henry's Farm and Hostel*

neighborhood. I passed neatly mowed lawns and two story wooden houses with paved driveways. I saw a woman dressed in spandex jogging down the street with her yellow Labrador. This seemed an unlikely place to find a wwoofing farm.

Then I spotted a house with three chickens pecking and scratching in the front yard. Without seeing the address, I knew this was Henry's Farm & Hostel. Abandoned tools, spare car parts, a totem pole, and several gnome statues mingled with the lush undergrowth of flowers and shrubs in the front yard. Small orange fruits studded the tall wet grass underneath a heavily loaded Clementine tree. I pulled my car onto a grass-flattened portion of the front yard that doubled as the driveway.

Before I had a chance to knock on the half-opened front door, four German shepherds filed out like a train, barking a loud baritone chorus. They pummeled me and began pawing at my chest. Quickly, my fear of being torn to shreds was replaced by the fear of getting muddy paw prints on my jacket. The dogs were fat and loving, behaving more like overgrown puppies than guard dogs.

Next, Henry appeared at the door -- a tough wiry man in his 80s, with a long white beard hanging to his waist. He resembled Father Time with his flowing white hair and a stern face. Henry didn't greet me, he stood in the doorway as if to say, "What the hell are you doing here?" Meanwhile, the overweight German shepherds licked my hands and begged me to pet them.

I introduced myself and reminded Henry we'd made arrangements a couple of months in advance. He said, "Okay, come on in," and then he called the dogs back in the house. That's all I received in the way of greeting.

"The bedroom's over there, bathroom's over there." Henry didn't give me a tour so much as he stood in one place and pointed in different directions. Stacks of paper, magazines, and books covered every available surface, and a layer of dust covered the stacks. "Curfew's 10 p.m. It's $18 a night or 2.5

hours of work."

I began to understand that Henry considered everyone a hostel guest.

"I only turn the hot water heater on if at least three people want a shower. Five to six p.m. is your time window. You snooze, you lose."

That was my tour from Father Time. Henry addressed one of his hostel guests, who sat at a picnic table that doubled as the kitchen table. "Shannon," he said. "Show Brian how to log in his work hours."

Shannon, a well-groomed and energetic young man from New York, showed me Henry's accounting system for balancing nightly fare against hours worked.

"He's really not so bad once you get used to him," Shannon said, smiling a radiant smile and providing the perfect counterbalance to Henry's gloom. "He's just a grumpy old man." Shannon said all this loud and clear, as Henry hunched over his keyboard just two feet away, typing a letter to the local newspaper, proposing a ban on ATVs at a nearby beach.

In the middle of Shannon telling me about his recent week in Tijuana, where a Mexican girl had seized him from behind and forced tequila down his throat and then demanded payment, Henry got up from his computer. He walked over to the wall and began tugging at a dog leash or a belt, trying to unhook it from a snag of keys and bags dangling from the same hook. He grumbled, "stupid motherfuckers," presumably at the tangle of objects. He pried the leash free and marched out the front door with the dogs trailing after him. That was my introduction to Henry.

## We'll Condition 'em

I awakened on my first morning to Henry blowing on his bugle at 8 a.m. sharp. Apparently, this was a morning ritual at Henry's Farm & Hostel. Henry stood at the end of the hallway and trumpeted a spirited wake-up call, as if we were in the military and he expected everyone to roll out of bed and start

*Henry's Farm and Hostel*

doing jumping jacks. I heard Shannon groan and pull the blanket over his head. He slept in the top bunk of our bunk beds.

Henry didn't demand a structured workday. He just liked to get everyone moving bright and early. After the bugle call I couldn't get back to sleep, so I dressed and asked Henry what he had on the agenda for the day.

Henry, ever-spry for his age, slipped on a pair of knee-high muck boots and led me into the backyard. The backyard was the "farm" of Henry's Farm & Hostel and occupied about a quarter acre, with a living room size pig pen, where two pigs lay motionless in a couple inches of mud. The enormous pigs were clearly alive, but the only time I saw them move was when I chucked a bucket of expired leftovers into their trough.

Most of the backyard served as goat pasture, with nearly every leaf and blade of grass stripped clean, leaving a brown yard spotted with mud puddles. Three goats roamed the fenced area, keeping any green growth mowed down to stubble. A flock of hens completed Henry's stock of backyard farm animals.

The animals were Henry's groceries. Everything on Henry's farm was for his own personal consumption. He shared the eggs with us, but the goat's milk and pork were his, as was the small garden situated near the chicken coop.

When I first laid eyes on the garden, I saw a ramshackle fence, hammered together haphazardly with a hodgepodge of old wooden boards. I saw the attempts of previous wwoofers and hostel-guests to keep the goats and chickens out of the vegetables, or at least an attempt to accumulate their 2.5 hours of daily work.

As Henry led me over to the garden fence, he said, "This is what we're doing today." I made sure to keep my distance from the rusty nails jutting out of the boards. "We need to fortify it against the chickens, and there's the chicken wire." He pointed to a pile of orange mesh fencing.

I studied the existing fence for a few minutes. Wooden boards jutted out and formed a kind of chicken staircase, practically

## Henry's Farm and Hostel

inviting the chickens into the garden. It seemed like no matter how I wrapped the chicken wire around it, the chickens would just hop up the steps and jump right over. *Should I just tear it down and start fresh?* I wondered. I figured I'd better ask Henry, who had already marched over to the other end of the backyard to round up the goats for their morning milking.

Asking Henry a question, *any question,* was not a good idea. After knowing him for one day, I'd already learned to limit my interaction with him. For one thing, he couldn't hear well. Even if I spoke loudly, and enunciated each word, Henry had a bad reaction.

Just moments before, while Henry and I untangled the chicken wire for the fence, I casually asked if he knew of any nature hikes in the area, and he flared back, "No! That's not what we're doing right now!" His face turned bright red with anger, looking like his beard was about to go up in flames.

In order to get Henry's attention, I knew I needed to do a little play-acting. I staged myself beside the wacky fence, my hammer aimed on a nail, and just as he walked by, I acted surprised to see him. "Oh, hey Henry," I said at full volume. "I have a question about the fence, the part I'm working on right here."

Henry shot down my proposal to rebuild the fence. He said, "We'll condition 'em." He planned to sit in a lawn chair with a pellet gun and every time a chicken hopped up on the fence he'd pelt it with a plastic bullet. Henry practiced the old school method of psychology – reinforcement through punishment.

That morning I watched Henry give the same treatment to his goats. Every day, when milking time rolled around, Henry unleashed a stream of profanity and fired his pellet gun at the animals until he got all three of them into the milking pen.

As I witnessed this crazed event for the first time, while I hammered chicken wire to the garden fence, Henry caught me watching with a big smile on my face. His cheeks flushed violently red and he yelled from across the backyard, "If you're working, work!"

## Henry of the Moment

Henry was the grumpiest man I've ever met. Despite a strong constitution, he didn't age with grace. Henry rebelled against the natural dulling of his senses. He flew into a rage when anybody noticed his loss of hearing and vision, and any interaction with him brought attention to those things.

During my ten days of meditation, I learned to accept the reality of each moment. If I felt good, I observed the pleasant sensation with a smile and the understanding that it wasn't forever. If I felt pain, I learned to observe the unpleasant sensation with a balanced mind and know that "this too will pass away." I observed my reality as it was, not as I wanted it to be. I observed reality through the lens of anicca – trillions of subatomic births and deaths every second, putting me in a constant state of flux.

I exited the meditation center with a greater capacity for accepting change. In the process, I also gained insight into why some people suffer more than others.

Henry was a good study. I thought back to the man with Lou Gehrig's disease at the meditation center in Texas. Once an avid hiker and rock climber, he was half Henry's age, yet in far worse physical condition. He could barely speak, walk, or swallow his food anymore, yet he radiated friendliness.

I wondered why Henry was so pissed off all the time, while my friend with Lou Gehrig's disease smiled at the world. The conclusion I came to was this: Henry rebelled against his own reality. Painful joints, loss of hearing, and failing vision brought double misery. He suffered first from the physical breakdown, and then he magnified his suffering many times by generating anger and frustration toward the unpleasant sensations. Henry, the man Shannon and I called Father Time, wanted to live in a timeless, painless state.

Henry was always pissed off because he didn't embrace the Henry of the moment. Men and women in far worse shape could smile at the world because they knew "this too will pass." No pain is eternal.

*Henry's Farm and Hostel*

## Dinner's in the Red Containers

On several occasions, usually after observing one of Henry's temper tantrums, I reminded myself of the simple truth, "This too will pass." Henry's Farm & Hostel wasn't forever. New farms and new hosts awaited me in the near future.

Henry only asked for 2.5 hours of work each day, which sounded like an excellent deal, but neither the food nor the lodging were all that good. Dinner consisted of leftovers from Henry's senior nutrition meal. He attended lunch at a senior community center and brought back leftovers in what he called "the red containers." Old Folgers coffee containers. The food resembled something you'd expect to find in a middle-school cafeteria.

"Dinner's in the red containers," Henry announced gruffly as he hurried through the kitchen and slid three plastic coffee containers into the fridge.

Henry only joined me and the other hostel guests for dinner on one occasion. In typical brusque manner, he pulled a leg of pork out of the microwave, a piece from last year's pig, and said "Move over!" as he squeezed up to the picnic table in his kitchen.

For a good ten minutes, Henry fell silent as he chewed bits of pork from the bone. About half-way through his greasy, tough looking hunk of pork, Henry suddenly turned thoughtful and said to me and the other guests, "You can have some if you want." Only the young man from France, we called T-bone, took him up on his offer. The rest of us continued eating the red container special – mushy spaghetti and meatballs with a side of steamed spinach, the food someone deemed nutritious for senior citizens.

As for sleeping accommodations, things appeared fairly neat and organized at a quick glance, but after I examined the interior of Henry's house a bit closer, unsettling details came into focus. Mouse poop, which appeared as random piles of broken up pencil lead, littered the carpet. A layer of grime and dust covered every surface. Aimed at any one place in the

> Henry's Farm and Hostel

house, a microscope probably would've revealed dead skin cells and fingerprints from thousands of hostel guests. Henry's Hostel contained genetic material from all over the world.

Shannon told me the previous guests left because of a bed bug infestation. With that thought in mind, after Henry moved me to the "couple's room," I decided to sleep on the floor and take my chances with the mice.

The couple's room had amusing décor; items showing a different side of Henry – Henry the Environmentalist. He stocked the couple's room with an ample supply of condoms. A large poster on the wall with a declining line graph promoted Negative Population Growth. Next to the poster a sticker pressed to the wall read, "Recreate not Procreate."

## Museum of Henry

Aside from being a grumpy old man, Henry cared deeply for the environment. This was his one redeeming quality. Throughout his life, Henry waged successful battles to save coastal habitats and wetlands.

His most recent battle pitted him against wealthy coastal developers, spanning several years and ending with the victorious preservation of Point Sal, a several mile stretch of pristine sand dunes and coastal habitat west of Santa Maria, California. After hiking Point Sal during my stay at Henry's Farm & Hostel, I understood why many locals saw Henry as a town hero. The magical stretch of coastline contained tide pools teeming with aquatic life, and birds and plants that seemed especially well-adapted to the sandy, salty habitat. Henry kept the area free of hotels and restaurants.

Henry may not have been an amiable fellow, but he was a friend of the earth, and I admired him for that.

Henry displayed his achievements in clear sight, for all his hostel guests to see. Every square inch of wall space in his house was dedicated to himself – a museum of Henry. Framed and laminated newspaper clippings chronicled Henry's battles to preserve Point Sal and coastal wetlands. One newspaper article focused on Henry's advocacy for medical marijuana. A portrait of Henry and his long white beard bordered the article with the caption, "local man uses marijuana to treat glaucoma."

Photographs and paintings of Henry plastered the walls in a kind of celebration of himself. He even had postcards made of himself posing in the sand dunes of Point Sal. One thing was clear. This man was proud of his life's work and he wasn't humble about it.

## Au revoir, Henry

Environmentalist Henry, the man who fought for the preservation of the natural world, did exist. Unfortunately, when I passed through Henry's Hostel, grumpy Henry reigned supreme. At first, I viewed his behavior as an observation into human suffering. I enjoyed some good laughs with Shannon, after the two of us witnessed one of Henry's flare-ups. But after awhile, the grumpiness, filthy conditions, and bugle wake-up calls became too much for me. I left Henry's Farm & Hostel earlier than planned, as did several other guests.

The bad vibrations also overwhelmed T-bone and his girlfriend, a sweet French couple in the process of hitchhiking from Montreal, Canada down to the southern tip of Argentina.

Henry handled the French-English language barrier with quite possibly the foulest attitude I'd ever seen. When T-bone or his girlfriend looked at Henry in puzzlement after he delivered a work order or an attempt at casual conversation, Henry turned red and yelled at them. He repeated himself like he was about to have a heart attack. Then he resorted to his usual refrain. "Brian, explain," or "Shannon, explain," and walked away.

So the French and I said fare-thee-well to Henry. We said, "So long and au revoir, Henry." The heavyset German shepherds followed me out to my car and, despite Henry's grumpy nature, he gave me a handshake and an uncharacteristic smile. I considered Henry's obvious suffering and thought, *this too*

*Henry's Farm and Hostel*

*will pass, Henry.* I smiled as I returned to my car, which felt more like home than ever. I knew I was on to something new.

# Chapter 8
## *Farm in the Canyon*

After a week of living with Henry, I began making desperate phone calls to other farms. No one had room for me, but one farm host gave me a promising lead. She said, "I already have enough volunteers, but a friend of mine needs a hand since her husband recently had a stroke."

The no-name farm, which I came to know as the Farm in the Canyon, was four hours inland, located in the foothills of the Sierra Nevada Mountains.

Over the phone, Anore, the friend who needed a hand, asked a few questions. Where was I coming from? Where was I going? Did have a dietary preference? I think she wanted to get a feel for my level of sanity, since I'd be living in close quarters with her husband and granddaughter.

Anore told me I'd be helping with the garden, chopping wood, and repairing the goat fence. "We have goats, chickens, and a few other farm animals," she said. "And we live in a very beautiful area." That was all I learned about the farm.

Knowing so little about the place, I had a moment of doubt when she asked, "When can you be here?"

But then I thought about the mouse poop on the bedroom floor and dinner from the red container. An image of Henry flashed through my head, white-bearded and swearing at the

## Farm in the Canyon

goats. I considered the seven a.m. bugle call, and I told Anore, "I can be there tonight."

She accepted.

I had never seen the Sierra Nevada Mountains, the mountain range encompassing Yosemite and Sequoia National Parks. Anore lived a mile from the western edge of Sequoia National Park, in Three Rivers.

I drove across the dry southern valley of California, leaving the ocean behind. After passing through Bakersfield, I passed through the brown rocky landscape for miles without seeing a house, farm animal, or crop. The land didn't have the character of true desert, nor did it possess the rugged beauty of jagged rock formations. The terrain was a featureless brown plateau that never flattened out.

I wondered if I'd made a mistake veering so far off the lush green path of California's coastland. *Would it be brown forever?*

My doubts were allayed when I climbed into the foothills of the Sierra Nevada Mountains. The air blowing in from my car window felt cool and dry, but I saw evidence of recent rainfall in the luxuriant green grass covering the hillsides. Splotches of purple and orange painted the rolling landscape, where spring lupines and poppies blossomed. A streak of yellow or white overtook the green grass where fiddleneck and popcorn flowers exploded in masses of tiny petals.

I saw families of cattle grazing on the steep slopes, keeping the grass mowed short for miles in both directions. Every so often I stepped on my brake pedal to pass over a cattle-guard, a widely spaced metal grating in the road that deterred cattle from migrating to somebody else's land. It seemed everyone in the foothills kept cattle or goats. The goats were less visible, but I did see a few herds near the tops of the hills.

Enormous boulders studded the green, mostly treeless landscape, and from afar snow capped mountains overlooked the entire canyon as it snaked through the foothills. After crossing the brown valley, I felt as though I'd entered a Zen garden of magnificent proportions.

*Farm in the Canyon*

## Caretakers

Snowmelt from the mountains poured into the ice-cold South Fork River, the crystal clear river that ran through the canyon and Anore's backyard. As I pulled into Anore's driveway I heard the river before I saw it. A steady rush filled my ears, as if a waterfall poured over the edge just around the canyon wall.

The first structure I saw was a wooden house surrounded by a white picket fence. The fence looked ornamental, as it had a permanent gap where the driveway entered onto a two-car garage. The house looked like something from a vacation brochure for a dude ranch, sitting atop a hill, with a stained wood finish to give it the look of a rustic cabin.

I never entered the house on the hill during my stay with Anore, nor did I see anybody else use the house. The owner, a wealthy businessman, lived in Los Angeles. He owned all of the Farm the Canyon, yet only visited to take his clients for a horseback ride or show off his flock of peacocks.

Anore and her husband Keith served as caretakers for the Farm in the Canyon. For nearly twenty years they'd taken care of the animals and carved out a living for themselves down by the river.

Financially speaking, the land didn't belong to Anore and Keith. Regardless, they'd cultivated a deep and long-lasting relationship with the land, river, and farm animals.

After I passed the driveway to the lord's vacation manor, I drove down a switchback gravel road to Anore and Keith's home – a one-story house surrounded by a functional wire fence. Two barking dogs patrolled the fenced in yard. A stack of chopped wood sat on the front porch, and a much larger pile of whole logs rested beside a chopping stump.

Farm animals idled and munched on their food, enjoying the sunshine and pasture outside their respective coop or barn. As I pulled into a parking area, I saw a flock twenty or so chickens pecking in the grass. A cat lounged on a wooden fence beam, resting its chin on one paw while watching the

## Farm in the Canyon

chickens with lazy interest. A dozen peacocks strutted around the barn entrance, free of any fencing. The steady cluck of hens was soothing compared to the sporadic trumpet calls of the ornately feathered male peacocks. The males carried several feet of brilliant green feathers in the dirt behind them, stopping frequently to prune their shiny blue neck feathers.

Before meeting my new farm hosts, I walked over to the barn and admired the diversity of farm animals. In a fenced in rocky enclosure, nineteen goats grazed on vines, grass, and the early leaf buds of trees. A billy goat with a long goatee stood perched on the tip of a tall rock, wearing a cowbell around his neck. Behind the goat yard, I caught my first glimpse of the fast-moving South Fork River, which raced over rocks, stirring up pockets of white froth.

On the other side of the barn, three horses eagerly stepped up to the fence and sniffed my hands. I stroked the forehead of one of them and when I made a move to pull my hand back through the fence she bumped my arm into the air, apparently telling me it wasn't time to stop petting her.

Later in my stay, I learned Anore and Keith also kept five cows, but the cows spent most of their time grazing on the hillside pasture somewhere out of sight.

On my way to the front door, a dog tied to one of the trees erupted into a burst of excited barking, drowning out the sound of hens, peacocks, and the rush of the river.

I heard the squeak of a screen door and a tall, slender woman stepped out on the porch. She had prominent cheekbones and a touch of platinum-grey in her short, light-brown hair. Creases radiated from the corners of her eyes, as if she'd spent much of her life smiling or squinting into the sun. Her piercing gaze and direct manner of speech alluded to an inner strength and confidence absent in most people. "If he lunges at you, kick him in the gut," she said, referring to the barking dog. I knew this must be Anore.

After I stepped onto the porch to greet her with a handshake, her eyes softened a bit and she gave me a warm smile, but

| Brian J. Bender

*Farm in the Canyon*

few words. Inside the house, I met her husband Keith, who lay on the couch next to a crackling fireplace. He managed to right himself to a sitting position and give me a handshake and smile, but I could tell this took serious effort for him. Despite his difficulties after a recent stroke, he retained a tough physical appearance. His sun-weathered face reminded me of a sailor who'd been out to sea for many years, his skin whipped and tightened by sun, wind, and salt water.

A beautiful young woman with nearly black hair sat at the kitchen table working on problems from a high school chemistry book. "This is Vanessa," Anore said, introducing the two of us. As I unpacked my stuff in a spacious computer room, which became my bedroom for the week, I heard Vanessa chat with her Grandma about swim practice, her long hair still wet and smelling of chlorine.

When I stepped into the kitchen to grab a glass of water, Keith called to Vanessa from the couch. In a slow measured voice he said, "Did you almost drown again?" Vanessa looked at me and blushed before stomping off to her bedroom and telling her grandpa to "shut up!" They clearly had a loving and playful relationship.

## Eskimos

Over a spaghetti dinner with ground beef from one of the farm's own cattle, Anore relayed a bit of her life story, shedding some light on their history. For thirty years, both of them lived in the remote Alaskan wilderness north of the Arctic Circle. They lived in Ambler, Alaska, an Inupiat village of 200. The Inupiat are one of many indigenous people we generically label Eskimos.

Anore learned from the Inupiat elders. They taught her traditional methods of fishing and harvesting wild plants from the stark yet "stunningly beautiful" countryside. Keith hunted caribou for food and clothing and worked as a commercial fisherman for part of the year.

The two of them built a sod-house in the middle of wind-

Farming Around the Country | 133

blown arctic wilderness and raised their two girls in this environment. A team of sled dogs lived outside their sod house year around. Anore didn't mention the treatment of their dogs, but judging by how she greeted me in their front yard, maybe she did have to occasionally "kick a dog in the gut" to establish dominance.

Anore told me Keith developed talent as a musher, or dogsled driver, and made a run in the famous Iditarod dogsled race. After a grueling two and half weeks and 1100 miles, Keith crossed the finish line in Nome, Alaska in the top twenty.

When I first met Keith, as he lay on the couch by the fire, I saw a man who refused to be taken down by a stroke. The stroke was so crippling that Keith lost a good deal of his capacity for speech. He also had constant difficulty getting around because of vertigo. I couldn't think of many things worse than being in a room that never stopped spinning.

Despite Keith's stroke, he showed incredible will power to walk on his own and carry on conversations without assistance. In carefully measured words, as I spun spaghetti noodles around my fork, Keith sat at the kitchen table with us and told me the brief history of his professional careers. In as concise a manner as possible, he told me he'd been a cowboy back in Wyoming, then a commercial fisherman, catching sockeye salmon in Alaska. Keith's fishing career was cut short after the Exxon Valdez oil tanker crashed and spilled crude oil all over the Alaskan shoreline. Keith was part of a class-action lawsuit that had been dragging on for two decades.

Enunciating each word carefully, Keith managed to say, "Even if we win, we'll end up owing the lawyers money."

## Climbing Mt. McKinley

Throughout dinner, as I listened to the amazing life stories of Keith and Anore, Vanessa pored over her chemistry book, trying to solve problems for class the next day. She'd probably heard about her grandparents' ascent of Mt. McKinley a thousand times. This wasn't news to her.

*Farm in the Canyon*

I, on the other hand, was awestruck, sitting across the table from the second woman to summit Mt. McKinley.

Anore told me that back in 1962, she and a group of four men, including Keith, made the ascent without oxygen masks or high-tech gear. "Moisture was our biggest threat," she said. "If we didn't keep our clothes completely dry, they'd freeze."

They ate dried meat, cheese, and trail mix along the way. Once they reached the top, a friend of theirs arranged for a wooden crate full of oranges to be dropped on the summit. Evidently this was a special treat in Alaska, not to mention the top of North America's tallest mountain.

The whole journey took Anore and the group of men seven weeks. One week to ski to the base of the mountain and another six weeks to climb a jagged glacier full of crevasses.

Anore gave an oral history of her Mt. McKinley experience to the U.S. Fish and Wildlife Service, and in it she commented on what it was like to be outside in the great wide-open space of Denali Park for seven weeks. She said, "You get a sense of peace and rightness and wholeness and satisfaction from being at home with the land, or in that case, the ice, for six weeks. I would wish it for the whole world. It seems like a human ought to have that by rights, as opposed to the chaos and political problems that are in the news every day."

As far as enduring harsh conditions, Anore and Keith were the strongest people I'd ever met. Even after Keith's stroke, they didn't show any signs of slowing down.

Serving as caretakers of the Farm in the Canyon seemed like a labor-intensive retirement for Anore and Keith. In reality, retirement wasn't in the picture for them. Anore chopped wood on a daily basis, milked goats, took care of chickens, cows, peacocks, horses, dogs and cats, and also tended to the needs of Keith and her energetic and scholarly granddaughter.

On top of that, Anore kept a garden and was in the middle of writing a book about the traditional food wisdom of Inupiat people. After a night of getting to know Anore and studying her weathered, yet attractive face, which remained full of vigor, I understood why she might need a hand to lighten her load a bit. I felt honored and happy to be that person.

## Leader of Goats

Every night I watched out my bedroom window as Anore led the goats back into their enclosure. During the day, the goats were allowed to roam freely over hundreds of acres of pasture on the other side of the South Fork River. They grazed on wild plants, climbed the rocky hillside, and did basically everything wild mountain goats do. As the sun settled, the goats dutifully returned to the bridge on the far side of the river and waited for Anore. The goats were punctual and routine-oriented, much like all farm animals. At sunset, they expected to reenter their safe enclosure and munch on the hay and grains that awaited them.

The nightly goat roundup was as ritualistic for Anore as for the goats. For her, this routine was as common as doing dishes or brushing her teeth. For me, the scene looked like something from a different age---a villager leading her herd down from the Swiss Alps.

From my window, I watched like a voyeur as Anore opened the gate on the far side of the river and attached a rope to the leather collar of the lead billy goat. The goat wore a bell around his neck, so when I heard the dull metal clanking resound off the canyon walls, I knew they were coming home. Anore led the procession, holding onto the rope with the billy goat trailing dutifully behind. The other eighteen goats followed in single file behind Anore and the billy.

The expression on Anore's face was stoic. She didn't appear giddy, as I probably would've been in her place. I would've been thinking to myself, "Wow! I can't believe all these goats are following me. I can't believe I'm walking alongside a crystal clear mountain river in the foothills of the Sierra Nevada Mountains!"

Anore had the face of experience. She led the goats calmly, meditatively through a cactus garden Keith had planted along the riverbank. Through the screen of my window, I heard the continual rush of the river. Colorful patches of wildflowers and vibrant green grass were visible on the other side of the river, but they grew dimmer and softer as the night washed in.

When I heard the clanking cowbell stop, I knew the goats were latched safely into their nightly enclosure, secure from the cougars and bears Anore and Keith frequently spotted on their side of the river. Anore, the leader of goats, had taken good care of her milk supply and the lives of nineteen animals for yet another night.

## Wave of Steel

The goats were so robust and accustomed to daily foraging freedom that they sometimes became greedy and successfully jumped the six-foot fence surrounding their nightly enclosure. To remedy this and prevent the goats from tearing their udders on the top of the fence, I helped Anore erect a higher section of fencing.

In the process of straightening a roll of wire fencing, I received the first bloody nose of my wwoofing adventure. The tightly coiled roll had so much tension locked into its formation that I had to unroll it a few feet at a time and stamp it to the ground. I didn't realize the full force of the tension until I absentmindedly looked over at a peacock and took my foot off the fence. No longer pinned down, the far end of the metal fence curled off the ground like a tidal wave of steel and pounded me in the face. Instantly, a stream of bright red blood rushed from my nose.

Luckily, my nose wasn't broken, and by the end of the day the goats had a nine-foot fence to reckon with.

Much of my work on the Farm in the Canyon involved daily chores that kept the place heated and invested in future food. I chopped firewood. I moved topsoil across the bridge and shoveled horse manure from the stables in order to form raised beds for a garden. And every night I helped Anore wash dishes and clean up the kitchen--a small favor in exchange for

*Farm in the Canyon*

the delicious array of food she whipped up during my stay.

## Weston A. Price

Every day for breakfast, Anore made me the most delicious smoothie I've ever had – a blended concoction of creamy raw goat's milk, two egg yolks, coconut oil, a frozen persimmon, and a sprinkle of powdered seaweed. No milkshake I'd ever had compared with that morning smoothie. After drinking it down to the last drop, I felt charged with long-lasting energy: ready to chop wood and shovel horse manure.

For dinner, Anore served up several unique meals. One night we rolled sushi, using slivers of raw trout shipped from a friend in Alaska. Anore and Keith ate the fish in its frozen state. "It's the Inupiat way," Anore said. Vanessa refused to touch the uncooked fish. She ate avocado and cream cheese rolls in between studying for a chemistry test.

One night we had beans simmered in a bone marrow broth with a side of steamed nettles Anore collected from the other side of the river. This was my first experience with *eating* nettles. I knew stinging nettles were to be avoided like poison oak, but Anore showed me how to strip the leaves off using a pair of gloves, and as soon as they boiled down to a wilted looking leaf, they lost their sting and acquired a buttery green tea flavor. I know it sounds cliché, but I felt the health course through my arteries. After eating a bowl of nettles, I honestly felt like I'd just popped five vitamin supplements.

Other nights we had Indian or Italian food, and every meal was accompanied by homemade sourdough bread slathered with copious amounts of butter. I'd come a long way since eating Henry's leftover senior nutrition meals.

Over the course of my farm tour, I sampled interesting diets. After Malcolm left, I tried eating nothing but bananas for the first half of the day. On Hector and Lucy's farm I ate a mostly vegetarian diet. In Maine and North Carolina I had ˜nal flesh taken right from the local sheep and deer. Many ⁷ dinners were vegan and downright delicious, despite the lack of real cheese and butter.

Except for the red container diet, all the diets I tried had their good sides. I'd never eaten such fresh vegetables, eggs, and milk in all my life. I knew everything on my plate came from top quality sources, right outside my bedroom window or tent flap.

The food I enjoyed at the Farm in the Canyon easily ranked among the best food of my life. Not only did I enjoy fresh eggs, milk, and meat from the happy free-range residents of the foothills, this natural food was prepared in such a way as to maximize digestibility and nutritional value. Anore derived most of her cooking techniques from the work of an anthropologist named Weston A. Price, a man who brought traditional food wisdom to western civilization.

Weston A. Price, an Ohio dentist from the early 1900s, became suspicious of refined foods after seeing decades of patients with awful teeth and stunted bone growth of the face and skull. He set off on a trip around the world to study the diets of so-called "primitive" societies. A small sampling of his subjects included Eskimos, the Maori of New Zealand, villagers in the Swiss Alps, Scotland, and Ireland, plus tribes in remote regions of Africa, Peru, the Andes, and the Pacific Islands.

Dr. Price's research found these so-called primitive people not only had perfect dental health, but also displayed a high degree of physical and mental health unrivaled by the people of Western society. Chronic diseases and mental health issues appeared to be absent.

The common dietary thread Dr. Price found in every primitive society was a diet that consisted of whole foods, never refined or processed. Raw dairy products served as a cornerstone in the diet of all tribes who had access to milking animals. None of the tribes Dr. Price studied practiced a strictly vegetarian diet. All consumed animal, fish, or insects. In addition, fermented foods played an important part in their diets – things such as sauerkraut, cheese, kefir and kvass.

*Farm in the Canyon*

Fermented foods not only solved the no-refrigerator problem, but also added the digestion-bonus of beneficial bacteria, the stuff marketing gurus now call probiotics.

## Kefir and Kvass

Anore had kefir on hand at all times. We sipped it after meals or ate it like yogurt, topped with honey or fruit. I watched her make it so many times that the process became burned into my memory.

First, she poured a recently fermented jar of kefir through a pasta strainer. She collected the finished kefir in a jar below the strainer and placed it in the fridge for us to drink. From the strainer, she spooned out several popcorn sized kefir grains and dropped them into a clean mason jar. The grains looked like cauliflower florets. They consisted of a gelatinous bacteria and yeast complex. In the new jar, Anore poured fresh goat's milk over the grains, stirred, and set the jar in a dark, warm place to ferment for a day. By the following morning, the milk thickened into a runny yogurt-like consistency and developed a slightly sour zing. If Anore wanted to separate the curds and whey in order to make goat's cheese, she simply let the kefir concoction sit for an extra day, then poured the milk solids over a cheesecloth. We used the whey, a clear yellowish liquid, in rice or oats, to make them more digestible after soaking in water over night.

Anore also made a fermented drink called beet kvass. She sliced several beets and allowed them to ferment in a jar of water for a few days, much like the kefir. The finished product resembled champagne – a purple effervescent drink. The beet champagne provided the same digestive powers as kefir, but with an added touch of alcohol from the fermented beet sugar. I always felt more alert and in a slightly more pleasant mood after chasing my dinner with a shot of kefir or kvass.

## d Fats, Bad Fats

favorite part about the Weston A. Price diet is its

J. Bender

foundation in traditional dietary wisdom: eating habits honed for thousands of years, rather than a new science-based diet or Hollywood fad. The diets of traditional cultures were linked to a long track record of physical and mental health.

Another thing I liked about the Weston A. Price diet was that it didn't shy away from fats. In fact, it encouraged them. Bacon and eggs? No problem, as long as they came from pastured hens and pigs raised on a natural diet. A stick of butter a day? No problem, as long as the cream came from a grass-fed animal, unpasteurized.

For almost my entire life I believed fats and cholesterol should be consumed in moderation. After reading several of Anore's books, I discovered an entire foundation had been erected in the name of Weston A. Price in order to disseminate traditional dietary wisdom and debunk theories that demonize fat and cholesterol.

According to the Weston A. Price Foundation, good fats should comprise the majority of one's calorie intake. What are the good fats? Animal fats, olive oil, coconut oil, and other nut oils. Bad fats, on the other hand, should be avoided like the plague. These include vegetable, canola, corn, and soybean oil, plus hydrogenated and pasteurized products.

After drinking my morning smoothie of raw egg yolks, raw milk, and coconut oil, I felt completely satisfied. Normally, I'm accustomed to eating a much larger breakfast, but a smoothie like the one Anore made for me, packed full of nutrient-dense fats, satiated all my stomach's cravings.

In reference to cholesterol, which serves as one of the body's main repair mechanisms, the Weston A. Price foundation draws the following analogy: "...just as a large police force is needed where crime occurs frequently, so cholesterol is needed in a poorly nourished body to protect the individual from heart disease and cancer. Blaming coronary heart disease on cholesterol is like blaming the police for murder and theft in a high crime area."

I left the Farm in the Canyon with a better understanding of

*Farm in the Canyon*

who my food allies are. Fat is my friend. I learned cholesterol is an ally in repairing my body, rather than the enemy it's often labeled. I decided to never take a cholesterol-lowering drug so long as I live. Butter, bacon, eggs, raw milk, and cheese are foods I no longer see as taboo, so long as they come from happy, healthy animals.

After my short stay at the Farm in the Canyon, essentially my temporary refuge from Henry's Farm, Anore sent me on my way with edible souvenirs: a bag of pink-fleshed oranges, dried persimmons, and my very own kefir grain. "Feed it with fresh milk whenever you get the chance," she told me.

I left the Farm in the Canyon with warm farewells from Keith, Vanessa, and Anore, and insight into two of the most adventurous and hard-lived people I'd ever met. I nestled my pet kefir into a cooler and set off toward the ocean once again.

## Road between Farms

Since the beginning of my wwoofing trip, I always experienced a sharp and sudden scenery change when I picked up and left a farm, especially one as beautiful as Anore's place.

I spent month-long segments of my life in idyllic settings: the crisp autumn mountains of North Carolina, the lush tropics of Lucy's Farm, and the rocky sheep pasture and primordial forest in Maine. I spent time in the peace and quiet of plants and farm animals, and then reentered the stream of fast cars and billboard-studded highways. I glanced frequently in my rearview mirror, careful to keep my speed up or stay to the right in order to prevent other drivers from flying into a rage.

Although my blood pressure shot up a bit on the highways, I did enjoy the scenery. I saw many interesting road signs along the way. In a construction area I saw an orange sign warning *Smokefog*. Another one said, *Men in Trees*. I didn't quite know what those signs meant. Slow down?

As I entered the dust blown regions of southern New Mexico a sign warned--*Dust Storms May Exist*. I saw my favorite of all the road signs in Texas. A cartoon turtle wearing a hard-hat

*Farm in the Canyon*

held his hand up to *Stop*. In a voice bubble, the turtle said, "Play it safe, kids. The oilfield is not a playground." I really wondered how many kids looked at the field of oil derricks and saw it as a giant jungle gym.

In Georgia, I saw banners that advertised, *Boiled Green Peanuts* hung along the tops of roadside stands. Pecan trading posts announced, *We Buy, Sell, and Crack.*

Each region had its own special scenery. Near Blacksburg, Virginia, I enjoyed the smooth rolling Appalachian Mountains, not a jagged edge to be seen for miles.

In California, the sheer bounty of agriculture impressed me most of all. Near Santa Barbara, Nipomo, and San Luis Obispo, expansive fields of artichokes and strawberries stretched out along Highway 101. Teams of Mexicans picked the strawberry fields, wearing improvised biohazard suits made from an assemblage of handkerchiefs, masks, and gloves. The fields were clearly coated with toxic pesticides.

On my way out of the Farm in the Canyon, as I headed west along a more northern route, I passed through the world's largest cache of almond trees – endless rows of neatly planted trees, all the same height and separated by strips of grass. Groves of pistachio, orange, and lemon trees broke up the almond monotony every so often.

The almond trees grew in California's central valley, often called the world's biggest garden. I admired the grand-scale of the farming operation, but I also doubted such a thing could go on for much longer. I imagined what would happen when the outside water source dried up and the land reverted back to its natural state – the semi-arid desert I'd seen driving into the Sierra Nevada Mountains from the south. The multibillion dollar almond economy would collapse if the beehives couldn't be imported for pollination. So many environmental factors seemed pitted against such a large-scale mono-crop operation.

Although most of the farms I drove past were saturated with toxic chemicals and represented the very picture of unsustainable agriculture, I did see a good deal of beauty in the land. The repeating rows of almond trees had a calming effect on me. They stirred up nostalgia for the long bike rides I used to take in Ohio, where just outside my hometown I pedaled alongside a sea of corn and soybeans, an unbroken stretch of gold and green rustling in the breeze.

## Factory Farm

Crowded plants can hold a sort of beauty, one of bounty and simplicity. But after leaving the great garden of the central valley, I came upon a far less appealing sight, dominated by tightly bunched animals rather than plants. About an hour east of Santa Cruz, I witnessed a cattle factory farm.

I didn't see a single blade of grass on the two-mile long ranch. Just tangled knots of cattle feeding from troughs of corn. I knew from reading about such places that "downer" cows were a big problem. Cows became so sick from an unnatural diet and lack of exercise that they simply collapsed and couldn't stand on their own legs.

The feedlot operation represented a stark contrast to cattle in the foothills of the Sierra Nevadas, where small bovine families grazed along the mountain pasture and moved from one patch of fresh grass to another. They dumped their cow pies in a mat of freshly mowed grass and wildflowers and moved on. The cattle I saw through my car window were forever confined in their own excrement.

The feedlot was a reality not depicted on the packaging of USDA prime cuts or Certified Angus beef. Nonetheless, most beef originated from similar crowded brown worlds. I wonder how many people would continue eating conventional grain-fed meats if they knew the health of the animals they consumed. For me, the unsavory sight served as yet another reminder to eat local and know the source of my food.

## Monterey

After I drove through the valley of almonds, I finally got to see familiar faces. My parents flew out from Ohio to visit me

*Farm in the Canyon*

in Monterey.

For once, I didn't have to pull weeds or shovel manure to earn my keep. My parents treated me to a week of seafood and bike rides along the rainy Pacific coast. One of my favorite memories of the trip was when the three of us rode into a stretch of torrential rains. We spotted a patch of trees on a coastal golf course and quickly took cover under the thick foliage. I pulled some of the pink-fleshed oranges out of my pouch, the gift from Anore, and while we waited for the rain to lighten we sat in the dry grass and enjoyed the sweet citrus of California.

The Monterey my parents and I experienced was different from the one immortalized by John Steinbeck in *Cannery Row*. He described it as a foul-smelling place filled with gamblers, thieves, and drunks. Whorehouses and flophouses lined the streets. Everything was in some way connected to the smelly fishing and canning industry.

My parents and I, on the other hand, saw hordes of well-dressed tourists gripping their cameras, walking the streets while drinking cappuccinos from Starbucks. Things had changed. The one thing still remaining from the old foul-smelling days was the dramatic coastal scenery. We sat on the beach and watched the waves smack against the rocky shoreline, sending up sprays of salt water. We ate clam chowder and watched sea otters swim on their backs through beds of kelp forest.

We drove north of Monterey to Ano Nuevo Point and watched 5000-pound elephant seals lounge in the sand with their pups. The pups, only a few months old, were already the size of morbidly obese humans. Every now and then a seal flipped some sand up on its back to reduce the sun's heat, but that was about all the action we saw of them.

Monterey was about as leisurely for me as for those elephant seals. My parents rented a hotel room for us, so for the first time in a while I slept amid pristine cleanliness. My boots, embedded with bits of muck and manure from farms around

*Farm in the Canyon*

the country, sat next to the door of my sterile bedroom.

The clean environment didn't last long, for after the week ended I hugged my parents goodbye and set off on a couchsurfing spree through the Bay Area.

## Spiny Lumpsucker

I made my first stop in Santa Cruz, where I stayed with an older couple with an empty nest. I surfed through San Jose, spent a couple of nights in the redwoods of Big Basin State Park, and then stopped in San Francisco for a few days.

The highlights of San Francisco were the best banana cream pie I'd ever had, sushi fresh from Japan's world-renowned Tsukiji Market, and a naked man walking down Baker Beach curling dumbbells.

An aquarium located in Golden Gate Park held perhaps my favorite part of the city. I saw a little fish about the size of a fishing bobber, called the Pacific Spiny lumpsucker. The lumpsucker had tiny side fins that fluttered, causing it to wobble though the water. The slightest change in current caused the fish to wobble out of control.

For some reason, the spiny lumpsucker made me happy. This fish was an amazingly poor swimmer, yet managed to survive on its own terms. The spiny lumpsucker spent most of its time gripping to rocks at the bottom of the aquarium tank. It puckered its pronounced red lips as if to say, *You don't need to be a good swimmer to be a fish. You just need a pair of aqualungs and a style that works for you.*

## Dhamma Servers

I made my final couchsurfing stop in Berkeley, where I slept in a backyard tree house. After living like a gypsy in the Bay Area for two weeks, I wanted to settle in one place and clear my head before starting at my next farm in April.

I located another meditation center, this one near Yosemite National Park, and signed on as a *dhamma server*, as helpers of the meditation center are called. Instead of sitting on a pillow

> Farm in the Canyon

in deep meditation for ten days, I assumed the position of head cook.

For a week and a half I cooked up ten-gallon pots of oatmeal and boiled prunes. I sautéed onions, garlic, and ginger with cumin and mustard seed for spicy Indian dishes, such as dhal and curried vegetables. With the help of nine other servers, I chopped massive piles of potatoes, cauliflower, carrots, cabbage, and broccoli. I made batches of four hundred cookies and enough gingerbread and whipped cream to satisfy the sweet tooth of a small army of meditators.

I discovered that cooking on such a large scale was more about logistics and timing than any real culinary art. I made sure not to burn the sautéed veggies or undercook the beans, but the most crucial skill was knowing when to slide the potatoes into the oven and when to start boiling the water.

Luckily, I had an intelligent and cooperative crew of young adults to work with. By the time we finished our ten-day stint together, I learned that every single one of them had spent time in the restaurant business, either as a server or cook, so naturally the kitchen was in good hands.

I also learned that, with the exception of a yoga instructor from San Francisco, each and every dhamma server was unemployed. We were all nomads, traveling, in-between jobs, or specifically seeking refuge in dhamma, the path to liberate oneself from suffering. Without intending to do so, I'd found a congregation of people just like myself. All of us tried the 40 hour/week plan-for-retirement-life, and we each gave it up in pursuit of something different.

I felt a new affinity for my journey as a nomadic farmer. Like the rest of the dhamma servers, I sought an alternative lifestyle – not in relation to sex or politics, but in relation to spiritual growth. I sought a heightened awareness of my own reality, the interconnectedness of my mind, body, and environment, and for once in my life I didn't look to books or lectures or drugs to achieve that goal. Instead, I looked to meditation, and I found peace and understanding like never before.

## Chapter 9
*Chestnut Hill*

The landscape of California varied sharply from east to west. As I zigzagged up the state, I experienced sand dunes on the beach, semi-arid desert, and snow-capped mountains – all within a three hour drive from one another. Rain-saturated foothills bordered the Great Central Valley on both sides and served as a watering can for a 400-mile long garden. Almonds, strawberries, oranges, avocados, and walnuts drank entire lakes and rivers to keep the valley green and productive.

After a rewarding ten days of cooking at the meditation center, I descended from the foothills of Yosemite and drove across the Central Valley one last time. I drove past cattle ranches, rice paddies, more almond orchards, and then as I reached the western edge of Sacramento Valley, I arrived in yet another agricultural region of California: wine country.

Four hours north of San Francisco, grapes dominated the scenery. Leafless grapevines grew in neat rows, like long strands of brown hair combed neatly over the hillside.

Chestnut Hill, my farm for April, was situated in the hills just east of Napa Valley. After following a set of directions from Sam, my farm-host-to-be, I arrived at a locked gate. I didn't have the combination, so I left my car parked in front of the gate and set off on foot. *How far up the gravel driveway could his house be?*

## Chestnut Hill

The answer to my question was: Far! I should've known from the driveways of past farms that Sam's house was more than just a stroll up the country lane. I regretted not wearing a jacket after I spent twenty minutes hiking up the steep, winding road.

A chilly breeze blew in from the dense evergreen forest along the driveway. I walked in full shade with only a narrow channel of clear blue sky directly overhead. Gravel crunched under my hiking boots as I picked up my pace in order to generate body heat. Normally a fairly patient person, I grew anxious, wondering if I should turn back.

About forty minutes past the gate, thinking I'd misread the address and hillbillies had probably broken into my car, I saw a small pick-up truck round the bend with its headlights on, kicking up a cloud of dust in its wake.

The man behind the wheel, with a neatly trimmed white beard, rolled down the passenger window and said, "My neighbors said they saw someone out here. Didn't you get the combination I sent you?"

"Sorry, I must've missed that," I told the man, clearly Sam, my new farm host. I tried to lighten the mood a bit by asking, "Is this how you condition your new wwoofers?"

He barely laughed. He seemed irritated that I didn't get the gate combination he sent me through e-mail. "Well, hop in," he said, "and I'll take you down to your car."

On the way back down the driveway, I got a better look at the man. He was heavy-set and heavy of breath, like a king who'd enjoyed too many years of sweet meats and wine. The carefully combed hair on the crown of his head resembled spaced out rows of grapevines, laying in distinct rows along his sun-reddened scalp.

I followed Sam back up the gravel driveway in my car, and discovered that I'd been close to reaching the top. Just around the bend from where Sam picked me up, the evergreen forest gave way to an open hilltop. I squinted in the sunlight that illuminated the full twenty acres of Chestnut Hill.

Tailing Sam's pick-up truck, I drove through the entrance of a tall, chain-link deer fence encircling the property. Inside the fence, hundreds of chestnut trees grew in terraced rows, hugging the east side of the hill. Each tree had its trunk painted white.

When I sat down to dinner with Sam that night over a glass casserole dish of chicken and wild rice, I asked the obvious question: "Why are your trees painted white?"

He told me, "Chestnuts aren't used to growing out in the open. For ages, their trunks have been in the shade of the forest understory." He said, "My trees are young. If I don't paint them, they'll get sunburned."

Sam took a mouthful of red wine and began explaining his vision for the orchard, which he referred to as his "hobby farm." "Soon enough, I won't need to paint them," he said. "In time, as the trees mature, their branches will merge with their neighbors and form a chestnut forest. The roots will become one mass underground."

I looked out the window from Sam's kitchen nook, where the two of us shared a small table and dined to the country blues music of Ry Cooder. I imagined hundreds of white-trunked trees intertwining their roots and branches to form a super-tree that rained down millions of chestnuts every fall.

## Garden of Eden

Sam's chestnut forest vision would take a decade or two to reach fruition. In the meantime, he'd already achieved a miniaturized version of California's Great Central Valley.

The moment I drove out of the permanent shade of the evergreen forest, ascending Sam's gravel driveway for the first time, I literally saw the light. Sunshine reflected off the white-painted chestnut trees, and I decided to pull a pair of sunglasses out of my glove box.

After driving past terraced rows of chestnut trees, I reached a hilltop garden that resembled a Garden of Eden, resplendent in fruit and nut trees, champagne grapes, rose bushes, and an open field of grass bursting with daffodils of all shades of orange and yellow. An ancient-looking live oak tree with gnarly branches and a twisted trunk covered with a thick mat of green moss, stood at the top of the hill. I strolled up to the live oak tree after Sam gave me a walking tour of his property. From its shade, I could peer down into the neighboring valleys and grape-covered hills that rolled gently toward the ocean twenty miles away.

The Book of Genesis didn't mention a modern A-frame wooden house with a 50-foot tall windmill and a Nissan pickup truck parked in the driveway. Nor did the Bible speak of solar panels to fuel Adam and Eve's electrical needs.

However, some parts of the Bible's Garden of Eden matched with my impression of Chestnut Hill. The Book of Genesis said, "The Lord God made all kinds of trees grow out of the ground – trees that were pleasing to the eye and good for food."

Sam had rivaled God's green thumb with Chestnut Hill. Aside from the orchard of chestnut trees, his forest garden included apple and peach trees, plums, apricots, cherries, pears, persimmons, walnuts, and almonds. A two-acre vineyard grew on the western slope of Chestnut Hill, where thick grape vines wrapped around their wooden trellis like snakes with flaking scales.

Sam's years of watering, weeding, and fertilizing his hilltop garden had paid off. His trees were at the point where they now took care of him, producing flowers and foliage that were "pleasing to the eye," and fruits and nuts "good for food."

Sam's network of underground irrigation pipes delivered a reliable source of water to the tree roots. During my stay on Chestnut Hill, Sam employed me to dig a 50-foot long trench in order to lay a new branch of water pipes from the main line. As I shoveled clay and gravel to a depth of three feet, digging my trench directly toward Sam's vegetable garden, I manifested another detail of Genesis: "A river watering the garden flowed from Eden." In my case, Eden was the main line and I was the peon bringing Sam's vision into reality.

"The Lord God took the man and put him in the Garden of Eden to work it and take care of it." In my experience, I contacted Sam by e-mail and he put me to work digging trenches, spreading fertilizer pellets, and removing pack rat nests from his rose bushes. I took care of the chestnuts trees by weeding and spreading leaf mulch around the white-painted base of each one. In exchange for a perfectly fair and leisurely schedule of 25 hours/week, I enjoyed lounging under the live oak tree and strolling through the garden.

The best privilege, of course, was articulated by the Lord God when he said, "You are free to eat from any tree in the garden." That was all well and good for Adam and Eve. In my case, I didn't get to enjoy the freshly picked fruits. I arrived on Chestnut Hill at the onset of spring, just as the trees unfurled new flower and leaf buds. I enjoyed a feast for the eyes, plus canned plums, pears, cherries, and tomatoes from the previous year's harvest. In addition, I had full access to a stash of chestnuts Sam kept in a chest freezer.

After my first day of work, sprinkling fertilizer pellets around the feeder roots of the chestnut trees and picking up sticks from last year's pruning, Sam roasted and pureed chestnuts with heavy cream. He sautéed leeks and shallots and added them to the sweet nutty concoction, along with cinnamon and nutmeg. I ate three bowls of the creamy chestnut porridge, glad to be back on a farm again. I knew Sam wasn't the Lord God, nor was Chestnut Hill the Garden of Eden, but I felt fortunate to find myself in such a beautiful landscape.

## Tree of Pessimism

If a Tree of Knowledge grew on Chestnut Hill, Sam had surely found it, for he showed remarkable intelligence. He could fix nearly anything machine-related. During my stay, he rebuilt the engine for his riding lawn mower, re-wired the electrical system for his solar batteries, and added to the irrigation network that fed nearly twenty acres of trees, vines, shrubs, and vegetable plants. He was a mechanic, electrician,

*Chestnut Hill*

plumber, and master gardener, all wrapped into one.

Sam had many gifts. However, he also carried a dark cloud. Whenever I saw Sam walking around the farm wearing his remote radio headphones, I wondered if he was tuning into some radio station that broadcast human misery 24 hours a day. Everything Sam said seemed to reflect a state of disappointment and frustration with the world. His disposition told me he ate heavily, not only from the Tree of Knowledge, but also from the Tree of Pessimism.

Throughout my month with Sam, I noticed a recurring theme. He trashed his own species, as if Earth hosted a game that could be won or lost and Homo sapiens had lost the game. On my second night on the farm, while I sipped from a bowl of chestnut porridge over dinner and Sam sipped from a glass of wine, he shared his feelings regarding the rest of humanity. "People are fundamentally stupid!"

He said this in reference to something he heard on the news earlier that day. Initially, I thought he meant, "People *act* stupidly sometimes." I offered my own viewpoint on the matter, which was that "people are fundamentally good, but often clouded by ignorance." To this he shook his head and repeated his original statement. Sam honestly believed the fundamental nature of humanity was stupidity.

Here was a man who raised a magnificent garden from the land, not just in a utilitarian way, but in the way an artist strokes his brush against the canvas. Sam clearly wasn't stupid, yet he thought the majority of humankind had a built-in engineering flaw.

Sam radiated displeasure. From the moment I woke up and began fixing my oatmeal, he looked at me as though I was doing something wrong. He must've thought something was inherently stupid about the way I poured hot water over my oats and stirred in honey and sliced bananas.

It took me a week to figure out that he didn't have anything against me personally, but felt disenchanted by humanity in general. Over the course of my month on Chestnut Hill, I had many dinners with Sam and served as the sole audience member to his trademark conversation-piece, always delivered hot on the breath of alcohol, and always containing the same core message: "People are fundamentally stupid," "Regan fucked up this country," "Today's youth aren't rising up like they should," and "Affluence will be the downfall of mankind." I think he liked to transfer the source of his own suffering to a failed politician or a dysfunctional society.

Upon hearing Sam's message the first few times, I thought we were having a conversation, so I offered my own view. I mentioned pockets of society that were breaking off from the mainstream and creating communities based on local economy, local food, and friendly neighbors. I mentioned all the people I'd met at meditation centers who appeared to be coming out of their suffering. I mentioned my own travels, through couchsurfing and wwoofing, where complete strangers took me into their homes and fed me.

I soon learned my attempts to converse with Sam were worthless. Sam plain didn't hear me. Or *couldn't* hear me. He said he had Lyme's disease and it affected his ability to listen and talk at the same time. In the rare moments when my words registered, he said something morbid like, "It doesn't matter. I'll be gone soon anyway."

I often wondered from where Sam's Tree of Pessimism drew its nourishment. What fed the roots?

I hypothesized that Sam's heavy consumption of booze, television, and newspapers had something to do with his attitude. Through his media input and belief-system, he positioned himself in the universe to guarantee a sense of isolation and hopelessness.

## Inner Landscape

Sam lived as a firm atheist. To him, this meant when his body died he would be erased. God from the Book of Genesis did not exist. Karma did not operate. The afterlife was a sham. For Sam, the moment he died, the forces of nature would become irrelevant. His soul would be extinguished forever.

Most atheists I'm friends with are open-minded, highly educated people. I think what they reject most of all is not God, but the blind faith and warfare that exists within organized religion. In that regard, I'm with the atheists. I think one can live a moral and decent life without vowing allegiance to a specific religion or God.

I like the rationality of atheists. However, I'm also a believer. I believe karma exists. I believe there is life after this one and my soul goes on forever. I believe God exists as the source of everything true, peaceful, loving, and compassionate, and as the gears that turn the universe. I believe each and every one of us is a particle of God, an expression of infinite possibility.

I think part of Sam's suffering came from the fact that he felt so alone in the universe. During one of his dinner soliloquies, Sam told me he didn't identify with any particular "tribe" of humanity. He belonged to a special breed of close-minded atheists, where he existed as the only member. Not only did he live in a godless world, he also lived in a world where morality and karma were worthless. If he drank too much, spoke badly of others, and killed animals, it didn't matter. For Sam, there were no repercussions or rewards beyond his very short existence on Earth.

One day while the two of us were driving back to Chestnut Hill after a trip to town, Sam forecasted his future. As he gripped the steering wheel to navigate the winding gravel road, he said, "I wouldn't be surprised if I was gone within the next decade." Then, as if to emphasize his point, he said, "Hell, I could have a heart attack right now." I grew nervous as I watched the speedometer needle waggle around 60 mph.

For the remainder of the month, I felt anxious every time I heard Sam make strange noises through the bedroom walls. Whenever he had a coughing fit or an uncommonly loud nose-blowing session, I thought, "Is this it? Should I go check?"

I often returned to the house to find Sam sitting in his rocking chair, sipping from a glass of wine and looking solemnly out the window at his chestnut trees, his Garden of Eden. *Here's a man filled with great suffering*, I thought. He's surrounded by natural beauty and an abundance of food and material comforts, yet no smile crosses his face and no joy fills his voice.

Sam served as a living example that happiness begins from within. One cannot expect real happiness while the inner landscape goes untended and overgrown with weeds.

## To Kill or Not to Kill

Coming to Chestnut Hill from the meditation center felt like going straight from a monastery to a bar. At the center, people beamed with good intentions. Everyone aimed to walk on the path of morality and purify their minds. The meditation operated like a science, eradicating mental defilement in a systematic way. Following each one-hour meditation, we remained on our pillows and practiced a less-scientific technique called "metta," which translates to "loving kindness." Metta served as a way of directing good vibrations outward, much as prayer works to focus one's thoughts.

As I worked in the kitchen of the meditation center, cooperating with nine strangers to prepare breakfast and lunch, everyone seemed to direct metta at one another. These were not monks or holy people, yet they shone with compassion. They smiled more, listened patiently, and appeared less tense than most people I'd met in my life.

When I stepped onto Chestnut Hill, the atmosphere changed. Sam-energy and the smell of frying bacon filled the kitchen. One night, Sam came back for dinner with wood chips clinging to the back of his sweatshirt. A pair of binoculars hung around his neck, and he smelled like a distillery.

"We're having BLTs tonight," he said in a slurred voice. As he carefully laid thick slices of bacon on the hot cast-iron skillet, he said, "You can't eat enough bacon." Above his white beard, his cheeks were flushed red from sunshine and alcohol.

He was so inebriated, that he only managed to criticize the world a couple of times. "There's no revolutionary spirit in college students nowadays," he said half-heartedly.

After about twelve pieces of crispy bacon and a pile of steaming potatoes fried in bacon grease, I gave Sam my compliment for such a tasty meal. He flashed me an uncharacteristic smile and said, "I have a lot of experience cooking those two things." Then he added with pride, "I'm an old potato man. I'm an old bacon man."

In the kitchen of the meditation center, meat and alcohol were prohibited. Sam, the old bacon man, would probably feel uncomfortable in such a place, being forced to eat vegetarian dishes and take tea as an after meal drink.

As for my own diet, I made it a point to be an adaptive eater as I traveled around the country. I wanted to experience the cuisine of choice. Therefore, I felt perfectly okay eating a plateful of bacon on Chestnut Hill, especially since I knew the pigs came from a small neighboring farm, fattened on Sam's chestnuts. I gladly traded a sliver of spiritual purity for a BLT.

For some reason, the carnivorous diet didn't bother me as much as when Sam ordered me to kill some of his garden pests.

I had prior experience killing cucumber beetles by drowning them in a jar of water and stomping them beneath my boot, and I didn't have savory memories of the task. So, when Sam told me, "Exterminate any snails and slugs you find in the garden," I felt disinclined to follow his orders.

For one, I didn't like the idea of killing such a slimy slow-moving creature. The same day Sam told me to exterminate the slugs, I saw a banana slug for the first time of my life. I watched in fascination as the slick, six-inch long, over-ripe looking banana glided slowly along Sam's concrete patio. The creature surveyed its surroundings with a pair of glistening retractable antennae. Two stubby finger-like projections probed the ground in front of it. How could I kill such a bizarre, slow-moving animal?

Maybe I refused to follow Sam's orders because the vibrations of the meditation center remained with me. When a server found a spider or insect crawling around the kitchen, they trapped it in a cup and released it outdoors. All life was sacred. No ant was smashed or washed down the sink. In the meditation hall, I saw a scorpion crawl out from underneath someone's meditation pillow. The thought of killing it didn't even cross my mind. I slid a piece of paper under the scorpion and relocated it to the woods.

I felt like I left the meditation center with a renewed sense of morality. I knew my bacon feast involved the killing of a pig, probably an immoral act. But at least I recycled the pig's flesh directly into my own. When Sam told me to kill slugs and snails I wouldn't even be eating, I didn't feel right about doing so. I expressed my feelings to Sam and he replied, "They're not animals. They're evil things!"

Fortunately, my job didn't depend on hunting down banana slugs. In a way, I felt Sam was joking when he called them, "evil things." Yet, I also think he wanted to believe that all his garden pests--snails, slugs, rodents, deer, and birds, *were* evil things. It's much easier to kill an evil creature than a sacred being.

## That Bird is a Loudmouth

Sometimes Sam killed animals not because they were evil per se, but because he perceived them as arrogant or downright annoying. One such incident happened with a crow eating from Sam's cherry tree.

"You get to know individual birds," Sam told me. "And this one was a loud-mouth."

During the previous summer a family of crows moved in and began picking nearly ripe fruit from Sam's cherry tree. Sam relayed the following details to me. He said he hollered in their direction and walked aggressively toward the tree waving a rake in the air. All the birds flew off except for one – the loudmouth. The bird perched stubbornly on one of the fruit-laden branches and called down to Sam in the way crows do, "Koww! Koww!"

Sam needed know further motivation. From a glass case in his living room, he took out a rifle, loaded, aimed, and extinguished the evil bird from his cherry tree.

Every gardener knows the frustration of a pest eating the fruits of their labor, but I think few would go as far as to protect their fruit and vegetables with a loaded gun.

For Sam, everything within his ten-foot tall deer fence had to be defended at all costs. His garden meant more than a yearly harvest of fruits, nuts, and vegetables. Sam's garden represented years of nurturing and caring for thousands of plants. Chestnut Hill reflected the only bit of beauty Sam cared to share with the world, and if an ugly slug or obnoxious crow attempted to mar the scenery, Sam squashed the opposition.

Any animal that drank or ate from Chestnut Hill without clearly giving anything in return, earned the mark of "evil thing," and had to be put down.

## Springtime

I took a big lesson away from Chestnut Hill: two people almost always experience the same phenomenon differently. I saw the banana slug as a beautiful, slow-motion creature. Sam saw it as a pest that needed to be destroyed. I saw heavy drinking as an obstacle to my own personal evolution. Sam saw a bottle of brandy as a refuge from his own suffering, something he wrapped around himself like a warm blanket.

Probably the biggest contrast of perception, between Sam and myself, happened when spring erupted on Chestnut Hill. In late April, after several weeks of peace and quiet and gradual unfurling of leaves and flowers, an especially warm morning induced billion of insects to hatch from their eggs all at once.

Suddenly, the calm air filled with clusters of flies, tracing loops and zigzag patterns in the sunlight. Beehives swung their doors open, and every patch of flowers buzzed with fuzzy yellow and black pollinators. Ants came out of the ground in full force, marching over the land in search of food.

# Chestnut Hill

I sat under the live oak tree at the top of the hill and admired the explosion of tiny life. Fairy-looking insects with transparent oversized wings and mosquito-shaped bodies fluttered through the air, more in a low-gravity state of hopping than in real flight. Dragonflies zoomed around my head like precision helicopters and hunted down newly hatched mosquitoes. My own heart pumped more rapidly, alerting me to the fact that some of these newly hatched bugs wanted to drink from my blood.

For the first time since Florida, I watched my bare arms and legs like a sentry. I tuned into the slightest ticklish sensation on my neck, wary of mosquitoes. Spring had come to Chestnut Hill like a Jack-in-the-Box, showing itself all at once.

I shared my observation with Sam, that "Spring is here! How about that?" Ever the pessimist, he acknowledged my observation with his own thoughts on the new explosion of life.

"I know. I always look forward to the first frost of fall, when it kills those little fuckers!"

Sam's comment reminded me everyone creates their own reality. He drove home the message that it isn't what's outside that matters, but rather, how we *perceive* the outside world.

## American Chestnut Tree

Underneath all of Sam's pessimism, he harbored a caring heart. Sam cared deeply for his trees. He didn't just care about the yearly chestnut harvest, he also wanted to help restore a piece of American History.

Like most American chestnut farmers nowadays, Sam grew Asian and European hybrids--bred for their blight-resistance. Regardless, *any* chestnut tree on American soil represented the revival of a tree that almost went extinct in this country.

The American chestnut tree once played a big part in the lives of early Americans. The woodlands stretching from Maine all the way down to Georgia were once full of chestnut trees. Old-timers used to say, "Where there be mountains, there be chestnuts."

During my stay on Chestnut Hill, Sam lent me a book titled *Mighty Giants: An American Chestnut Anthology*, from which I learned all sorts of interesting stories about the tree. Every fall, people from the cities headed to the country to harvest chestnuts and participate in the annual chestnut festival.

In one newspaper clipping dated 1902, I read about a boy who fell from a chestnut tree and broke his hand. "Physicians feared his hand would have to be amputated," the article stated. What a difference a hundred years of medical advancement meant.

While fearless young boys climbed out on high branches to collect the sweet nuts, the younger girls participated in a more intelligent means of gathering nuts. The girls held "nutting parties," where they'd run around collecting nuts from the forest floor. The girl who collected the most nuts earned the title, "the busiest squirrel," which entitled her to boss around the other girls for the rest of the day.

According to people who lived in the late 1800s, the mountains of Tennessee, North Carolina, and West Virginia were once "covered with snow in July," when the emergent chestnut trees bloomed and showered the mountainsides with their white flower petals.

Just about every living being on the East Coast was connected to the chestnut tree. Creatures of the forest depended on the chestnut as their main source of food. Carpenters and lumber mills practically built their industry on the rot-resistant chestnut wood, favored in furniture and fencing.

Then sometime around the turn of the century, a fungus, known simply as "the blight," arrived from Asia. The blight wiped out 99% of the American chestnut population. Some four billion trees stopped producing leaves and nuts. The fungus strangled the trunks and starved the tree of its own sap.

People alive during the height of the blight called the trees that remained standing, "ghosts." The bark turned a blackish

## Chestnut Hill

color and all that remained below the soil was dead roots. The once mighty trees that rose above the forest canopy and fed millions of animals and humans died off within one generation. The economy and yearly festival surrounding the tree dried up just as the roots did.

Not until recently, when former president Jimmy Carter gave birth to the American Chestnut Foundation, did a movement arise to revive the tree. Now, in the early 21st century, a blight-resistant strain of the American chestnut tree has already been developed. There is still hope for the tree once called "the emperor of the forest." I think that is something even a pessimist like Sam can be optimistic about.

# Chapter 10
## *Rock n'Ridge Ranch*

My gas needle dropped a half tank by the time I reached the mountaintop estate, Rock n'Ridge Ranch. The drive to the ranch was easy, only an hour north of Chestnut Hill, but the gravel road leading up the small, steep mountain put serious strain on my old '93 Ford Taurus.

I parked my car next to a row of three RVs and warmed my hands over my car's engine. I knew I wouldn't be taking any frivolous trips to town from Rock n'Ridge Ranch. Like all the previous farms with epic driveways, I planned to enjoy the country life in all its slowness, traveling only as far as my hiking boots would take me.

### Lion Rock

On my way up the mountain I passed a mailbox bearing the names Kitty and Creek. These were my new wwoofing hosts. I unrolled my window and typed in a string numbers on an electronic keypad. Luckily, I'd remembered to write down the combination this time, and the yellow gate swung open for me. As I continued up the driveway, I drove into the shadow of a 50-foot tall rock. An overhang from the rock completely shadowed my car for the length of two city blocks.

Later in the day, after I unpacked and met Kitty and Creek, I learned the colossal rock had a name: Lion Rock. Kitty advised

Rock n'Ridge Ranch

me to take a closer look at it. Heeding her advice, I put on my hiking boots and walked back down the driveway. Standing in the rock's shadow, I gazed upward and saw the unmistakable features of a lion's face, engraved by millennia of wind and rain erosion. A pale green skin of lichens covered the entire face of the rock. Scrub-like bushes grew out of its ears, and mats of wiry grass poured from its mouth. The lion was old. With a stretch of the imagination, I could make out a set of front paws resting in a forward sphinx-like position.

After I admired Lion Rock from the driveway, I climbed to the top. Creek had told me, "If you hike to the very tip of the lion's head, you'll get the best view we have. On a clear day, you can see the ocean."

I made the easy fifteen-minute climb, stood on the pale green skin of the lion's head, and looked west. The lion's ear, the overhang that had shadowed my car, blocked all view of the driveway below. I imagined the ear as a runway. With a hang glider, I could've leapt into the air and sailed off toward the ocean, peering into the valley below.

From my vantage point on the Lion's head, I viewed rolling hills blanketed by a continuous stretch of forest. I only saw six or seven clearings in the surrounding hill country, chopped out for a spacious housing estate or small farm. An occasional redwood tree emerged above the tops of manzanita, madrone, and evergreen trees. I looked long and hard toward the Pacific Ocean a good twenty miles away, but could only make out a wavy blue line on the horizon.

## Creek

My first day on Rock n'Ridge Ranch was one of the easiest wwoofing transitions of my entire trip. The scenery and climate were pleasant, and my hosts, Kitty and Creek, welcomed me with open arms.

During the first minutes of my arrival, after I passed through the shadow of Lion Rock, I drove into the warm, dappled light produced by a forest canopy overhead and parked my car next to a threesome of RVs.

Madrone trees, a species I'd never seen before, comprised most of the forest encircling the RVs and a 500-gallon propane tank. The tall, straight madrones were sheathed in a smooth reddish-orange bark that felt like finely sanded wood when I ran my hand over one of the trunks. The trees in the distance resembled unsalted pretzel sticks.

After I unloaded a few bags from my car's trunk, a solar-powered golf cart raced down the driveway, kicking up a cloud of dust. Gravel crunched under the tires as the driver pulled in next to the RVs with a braking skid.

Creek, a tall graceful man, sprang from the golf cart like a man half his age. "You must be Brian," he said. "I hear we're in good hands." He told me a wwoofer from Chestnut Hill I'd worked with during her brief two-day visit, had spread kind words about me.

Creek gave me a knowing smile as if to say, *I know all about Sam. Don't worry, you're in better hands here.* He pointed to the nearest RV, named *The Weekender*.

"This one's all yours," Creek said. Creek and his wife, Kitty, used the RVs to house wwoofers. Creek showed me how to refill the propane tank in order to power all my kitchen appliances and run the heater. Inside the RV, I discovered a housewarming present--- an oatmeal canister with a note taped to the lid that read *Brian's Granola*. "Kitty's homemade granola," Creek said.

Creek handed me a square magnet with the following inscription: "Be the Change You Wish to See in the World." Those very words hung from the outdoor kitchen back at Salamander Springs.

"We thought you'd like that one," Creek said.

"It's perfect," I told him. I slapped the magnet on the fridge and *The Weekender* was complete.

The magnet proved to be more than just a housewarming gift – it served as a symbol of Kitty & Creek's livelihood. They owned and operated a successful magnet business called

## Rock n'Ridge Ranch

Magnetic Graffiti. Kitty and Creek manufactured magnets with meaningful quotes like the one I'd received, or quirky sayings like *Everyday is a Gift, That's Why it's Called the Present* and *Is There Life Before Coffee?* Inside *The Weekender,* magnets from previous wwoofers remained on my fridge door. One of them said, *If Mom Says No, Call 1-800-Grandma.*

Magnetic Graffiti provided the financial power for Rock n'Ridge Ranch. After many years of living frugally and choosing not to have children, Kitty and Creek had attained a level of self-sufficiency where they could work from home, host travelers, and tend to their homestead.

After Creek and I stepped out of *The Weekender,* we jumped in the golf-cart and headed up to the main house. Along the way, he stopped to show me an array of 80 solar panels and demonstrated how to adjust the angle of the panels to face the sun more directly.

"Feel free to rotate them," Creek said.

Almost every day throughout my stay on Rock n'Ridge, Creek said, "Feel free to rotate the panels." He said this in a friendly tone, but said it consistently enough for me to know the true meaning, which was, "Feel *compelled* to rotate them."

Rotating the panels required no more than five seconds, two or three times a day, but the slight adjustment made a huge difference in the amount of electricity generated. Creek made frequent trips to town, where he helped with the local theatre and public radio station, and his mood upon returning home was often directly correlated to how closely his solar panels were tracking the sun.

For Creek, a wwoofer forgetting to rotate the panels meant unharnessed potential, like letting a ripe tomato drop to the ground and rot. During my stay on Rock n'Ridge Ranch I did my best to keep Creek's solar power at peak capacity. I thought like a sunflower. When I walked by the solar array I angled the panels a bit to the west, so the shiny silicon surface aimed an hour or two ahead of the sun's trajectory. When Creek's solar batteries were fully charged, he was a happy man.

*Rock n'Ridge Ranch*

## Pleasure Garden

Fruit trees, including cherry, plum, and blood peach, grew on a terraced hillside below the solar array. Their leaves never had to be rotated. Behind the solar panels, Kitty and Creek kept a small vineyard of Concord grapes, surrounded by a 10-foot tall deer fence. The fruit trees, grapes, and a large vegetable garden served to feed Kitty and Creek, as well as their friends and wwoofing guests.

The food production on Rock n'Ridge was impressive, but the real botanical highlight was the garden that didn't produce any food. After Creek reminded me a second time, "Feel free to rotate the solar panels," he took me to the pleasure garden that surrounded his house.

A stone footpath meandered through the garden. Unlike the neat rows of grapes, fruit trees, and vegetable crops, this garden had a more natural design. Shade-loving ivy and ferns grew beneath the leafy canopy of sun-loving shrubs. Water lilies and water chestnuts grew in a low-lying depression of standing-water. Hundreds of different plant species settled into their favorite microclimate in this one garden.

As Creek led me by a daphne in full blossom, Kitty overheard us talking and stepped out of the house to relieve Creek of his tour guide duties. Right away, she gave me a hug and looked deep into my eyes as though we'd met before. I could tell from the start she was a light-hearted and soulful woman.

She led me through the garden, rattling off the incredible array of plants that surrounded me. The garden was a treasure trove of medicinal and culinary herbs.

"That's sage," Kitty said, pointing out specimens as we strolled through the garden. "Rosemary, thyme, and oregano. If you ever have a stomach ache you might want to pick some mint leaves and brew yourself some tea." She pointed out the different kinds of mint growing next to a stone wall: "Spearmint, pineapple mint, peppermint, moroccan mint, and yerba Buena. If you ever want to pick mint in the wild, just feel for the square stem."

*Rock n'Ridge Ranch*

Kitty pointed to a tree that could be used to soothe a poison oak rash. "Manzanita," she said. "The plant next to that will treat cold and flu symptoms."

The medicinal plants were only a fraction of the garden. Flowering bushes, native ferns and huckleberry, and several exotic trees occupied their own bit of garden real estate. "This one originated in central China," Kitty said, pointing to a slender young tree. "It's called a dawn redwood, the only *deciduous* redwood on the planet."

A plant called a bleeding heart bordered the stone stepping path. "Also from China," Kitty said, noticing I'd stopped to stare at the bizarre flowers hanging from the plant. A row of dime-sized pink hearts hung from each branch, with a white tear-shaped drop of blood dangling from the tip of each heart.

Throughout my tour of the garden, hummingbirds buzzed around and sipped on sugar water from three dispensers hanging from Kitty and Creek's porch.

Unlike the CSA farms I'd worked on, where speed and production defined the atmosphere, the pleasure garden around Kitty and Creek's house where I spent time pulling weeds and planting trees, filled me with calmness. A babbling creek ran through the garden, adding to the peaceful atmosphere. The creek wove through artfully placed boulders and emptied into a goldfish pond.

The only thing that seemed remotely out of place was a giant black monolith. "What's that?" I asked Kitty, surprised I hadn't noticed the several hundred pound, eight-foot tall slab of rock. The enormous phallus of black marble sat amid a patch of goji berries and fava beans.

"It was for the Space Odyssey party back in 2001," she said. "We had to lower it in with a crane."

"Well it makes a nice addition," I added politely, figuring that since the party had ended seven years earlier, Kitty had no intention of removing the monolith.

"Yeah," she added. "Plus it draws cosmic energy. It's been wonderful for the plants!"

## Green Flash

Kitty and Creek invited me up to their house for dinner my first night. From an architectural standpoint, the house was as remarkable as the garden that surrounded it. One of Frank Lloyd Wright's students designed it. The main room, probably as spacious as fifteen of *The Weekenders*, had a kitchen along one side and a lowered pit in the center with a day bed, couches, and two computer desks. Two black cats with Japanese names lounged on the day bed.

A floor-to-ceiling window made the entire west side of the house transparent. Outside the window, Kitty and Creek kept cactus, aloe vera, agave, and jade plants in a greenhouse style sun porch. The sun porch doubled as an observation deck, looking out toward the ocean.

Midway through dinner that first night, Creek called me, Kitty, and two other wwoofers out to the sun porch to watch the sunset.

As the sun settled into a thin shroud of clouds that covered the horizon, the ocean turned a deep magenta and a beam of pink light shot up from the sun. The pink light radiated outward, like something you'd see in a child's depiction of the sun.

"Watch for the green flash," Creek said, his eyes glued to the horizon.

As the sun sank into the shroud of pink clouds on the Pacific Ocean, Creek explained himself. "Just after the sun completely sets, the last bit of sunlight that reaches our eyes has a higher frequency. This appears as a green halo, flashing directly above the sun."

We fixed our eyes on the horizon as the half-eaten dinner of cornbread and split pea soup cooled on the table. The clouds on the horizon turned peach and plum, then slowly faded into a deep blue. I didn't see a green flash. But I did see the first of many stunning sunsets, which gave credence to the saying, "The west is the best." As far as sunsets go, I have to agree.

*Rock n'Ridge Ranch*

## Mamma Bird Nesting

Rock n'Ridge and Chestnut Hill shared minor similarities. They both asked for a fair exchange of work hours. Both places sat perched on top of a small mountain, surrounded for miles in every direction by the two main cash crops of Northern California – grapes and marijuana. However, aside from common geography and work schedule, the two places couldn't have been more different.

Sam, the most pessimistic person I'd ever met, tended Chestnut Hill. He saw no future for himself or the species he belonged to, and any animal that nibbled from his garden, he shot, poisoned, drowned, or cursed.

Kitty and Creek, on the other hand, treated the local wildlife with a level of compassion and nurturing most people reserve for their own children. They regularly put dead mice on their porch to feed the ravens. They diligently refilled three sugar water dispensers to keep the hummingbirds fueled year around.

I mentioned my appreciation for the way Kitty and Creek lived, and Kitty said in complete sincerity, "We're the guests here." That explained it perfectly. Kitty and Creek viewed the local rattlesnakes, bobcats, birds, and deer as the true residents of Rock n'Ridge.

One day, while turning the compost pile with a pitchfork, I uncovered a large rattlesnake. The snake lay coiled under a layer of branches and showed no sign of defending itself, even with the end of my pitchfork just a few inches from its body. The snake was clearly in a state of torpor, as the spring sun was slow to heat up Rock n'Ridge, even in May.

I excitedly reported my news to Kitty, and she kindly instructed me to "leave the rattlesnake alone." Not for my own safety, but because it would "create stress for the snake."

Another day, while retrieving a shovel from the barn, I noticed the entrance to the barn was roped off. Kitty pointed out a songbird that had made her nest above the barn door and was in the process of feeding three hatchlings. On the rope, Kitty had hung a sign that read, "Mamma bird nesting. Please be quiet!"

Kitty's message compelled me to tiptoe around the nest. Over the course of the following week, whenever I fetched a tool from the barn, I felt like an intruder, breaking and entering the bird's private residence. I felt the way Kitty and Creek did: *I'm just a guest here.*

## Living Outside of Time

Kitty's reverence toward nature seemed familial and spiritual. She bonded with the animals that visited her garden on a deeper level than mere admiration.

If a stranger looked at Kitty in a grocery store they might see a good-looking white woman in her 50s, with long brown hair and stylish clothing. I don't think an average person would look at Kitty and think, *Now that's a Shaman*. After all, when most people think of a shaman, they conjure up the image of a brown-skinned indigenous man living in the middle of a rainforest.

Kitty didn't fit the image of a traditional shaman, but she entered the spirit realm to fix human ailments nonetheless. She'd trained under experienced shamans in Central and South America. She learned the ways of shamanism to such a degree that she served as an experienced medium to the spirit world. Loyal clients came up to Rock n'Ridge and sought out Kitty's ability to enter the spirit world and diffuse bad energy.

Whenever a client came up to the Ranch, me and the other wwoofers were asked to refrain from entering Kitty and Creek's house, for Kitty needed a private atmosphere and uninterrupted session with her client. After a client departed, Kitty often appeared physically and mentally drained, like she'd jogged a marathon.

From what I learned, shamanic healing operated a bit like acupuncture. Pathways throughout the mind, body, and soul are opened so good energy can rush through the spiritual arteries and cleanse a person of impurities.

Admittedly, I was a bit skeptical of shamanic healing. My upbringing in Ohio limited my exposure to alternative forms of healing, so naturally anything that involved "traveling through wormholes to communicate with animal and plant spirits" sounded farfetched and crazy.

However, after spending a few weeks in Kitty's company, I discovered she was far from crazy. She beamed with positive energy and clear mindedness nearly every moment of the day. Of course, like anyone, she had a few quirks. Things like "living outside of time" and talking to the birds.

"I live in shamanic time," Kitty told me one day as we pulled weeds from the pleasure garden. When I asked her what that meant, she explained that she lived "outside of time," a state of being in tune with the physical and spiritual world unfolding all around us.

I interpreted Kitty's "living in shamanic time" as a state of being unchained to clocks and calendars, because later that day, around two in the afternoon, she dropped her trowel on the ground and said in a fatigued voice, "I better go eat something. I completely forgot about breakfast."

When I asked Kitty if I should write down my work hours, she laughed and said, "Oh, nobody does that around here."

Not only did she live outside of time, but she also communicated with the local wildlife. When Kitty walked by the goldfish pond, she said affectionately, "How're my little fish people doing today?" If a bird flew by and sang a few notes, Kitty called right back in bird language. To my ears, the string of chirps emanating from Kitty's mouth sounded authentic. Who knows what the birds thought?

## Sunsets

I gave up on trying to find new ways of saying *that's beautiful* during my stay on Rock n'Ridge. Everywhere I turned, a view of the hills, valley, or garden inspired me to say, "Wow, that's beautiful!" *What a view. Stunning. Gorgeous. How beautiful.* After awhile I resorted to a nod of the head and said, *oh yeah.*

## Rock n'Ridge Ranch

The hummingbirds, their chest feathers flashing iridescent green and pink in the sunlight, became a normal part of my daily scenery. I came to expect beauty every time I walked past Kitty and Creek's house. Bleeding hearts, purple hyacinths, and cherry blossoms met my eyes. Sweet smells filled the air. I inhaled an aromatic breeze of winter daphne, then strolled by a rosemary plant and plucked some of its green needles. I rolled the resin-coated needles between my fingers and breathed in the sweet rosemary scent.

The madrone trees felt as smooth as silk when I leaned against their naturally polished trunks. Unlike the bleeding hearts and hummingbirds, the madrones always appeared foreign to my eyes, especially when they glistened in the soft light after a heavy rain.

I experienced a disproportionate amount of beauty on Rock n'Ridge. Yet, some things never ceased to amaze me. One particular sunset stood out in my memory as the most beautiful I'd ever seen.

From a perch on Lion Rock, I watched as the sun grew dimmer and descended toward the ocean twenty miles away, sending the last of it's energy to Creek's solar panels. I ran my hand over the rough pale green lichens that covered the lion's mane.

Up until that point, a thin layer of clouds shrouded nearly every sunset I'd seen on the west coast. Finally, as I sat in a bowl-shaped crater on the Lion's head, I saw my first full sunset.

The sun went through several phases as it approached the horizon. First it swelled in size, then it turned blood red and became easy to look at straight on. Next, it melted into a puddle over the horizon. For several minutes the sun appeared as a wavy band of reddish-orange light, as though the ocean caught fire in that one little spot.

After the fire faded, dim light diffused over the landscape and my focus withdrew to the hills and valleys that separated me from the ocean.

*Rock n'Ridge Ranch*

The sun had set, and I remained seated. I bundled up against the cold wind, and watched as a dense fog poured in from the ocean and filled the valley.

The fog lay so flat it looked as though the ocean spilled over and froze into a vast ice-skating rink. Only rounded green hilltops poked through the mist, their green tops quickly turning black in the approaching night.

That moment needed no label. Even if someone had been with me, no words would have done justice to the view. Not *beautiful* or *stunning* or *magical*. I looked in the direction where the sun used to be. A giant soup bowl of fog and hilltops filled the valley. I felt the immensity of Lion Rock, turning cold beneath me, and I simply nodded my head and enjoyed the moment.

## My Best is Good Enough

Kitty and Creek were the ideal farm hosts. They participated in wwoofing for the cultural exchange rather than the allure of free labor. They didn't expect expert farmers or thoroughbred workhorses. They simply wanted to meet world travelers.

In exchange for a few hours of work each day, they offered lavish accommodations. I had *The Weekender* all to myself, stocked with Kitty's homemade granola, raw milk at $10 a gallon, and any other groceries I requested. I did my share of work---shoveling manure, planting fruit trees, and tending the greenhouse---but I lived in comfort.

The thought of being a professional wwoofer crossed my mind. Eating wonderful food. Working outside everyday. Never having to fill out another piece of paperwork. This all sounded tempting. But in reality, I knew all farms wouldn't be like Rock n'Ridge, nor did I relish the fact of living like a nomad for the rest of my life.

Besides, I didn't want to stink up the place, as overstayed guests often do. In my case, I knew it was time to leave when I started farting propane. The propane tank on the *The Weekender* sprung a leak one night, and I must've inhaled several hours worth of the gas before I pinpointed the source of my dizziness.

Other than that one incident, everything went wonderfully on Rock n' Ridge Ranch. The scenery was beautiful. Kitty and Creek were a breath of fresh air.

On my way out, Kitty left me with some wise words. She hugged me goodbye and said, "Do the best you can, Brian. And that's good enough." She added, "Do it with love and compassion," but the first part is what really stuck with me. To this day, anytime I have a moment of doubt or regret, I replay Kitty's words. *I'm doing the best I can, and that's good enough.*

## Farmers Markets

Rock n'Ridge marked the end of my California farming experience, but not the end of my tour through the Golden State. Before I drove to my next farm, in Oregon, I pitched my tent in the redwoods for a week.

One of my most vivid memories of Rock n'Ridge was when I stumbled upon an old redwood stump in the middle of the forest. For a few minutes I sat on the 15-foot wide stump and counted the tree rings. The tree was 368 years old according to my count, only an adolescent on the redwood timescale.

After I departed Rock n'Ridge, I saw more than just stumps. I saw the living giants themselves. As I drove north on Highway 101, I took a detour through The Avenue of Giants, the most humbling stretch of highway I've ever driven.

My car felt like a toy as I drove along the paved road, in the shade of 300-foot trees. The thousand-year-old redwood trees that bordered the road formed the pillars of a living cathedral.

I came into the sunlight on the other side feeling exposed. I felt I'd just committed a sacrilegious act by zooming through the ancient forest, leaving an exhaust trail in my wake.

I planned to return to Humboldt Redwood State Park, which the Avenue of Giants bisected, and enjoy the forest on foot rather than through the windows of my car. But before I set up camp, I made a detour through Arcata, California, a hip

Rock n'Ridge Ranch

little college town in Humboldt County. Kitty and Creek told me Arcata hosted a top-notch farmer's market.

As I traveled across the country, I made it a point to stop at as many farmers markets as I could. In doing so, I discovered each farmers market has a personality of its own, characterized by unique food and atmosphere.

At the farmers market in Austin, Texas I felt like I was at a friend's house for dinner. Children ran around picnic tables with balloons and slices of pizza. A colorfully dressed Oaxacan woman served up delicious black bean and cheese tamales, steamed in a banana leaf. I slid into a picnic table and ate with several boisterous and laughing families.

The farmers market in Bloomington, Indiana felt more like a mild hangover. College students dressed in sweat pants, with tousled hair, moseyed around drinking coffee and popping free samples of goat cheese into their mouths. Music, caffeine, and bright-eyed farmers slowly brought life and sobriety back into the Saturday morning.

The spring market in Manchester, Vermont felt like a celebration. Another harsh winter survived. Maple trees had been tapped and turned into syrup, and the farmers sat proudly at their booths with baskets full of leafy greens, farm-fresh eggs, and mason jars of maple syrup. A banjo player plucked his strings, providing a quick bouncy rhythm for all the customers. High school students and close friends stood in the grass, looking more like festival-goers than grocery shoppers. The rounded tops of the Green Mountains overlooked the whole scene.

The farmers market in my hometown felt more like a roadside fruit stand, an anomaly in a county filled with endless fields of corn and soybeans. The farmers didn't display colorful signs or advertise organic goods. No musician played. But the simple display of produce sold at rock bottom prices. The farmers smiled and kept their tables filled with produce from the back of pick-up trucks. The farmers market of my hometown, of nearly 60,000 people, was in its infancy. My community was still waking up to the value of local food.

The small town of Arcata, California, on the other hand, was fully awakened, if not a little stoned. An hour north of the Avenue of Giants, I came upon the Saturday market in Arcata. Everything for sale was organic. Organic meat. Organic eggs, milk, veggies. Organic t-shirts and hemp tennis shoes.

Everybody seemed to be high. After I parked my car, I walked past an old man who rested his back against the tire of a classic VW bus. The man displayed his wares on a Navajo patterned blanket: vinyl records and Jimi Hendrix apparel. Another man, wearing a multi-colored head band, flipped through the records, and upon seeing Jefferson Airplane, he said, "Yeah man, far out."

When I arrived at the center of the farmers market I witnessed an amazing selection of local food, with nearly 80 vendors facing toward the town square. Around a music stage, people dressed in tie-die swung their hips inside hula-hoops. Other exhibitionists juggled psychedelic bowling pins or ropes with balls on either end. A barefooted girl ran through the grass, waving rainbow streamers through the air. I watched all this while I ate a bowl of organic strawberries.

## Moonstone Beach

I observed the Arcata farmer's market more as an outsider. However, shortly after the farmers market, I serendipitously found myself participating in a Native American ritual on a local beach.

I stopped at the beach, called Moonstone Beach, as a nice place to meditate before heading off into the redwoods. As I sat in the sand with my eyes closed, enjoying the sound of the ocean lapping against the shore, my senses perked up when I smelled sage and rosemary incense wafting my way. I opened my eyes. Next to a rocky enclave by the ocean I saw a group of people mingling. Half of them stood in line and took turns stepping up to a man who blanketed them in a silhouette of incense and then tapped their heads. This appeared to be some sort of blessing or new-age ritual.

After witnessing the free-spirited farmers market in Arcata, I figured this was just another public event, so I walked over and stood in line. Nobody questioned me. The man traced my body with a stream of herb smoke and gave me a hard two-finger tap on my forehead, signifying the blessing was complete.

The next thing I knew, I found myself standing around a pile of crystals with the rest of the crowd. Tribal drumming began. A man started chanting like an old Indian chief. And people began dancing as we spiraled in single file, circling inward toward the crystals. I felt a bit unsure about where I'd found myself, but I thought it would be rude to step out in the middle of the ritual.

After the dancing and drumming stopped, we went around the circle introducing ourselves and saying prayers to Mother Earth. By that point, I knew I was the lone outsider.

Each person started by saying "Oh, Creator," followed by a blessing for health or strength, and then their name. The man two places down from me announced himself as Running Wolf. The woman right next to me said, "Hello, I'm Soaring Eagle." I thought about making a name for myself like "Quiet Monkey," or "Basking Lizard," but I didn't want to offend or belittle their custom. Besides, they surely knew I was an outsider.

When my turn came, I told them my ordinary name and what had happened—that "I was meditating and had just wandered over." They all laughed and welcomed me, so I stayed for the rest of the ceremony.

After a peace pipe passed around the circle and I puffed a cloud of scented tobacco, the real purpose of the gathering was explained to me by Soaring Eagle. I had stumbled upon an old Native American ritual, meant to honor an older woman who was present. The idea was to honor the woman and give her blessings while she was still alive. After everyone shared a memory about the woman or paid her some sort of compliment or respect, the circle unraveled and the woman walked over to the ocean and tossed an eagle feather into the tide to symbolize the soul's return to the Great Spirit.

We ended the ritual by sitting around a fire while some of the elders sang enchanting Iroquois songs set to the rhythm of drumming and gourd shakers.

I felt honored they so readily accepted me and let me join what was probably a sacred ritual for many of them. They sent me on my way with a renewed sense of togetherness, the same feeling I'd experienced through couchsurfing. I felt a sense of familiarity with these so-called strangers.

## Redwoods

The redwoods sobered me up, though I didn't have a drop of alcohol in me. When I first set foot on a hiking trail in the Humboldt Redwoods State Park, I awoke to the reality of being surrounded by 800-year-old giants.

The first thing I learned was to stop trying to see the top of every tree I passed. I knew this would cause neck problems. The red bark of the trees twisted gradually upward. From the mammoth base, wide as a two-car garage in many cases, the tree tightened into a slender branchless body. *This is a redwood version of Jack's Beanstalk,* I thought.

When I tilted my head back to the sky, I saw a spray of branches at the very top, joining with neighboring trees to form a ceiling made of green needles. Very little light penetrated the canopy. Three hundred feet of dank cool air filled the space between the fern-covered forest floor and the top, where the slender redwood trunks supported the world's highest forest canopy.

Bird whistles echoed as if coming from a distant mountaintop, but I knew they occupied the canopy directly overhead. On one of my hikes I saw a place where an old tree had fallen over, leaving a gaping hole in the canopy. Several young trees, no thicker than lampposts, leaned toward the hole, attempting to tap into the sudden wealth of sunshine.

## Rock n' Ridge Ranch

Aside from bird whistles, the ancient forest felt eerily quiet. This was not the kind of forest where someone could feel claustrophobic. Agoraphobia would be more likely. The immense space made me feel tiny and vulnerable.

At times I felt transported to an ancient forest, with small dinosaurs lurking in the thick groundcover of ferns. This was the only warm-weather forest I'd ever walked in without seeing a single squirrel. I half expected a pterodactyl to swoop in from the canopy.

Mosquitoes and tourists brought me back to the present moment. The quick jolt of a mosquito bite interrupted my imagination. On one occasion, I crossed paths with a retired couple from Italy. They wore colorful windbreaker suits that swooshed when they walked, and they asked me, "Where is your girlfriend!?" They served as a clear reminder that I was in no threat of being attacked by a dinosaur.

All of the camera-toting tourists reminded me when and where I was. I was in two places at once-- a tourist attraction of big trees, and at the same time, a guest of those humbling pillars of nature that communed with the sun far above me.

When I came upon the tourist hot spots, I did some neck stretches and tilted my head back to admire the tallest and oldest of the trees, given nicknames such as Giant Tree and Founders Tree. I gazed in awe at these trees that pre-dated the Roman Empire. For millennia, they'd been silently and imperceptibly moving toward the sun. As Indian tribes and Spanish conquistadors and pioneers hustled around on the ground, looking for food or gold or land, the trees drank from the wet coastal air and extended their top branches above their neighbors. As mosquitoes hovered around the colorfully dressed Italian couple and vacationers arrived in droves to photograph everything in sight, the trees steadily grew taller.

I thought about Kitty as I stood at the base of the red giants. I thought about her belief that all plants and animals have a spirit, just as humans do. I placed my hand on the coarse bark of one of the trees, almost as if to feel for a pulse. I knew sap ran through the tree, feeding it's cells, but I wondered if Kitty and every other shaman on the planet was right, and a Redwood Spirit embodied this tree.

If Kitty could communicate with the tree, I wondered what it would say. I've been watching you? Or It sure is tough being a tree. Maybe it'd say, Thanks for breathing in all that poisonous oxygen I've been exhaling.

Regardless of whether those red giants harbored a spirit or plant soul, I enjoyed walking in their shadow. I left the redwoods feeling sober, as if I'd just witnessed the greatest natural history museum on the planet.

## Lost Coast

After visiting the redwoods, I drove west until I could go no farther and parked next to the wavy band of blue light I'd peered at many times from the head of Lion Rock. For three nights, I camped on California's Lost Coast.

The Lost Coast proved to be unlike any beach experience I'd ever had. Aside from the sand, I wouldn't call it a beach. No lifeguards or well-oiled sunbathers basked on the Lost Coast. Sunlight was scarce on the cloudy, windblown landscape. Cold and rocky waters made the shoreline inhospitable to swimmers and surfers.

This was a place for hiking. The Lost Coast is a national treasure, one of the longest stretches of pristine coastline still remaining on the Pacific Ocean. With the exception of an old 1910s lighthouse called Punta Gorda, the place was devoid of all things human during my visit. Even the boot-prints of hikers were quickly erased, either by the tide or the gusty winds that whipped the sandy shoreline.

Really, the only imprint of humanity was a narrow, but well-beaten path that snaked through the coastal prairie. In the redwoods, I felt like I'd found myself in a prehistoric forest. On the coastal prairie of the Lost Coast, I felt as though I'd ventured inside a Dr. Seuss illustration.

Tall, single-stemmed plants ending in tennis ball looking

# Rock n'Ridge Ranch

flowers stood alongside the trail. Lupines, poppies, and waist-high prairie grass bowed gently in the strong wind, and every so often, a handful of lemon birds burst out of the prairie grass and settled into a new spot. I didn't know the actual name of the birds, but they resembled the size, shape, and color of a lemon, with black wings.

Tidepools were just a stone's throw from the hiking trail. Every so often I wandered down to the ocean and hopped over the ebb and flow of little streams that cut through giant slabs of rock. The rock slabs kept me a few feet above the ocean's tide. I peered into tidepools, each one an isolated pocket of ocean water—like it's own aquarium, filled with swaying bands of kelp, sea anemones, and starfish. Tiny-shelled creatures hustled around in their underwater world.

The few people with whom I crossed paths had come to the Lost Coast to harvest food from the ocean. Two men dressed in full body wet suits told me they were after abalone. Next to my campground, a large group of women gathered seaweed from the tidepools. They carried five-gallon ziplock bags of the stuff and told me they simply dried it out and used it for soups and sushi, or baked and salted it into seaweed chips.

The seaweed people waved me out to join them, but I chose to sit on the wind-sculpted sand dunes and watch. I watched the turbulent ocean, slapping the rocks and churning up white froth. I watched seabirds run toward the receding tide and peck little creatures out of the sand, then take flight in unison as the next wave slid in toward their feet.

I watched women reach into tidepools with scissors and pull out strips of seaweed. This was my last view of California. I breathed in the salty sea air, taking a bit of the ocean into my lungs. In my own way, with a smile and a nod, I said goodbye to the Golden State and moved on.

## Chapter 11
### *Runnymede Farm*

Each farm I visited had a specialty. Chestnut Hill grew chestnuts. Applesauce Hill raised Icelandic Sheep. Lucy's Farm specialized in growing baby salad greens for Miami's elite restaurants, while the non-profit farms and homesteads focused on living off the grid.

The final farm of my wwoofing tour, located near Rogue River in southern Oregon, didn't concentrate on any one thing. Art and Teri, the husband and wife farmers of Runnymede Farm, put their eggs into many different baskets. Aside from keeping a flock of two hundred laying hens, they also milked two cows, harvested honey from six beehives, and fattened up two pigs each year for butchering.

Art and Teri also tended a one-acre orchard of pear and apple trees, and farmed flowers and a wide-range of vegetables, including onions, peas, garlic, leafy greens, tomatoes, squash, and sweet potatoes.

A patrol donkey named Sassy kept predators and foragers from penetrating the perimeter fence and devouring Art and Teri's edible merchandise.

Runnymede Farm maintained a high level of diversity. If the pear trees failed to set fruit, which happened the summer I arrived due to an unexpected late frost, Art and Teri had a

## Runnymede Farm

financial cushion from the milk, eggs, and vegetables. If the farmers market didn't yield a tremendous profit, then Art and Teri still had income from their direct-from-the-farm raw milk and egg sales.

Runnymede was the polar opposite of Ireland's potato fields of the 1800s and America's present day factory farms. Art and Teri didn't gamble on one product. They nurtured a symbiotic farm. Bees pollinated the fruits of the garden. Animals pooped fertilizer for the crops, and vegetable scraps and weeds fed the chickens. The farm produced no waste – only a nature-mimicking web of life, where the death or excrement of one being turned into life-giving food for another.

## Art and Teri

While driving alongside the crystal clear Rogue River on my way to the farm, I spotted an occasional group of white-water rafters paddling over the rapids. Men in chest-high waders fly-fished along the rocky banks.

The distant view consisted of pine covered mountains. The mountains weren't huge, but to a flatlander like me, anything more than a bump on the earth's surface is an impressive mountain.

I followed Rogue River upstream, nearly a hundred miles inland from the point where it emptied into the ocean. At the town of Rogue River, a tributary called Evans Creek led me directly to Runnymede Farm.

When I pulled into the driveway of Runnymede, ten feet across the road from Evans Creek, I saw the first indication that I'd arrived on a for-profit farm. A walk-in cooler with sliding glass doors faced the driveway, resembling a display cooler in a convenience store. Instead of being packed full of Pepsi, Gatorade, and flavored water, the shelves were stocked with Runnymede's two finest products: fresh eggs and one gallon glass jars filled with raw milk.

A couple hundred feet after I passed the milk cooler, the driveway ended at a red barn. The farm was compact. I could

*Runnymede Farm*

see most of the five acres from the end of the driveway. Three tents were pitched in the shade of Douglas fir trees, and a two-room carriage house equipped with a bathroom, kitchen, and laundry facilities, stood directly behind Art and Teri's house.

A young man named Taylor greeted me outside the carriage house. He and his girlfriend, a good-looking couple recently graduated from the University of Arizona, were Art and Teri's full-season interns. Taylor had won a Fulbright Scholarship, and wanted to get hands on experience before furthering his research in sustainable agriculture.

As Taylor led me around the farm, showing me the chickens, beehives, cows, fruit trees, greenhouses, and vegetable patches, he pointed to the stand of Douglas firs that formed a living canopy over the tents. "This all used to be a Christmas tree farm," he said. He called the previous operation a "ridiculous enterprise," and said Art and Teri had purchased the land over a decade earlier.

Taylor helped me pitch my tent in the cool shade of a 70 foot tall Douglas fir, one of the few Christmas trees allowed to reach full potential.

As I unloaded my bags from the car I crossed paths with Teri, a short woman who moved with balance and strength. She carried a five-gallon plastic pail filled to the brim with snow peas and sugar snap peas. "We're harvesting for the farmers market tomorrow," she told me cheerfully. "Help yourself."

I grabbed a handful of freshly picked peas and munched on their sweet, tender pods as Teri filled me in on the farm schedule during my stay. "We'll be harvesting onions, peas, salad mix and garlic while you're here," she told me. "Almost everything but the sweet potatoes is already planted."

Despite being in the middle of harvesting peas, Teri didn't act rushed or impatient. She smiled and wanted to know if I had any questions. I could tell right away she managed the farm with efficiency and an easy-going spirit. I took an immediate liking to Teri.

"Art's in the barn if you'd like to meet him," she told me.

## Runnymede Farm

Teri and I parted ways. She continued on toward the walk-in cooler to store the peas, while I headed toward an enormous pile of compost outside the barn. The pile consisted of straw bedding saturated with cow manure, but I didn't smell any unpleasant odors. The sweet grassy smell of hay filled the air.

I stepped inside the red barn. To my right, an entire room was filled with bales of alfalfa hay. On the other side of a wooden fence I saw Art, a sturdily built man with graying hair. It wasn't time for milking, but one of the cows had stepped inside from the pasture, and Art brushed the cow's coat with a stiff bristled brush.

When I walked into the barn, which served as the cow's shelter and milking parlor, Art continued brushing. He studied me over the tops of his glasses, then coolly slid the brush off his hand and stepped over to give me a firm handshake. We both turned around to admire the cow.

"This is Daisy," he said. "Our Guernsey."

Daisy looked at us as she chewed her cud from the pasture. She was a fine specimen, with a light brown coat and large, irregular white spots. The white markings looked like a map of unfamiliar continents set on a fawn colored ocean. After I admired her shiny coat, my eyes dropped to her udders. They were engorged, like an inflated latex glove ready to burst.

"Look at the udders on her!" I said.

Art met my comment with enthusiasm. "You bet," he said. "We get nearly seven gallons a day from her." He resumed brushing her coat and rattled off facts about Daisy's milk. "Her milk has an exceptionally high butter fat content," he said proudly. "Close to five percent." Then he pointed outside the milking parlor to a smaller cow grazing in the pasture. "That's Hayden," he said. "She's our Brown Swiss."

Art, a Vietnam veteran, struck me as a man of intelligence and old school work ethic. He kept the cows well groomed and in good health.

All of Runnymede was kept in orderly fashion. No broken down cars or rusted tools occupied the premises. Art and Teri

*Runnymede Farm*

had a German sensibility in the way they kept the farm clean, efficient, and working in harmony.

Neither Art nor Teri had any over-the-top eccentricities like some of my previous hosts. They didn't communicate with animal spirits or embody extreme personality traits. They were down to earth – a friendly couple concerned about their cow's milk production and how many onions they sold at the farmers market. They didn't demand extreme work hours or offer a vacation setup. They lived a balanced life.

During my stay on Runnymede, Art and Teri exposed me to a wide array of farm chores. I worked with the animals and harvested and planted crops. I spent time on the farm and at the farmers market. I gathered eggs and drank gallons of the fattest and freshest milk of my life. Runnymede was exactly the kind of farm I pictured when I sat behind my teacher's desk a year before, yearning for a change of pace.

## Sammy the Bull

Three chickens greeted me when I first pulled into the farm. They paused momentarily to cluck in my direction, then resumed pecking around in the tall grass next to a greenhouse. Chickens were the common thread of nearly every farm I visited. The clucking of hens had become the soundtrack of my life, as common as bird song and chattering squirrels.

Cows on the other hand, were still new to me. When Taylor took me for a walk around the farm, I paused to stare at the cows for quite some time. I leaned against the solid wooden beams of the fence and watched the massive animals graze. Daisy the Guernsey who gave milk with five percent butterfat, clipped the grass short with her powerful jaws. She ate more like a high-powered vacuum than a lawn mower. She lowered her mouth to the ground and sucked up patches of grass.

Hayden, the smaller of Art and Teri's dairy cows, stood a few yards from Daisy and watched Taylor and I patiently, choosing not to eat for the time being. A brown Swiss breed, Hayden had a solid light brown coat with a streak of blond fur

## Runnymede Farm

along her spine. She and Daisy's well-groomed coats shone in the sunlight. They looked as if they'd been shampooed and conditioned.

While Taylor and I watched the cows, I plucked a handful of tall grass from our side of the fence and held it out for Daisy. "Here Daisy," I said. "Come and get it." She looked at me from the corner of her eye and continued her vacuum-style grazing. Daisy clearly had enough fresh grass to eat. She didn't need my meager offering. I felt slightly rejected, so I put a stalk of grass in my own mouth and chewed the sweet wheat-grass juice from its stem.

Daisy and Hayden were beautiful animals—large, yet docile. They ate grass all day and essentially turned sunlight into milk. In addition, their manure had value. Daisy and Hayden's four-chambered stomachs acted like compost machines, turning grass and hay into concentrated fertilizer for Art and Teri's vegetable gardens and orchard.

Everyone on the farm enjoyed Daisy and Hayden, but no one enjoyed them as much as Sammy the Bull. Sammy was on loan from a neighboring farmer, with the intended purpose of impregnating the two cows.

As Taylor and I leaned against the fence and tried to summon the cows to eat from our hands, a small black bull followed the big ladies around. Sammy had a one-track mind. He played the same tune in his head on repeat: Daisy, Daisy, Daisy. He couldn't take his eyes off her.

Sammy didn't have the typical traits one would expect in a bull. He was small, black, and cute, about half the size of Daisy. However, he had one thing going for him – zero competition.

As I chewed on the stem of another piece of grass, I witnessed an unforgettable portrait of Sammy the Bull. Daisy stopped to vacuum more grass, and the moment she stopped, Sammy moved his face in toward her large behind and inhaled. He must've gotten a powerful dose of Daisy perfume, because he immediately curled his upper lip over his wet nostrils and tilted his head back to the sky. His eyes rolled back in his head.

Runnymede Farm

For a few seconds, he remained in that pose, his lip curled over his wet nostrils and his mind clearly in another place, enjoying ecstasy only Sammy the Bull could know.

"Oh my God!" said Taylor's girlfriend, who'd just stepped up to the fence to join us in cow-watching. "Did you see that?"

We all laughed at Sammy's shameless display. Oddly enough, none of us ever saw Sammy try to mate with the cows. He seemed content sniffing them. During Sammy's moment of sampling Daisy's perfume, she calmly continued eating her patch of grass, oblivious to the small black bull behind her.

## Whole Milk

When I first arrived on Runnymede, I thought the two hundred laying hens played a significant role in paying Art and Teri's bills. This was not the case. The chicken eggs didn't come anywhere close to matching the revenue from Daisy and Hayden's milk.

Back in Maine, when I milked Jane the Goat, I was lucky to get a pint each milking-session. Jane was a hobby goat. An occasional-round-of-cheese goat. Daisy and Hayden gave a whopping 15 gallons a day between the two of them. Each gallon sold directly from the farm at premium raw milk prices of seven dollars per gallon.

Runnymede's milk sold for almost twice the price of conventional milk. However, by raw milk standards, Art and Teri priced their milk at the bare minimum in order to sustain their farming operation. Those who know the value of fresh raw milk from grass-fed cows understand that seven dollars a gallon is a bargain.

Unsold milk wasn't a problem for Art and Teri. In fact, they had a waiting list. Families from all around the Rogue River Valley lined up to buy Daisy and Hayden's fine product.

Twice a day, after breakfast and dinner, Art put on his mucking boots and headed to the barn. He turned the radio dial to country and blues music, then lured Daisy and Hayden back into the barn with a scoop of sweet grains for each. This

## Runnymede Farm

was their milking music and snack time.

Art milked the cows by hand. When he finished, he carried the milk in large metal pails back to the house and poured it through a filter. He didn't pasteurize or homogenize the cow's milk. He simply filled seven or eight one-gallon glass jars, screwed the lids on, and placed them in the walk-in cooler next to the driveway.

Regular customers drove to the farm and exchanged a clean empty bottle for a fresh one. Since raw milk is a highly perishable commodity, customers chose a specific day of the week to pick-up their milk. This ensured everyone got milk at its peak freshness, taken from the cows the same day.

Art was the head milkman. Occasionally Taylor and his girlfriend helped out, since they had six months to hone their milking skills. Personally, I never pursued the chore. Unlike Jane the goat, Daisy and Hayden represented the source of Art and Teri's income. Art mentioned that first time milkers put stress on the cows, resulting in a dramatically lower milk output. Thus, I didn't want to risk cheating some eager raw-milk drinker out of their weekly gallon. Instead, I took the more satisfying task of drinking copious amounts of Daisy and Hayden's milk.

When I reached into the fridge for a jar of milk the first time, I noticed something I wasn't accustomed to. Unlike the conventional milk I'd drunk my entire life, and even raw goat's milk, which remained in a naturally homogenized state, I saw a thick layer of yellowish cream on the surface. I had to swirl the jar to mix the rich butterfat into the rest of the milk.

Occasionally I skimmed some cream to put on my oatmeal, or Teri ladled a few cups worth and whipped it with maple syrup to compliment one of her homemade pies or strudels. Mostly, I blended the whole milk with a frozen banana and a couple of raw egg yolks as my breakfast for the day. With nearly five percent butterfat, the smoothie kept me going for hours without hunger pangs.

Art told me that for most of human history cream has

been the most valuable part of the milk. Cream is where fat-soluble vitamins A and D are found, plus energy rich butterfat. Traditionally, dairy farmers skimmed cream from their milk to make butter and cheese, and the skimmed fat-free milk was fed to their pigs for its protein value.

After my month of drinking rich, creamy milk from Runnymede's own pastures, I'll never look at skim milk the same way. Skim milk is nothing more than the watery leftovers. Combine that with the fact that all conventional milk is cooked and homogenized before being placed on the shelf, and I think one could make a case for tap water being an equally nutritious and satisfying addition to breakfast cereal.

## Raw Milk

Historically, all milk was drunk raw. Pasteurization didn't arise until the late 1800s, when milk from sick cows led to an equally sick populace in Boston and New York City. The problem began with distillery dairies. Cows were kept on the premises of whiskey distilleries and fed spent grains and leftovers from the liquor production.

The cows in distillery dairies lived without grass, sunlight, and exercise. They averaged a life span of less than a year, and gave a pale, bluish milk devoid of fat, protein, vitamins, and minerals. The sickly cows, dirty milkmen, and lack of refrigeration turned into a recipe for disaster. Infant mortality skyrocketed and millions in the city died from tuberculosis.

Pasteurization saved the day, extending the shelf life of milk by cooking it free of pathogens. No wonder people touted pasteurization as a wonderful thing.

However, during the same time low-income city folks were drinking chalky blue milk from sick cows, a whole different product was being sold in the countryside. Milk taken from healthy, grass-fed cows was viewed as the best medicine of the day. The Mayo Clinic used this high quality country milk as the basis for many of its disease curing therapies.

The "milk cure" was common knowledge to most doctors

of the day. Raw milk from grass-fed cows was used to treat asthma, arthritis, allergies, depression, diabetes, kidney and prostate disease, tuberculosis, and just about every other chronic disease imaginable. Milk as medicine extends all the way back to the time of Hippocrates in ancient Greece.

Nowadays, all milk found in grocery stores, including organic milk, is of the pasteurized, homogenized, glow-in-the-dark variety. All of its healing properties---vitamins, digestive enzymes, and beneficial bacteria---are destroyed. That's the major difference between store-bought milk and raw milk. One is half the price and cooked clean of its natural goodness. Raw milk, on the other hand, is expensive but practically a health food.

Art and Teri had a waiting list for their raw milk because their customers were willing to pay a premium in order to get the real thing: wholesome raw milk with cream that rose to the surface. They were willing to pay extra for the high butterfat content, and they understood that diseased food only comes from diseased animals.

Most of all, Art and Teri's customers enjoyed knowing where their food came from. When a Runnymede customer stopped by the farm to pick up a fresh milk bottle, they could walk up the driveway and spend a few minutes leaning against the fence, watching Daisy and Hayden tear fresh wads of grass from the pasture. If that customer had a family, they were feeding their children the healthiest milk around.

## Collecting Eggs

Although I never milked the cows, I became well acquainted with the chickens. They were easy to care for. Twice a day I gave them fresh water and grains, and every so often I changed their straw bedding and tossed an escaped chicken back into the coop. When I weeded the salad beds or saw the compost bucket in the kitchen was full, I pitched the unwanted plant material over the fence, and the chickens flocked to the pile of apple cores and dandelions like they'd just hit the jackpot.

> Runnymede Farm

In exchange for meeting the chickens' basic needs, each hen laid about one egg per day. This translated to well over a thousand eggs per week from the entire flock.

The first time I collected eggs, I walked into the sheltered chicken coop with a large wicker basket and approached the row of wooden laying boxes fixed to the wall a few feet off the ground. As I reached into the first hen's laying box and attempted to slide my hand under her and steal her egg, she challenged me. The white-feathered hen puffed up her chest, appearing large and menacing. She jerked her head sideways and stared at my hand with beady red eyes, as if to say, "Are you crazy? I'll tear your hand off!" She filled me with fear.

I sensed the dinosaur blood in her predatory machine-like movements. A warning sound resonated from her chest, growing louder as I moved my hand closer. I felt like she would snap at any moment and start pecking at my face.

Taylor, who stood behind me, overseeing my first round as the egg collector, intervened. "Here's how you do it," he said, noticing how slowly and cautiously I approached the hen.

He deftly grabbed the hen by her tail feathers, lifted her from her laying box, and dropped her to the ground. The hen flapped her wings and clucked in protest, but the second she landed on her feet she seemed to forget all about the egg she'd just spent the morning incubating. She ran out of the coop and joined her sisters in the yard.

"Isn't that inhumane?" I asked Taylor.

"Not at all. They don't feel a thing," he said.

Over dinner that night, Art confirmed what Taylor had said. "You have to handle the chickens firmly. That's what they want."

Taylor repeated his demonstration on the next two laying boxes, and I quickly grabbed the eggs and put them in my basket before a new hen jumped in and claimed the vacant box.

After watching how easily Taylor managed the first few hens, my confidence returned and I made another attempt.

> Runnymede Farm

This time the hen followed through on her threat. Sensing weakness, she pecked my hand. Instantly, my fear dissolved. The peck felt like someone had jabbed my hand with a pencil eraser.

I quickly turned into a skilled egg collector. I picked a hen up by her tail feathers, gently tossed her from her laying box, and delicately placed her eggs in my basket. When I tossed a hen from her box, the whole coop temporarily turned into a madhouse. The evicted hen squawked and flapped her wings, sending the surrounding chickens into a frenzy of clucking. Loose feathers floated around my head.

I thought for sure I was doing something wrong, but Art and Teri assured me that "It didn't hurt the hens at all."

In some laying boxes I removed the hen to find no eggs at all. In others, I uncovered a cache of six or seven eggs. All of the wooden laying boxes were identical, yet the hens preferred certain ones. I sometimes found five hens piled on top of each other with the laying box on either side completely empty. In this overcrowded situation, the bottom hen always looked completely content with her position, while the hen at the top of the heap looked uneasy, clucking nervously, obviously aware something was wrong with this picture.

I never understood why certain laying boxes were so popular. Maybe hens are prone to advertising, just like humans. They figured since every other chicken wanted *that one box*, then it must be the best.

## Egg Oddities

Chickens share many personality traits with humans. They're defensive, stubborn animals, and when not laying eggs, eating, or having sex, they congregate in little gangs and show off their social status.

A hen proved her place in the pecking order by flapping her wings and pecking aggressively at lesser hens who encroached on prized food and water territory. The three roosters spent the entire day thrusting their chests out, pinning hens to the ground in rough chicken sex, and sounding off the strength of their cock-a-doodle-doo.

After I honed the art of collecting eggs and jettisoning hens from their laying boxes, I developed affection for the birds. I took pleasure in the way each hen appeared set in her ways. One hen decided to lay her eggs on the dirt floor. Another one, talented in the ways of escaping from the chicken coop, preferred to lay her daily egg in a roll of duct tape.

Each chicken had a personality. In addition, each egg I collected was unique in its own way. One robust hen laid mammoth eggs. For lunch, I cracked one of her eggs into the skillet and three yolks spilled out.

I collected tiny eggs no bigger than an almond. One day, Teri found an egg without a shell. A paper mache membrane surrounded the egg, and I could squish and deform the inside without tearing it. Another time, I found an egg with a hardened nipple on one end.

Regardless of the shape, size, and color of the egg, every chicken laid eggs with a rich golden yolk, unlike anything found in a carton of conventional eggs. Teri scrubbed and sorted the eggs, then sold the uniform ones for four dollars a dozen, either at the farmers market or directly from the milk cooler.

The odd eggs typically found their way into the wwoofer fridge. I blended the eggs into my breakfast smoothie and fried up a couple for lunch. I was an egg and milk powered machine on Runnymede Farm.

## Dirty Jobs

Working on the farm sometimes involved performing unsavory jobs. One day, Taylor and I found a half-dead chicken lying in the yard. The hen lay on her side, still breathing. She looked terrible. Her eyes were missing and a thick translucent goo covered the feathers on her chest.

My heart raced when I saw the sick hen. I thought I'd arrived at ground zero for the avian flu virus, a potential epidemic

*Runnymede Farm*

making big headlines around that time.

I didn't know the proper way to put the chicken out of her misery. Besides, I didn't want to get anywhere near her, even with a pair of gloves and a shovel. Luckily, Taylor the Fulbright scholar had been pent up in the classroom for so long he was eager for real-world experience. "I'll take care of it," he volunteered. I didn't argue with him.

"Thank you," I told him, with the utmost sincerity.

Taylor shoveled the sickly bird onto a wooden board, brought an axe down on its neck, and stuffed it into a burlap feed bag. And that was that.

Later that night, with the topic of chickens raised at the dinner table, Teri mentioned, "The chicken coop could probably use a cleaning."

I thought about what Taylor had done earlier that day and figured that cleaning the chicken coop was the least I could do in return. "I'll do it!" I said eagerly. I didn't realize I'd volunteered for the dirtiest, noisiest job on the farm.

I had come to enjoy the chickens. I loved watching them make little dust beds in the chicken yard. I enjoyed watching them run in excited flocks for weeds or food scraps I chucked over the fence. I even empathized with their stubborn personalities. They took after many of my family members in that regard.

However, for the duration of cleaning the hen house, my attitude toward the chickens changed. *These are the filthiest most annoying animals on the planet!* I thought.

Cleaning the chicken coop was without a doubt the nastiest job I'd ever performed. It wasn't filthy in a wading through muck kind of way. I didn't get dirt under my fingernails. The job was filthy because I had to work in a thick cloud of dust – and this wasn't ordinary dust. It was fecal matter ground into a fine powder. I literally worked in a cloud of shit.

It's one thing to wade through a pile of manure and get it all over your boots. It's quite another to breathe chicken excrement directly into your lungs and have it settle over your entire body.

*Runnymede Farm*

I probably should've worn goggles. Instead, I opted for a surgical mask, gloves, and a hood. Surprisingly, I got used to working in the cloud. The mask did a fairly good job of filtering the smell. I also got used to the physical act of scraping dried chicken poop from the floor, like scraping plaque off a giant tooth. It didn't even bother me that the hens were totally unappreciative of what I was doing to improve their standard of living.

The one thing I *never* got used to was the noise. For three consecutive hours, the hens made an absolute raucous, squawking, and screeching. I probably looked like an executioner to them, with my mask, hood, and a sharp scraping implement.

The entire flock of two hundred birds had a conniption fit. I tried various types of music to quiet them, or at least drown out their deafening squawks. I tried the band *The Talking Heads*. The hens seemed to harmonize with the music, and when a song ended the entire flock fell silent for one blissful moment.

I didn't regret leaving my teaching profession, but if I could trade one job for a classroom full of rowdy ill-mannered teenagers, I'd gladly trade cleaning the chicken coop.

## A Donkey and Her Peas

Most of the farm work on Runnymede was pleasant. I worked in the sunshine and clean country air, and the distant cluck of the hens blended with the sound of crickets and bees. I planted lettuce and sweet potatoes. I pulled onions from the ground. I shoveled steaming horse manure from the bed of a pick-up truck and performed the ever-present task on all organic farms of pulling weeds.

I volunteered on Runnymede in early June, during the height of pea season. Six fifty-foot rows contained a variety of sugar snap and snow peas. Teri also planted one row of purple peas.

I spent many-a-morning sitting on a burlap sack in the wet grass, reaching my hands into a thicket of pea vines to harvest ripe pods. The cattle fencing that served as a trellis for the pea plants was invisible in the mass of leaves and tendrils. Each row appeared as a freestanding pea forest.

The ripe purple peas were easy to spot, because they stood out against the green backdrop. I plucked a handful of pods from the vines and dropped them into a large rubber harvest bucket.

The sugar snaps and snow peas were more difficult to see. Even with my head practically in the pea forest, they remained camouflaged, each pod framed in a tangle of same-colored green vines. After I picked one section and slid my dry burlap sack down the row a few feet, I often looked back from the new angle and realized I'd missed about twenty perfectly plump pea pods. Either the peas were growing faster than I could pick them, or the peas were hiding better than I could seek them out.

The best perk of harvesting peas was snacking directly from the vine as I went along. Sugar snap peas are nature's finest green candy. The crunchy walls of the fat pods pack just enough sweet juice to balance out the tender peas within. The more flattened snow peas were also good and crunchy when eaten raw, but I preferred the sugar snaps. I polished off close to a pound of sugar snaps every day.

Only Sassy the patrol donkey rivaled my appetite for sugar snaps. Sassy lived outside the perimeter fence and kept deer, raccoons, and wild cats at bay. Art told me donkeys are notorious for driving off predators. He said a neighbor brought two doberman pinchers to the farm one day and Sassy charged them, sending them running in the opposite direction. In combination with a secure fence, Sassy was the best cow, chicken, and vegetable protection Art and Teri could hope for.

When I picked peas, Sassy watched from the other side of the fence, patiently waiting for me to stand up and bring her a handful, as I often did. I walked over to the fence and handfed her one sugar snap pea at a time.

*Runnymede Farm*

Sassy displayed all of the symptoms of a pea addict. As soon as I got remotely close, she stuck her mouth through the chain-linked fence and showed her big yellow donkey-teeth. It didn't matter how many peas she had in her mouth at one time, she could always take an 8th or 9th or 20th sugar snap. I honestly think Sassy would've eaten herself to death if she found a way through the fence and into the pea rows.

When I decided to go back to work filling up my harvest bucket, Sassy threw a fit, "hee-hawing" desperately like a swing set in need of oiling. I showed her my hand was empty. "No more peas, Sassy," I told her. But that didn't calm her one bit. She knew there were more, and she knew I'd bring them to her. That donkey loved peas.

## Selling Purple Peas

We harvested peas, onions, lettuce, and garlic scapes the day before going to the local farmers market. Before putting the 80 or so onions in the walk-in fridge, I used a pair of scissors to cut the tops and root hairs off, and then I submerged them in a water bath to rinse off any dirt.

One morning, in the middle of making the onions look presentable, Art stopped at the water basin I was using and told me *how things used to be*. "We used to sell the onions just how they came out of the ground," he said. "Covered in dirt, with their tops still on. Now everyone wants them to look just like they do in the grocery store."

I agreed with him. From my perspective vegetables are more alluring when they have a straight-from-the-ground look. But Teri knew what the customers wanted, and it wasn't a carrot covered with dirt.

The following day, Teri took me to Medford, Oregon, where I experienced the Rogue Valley Growers Market from the farmer's side of the table.

I watched an empty parking lot turn into a village of food. Vans and trucks from all over the countryside unloaded freshly harvested vegetables and fruits, cartons of eggs, baked

## Runnymede Farm

goods, flowers, potted vegetables and trees, as well as jewelry and crafts. Teri and I set up a long table with a canopy on our designated site. We arranged the peas, salad greens, and Walla Walla onions in wicker baskets next to a stack of plastic bags and an electronic scale.

The woman in the booth next to ours unloaded a station wagon full of baked goods. She and Teri were good friends, having shared neighboring sites at the farmers market for many years. The baked goods woman handed Teri and I a plate of oatmeal raisin cookies and strawberry rhubarb turnovers.

After Teri and I set up, I ate a few cookies and watched the market come to life. A man rang a bell at 8:30 a.m. and the customers started drifting in.

Within minutes, a line formed in front of the donut stand across the way from us. The donut stand was a family operation, as were most of the booths at the market. An old couple and their three granddaughters stayed busy for the next five hours, dropping dough into the deep fryer.

I walked over to the donut stand to get a better look, and the next thing I knew, I found myself standing in line with a handful of dollars. I watched as a little conveyor belt carried hot donuts out of the deep fryer and dropped them into a bin of sugar and cinnamon. A pretty Mexican girl, probably fifteen years old, used a pair of tongs to bag the fresh donuts. "I'll take four," I told her, hoping to share a couple with Teri.

Over the course of the day, I felt like Sassy set loose in a field of peas. I lost all self-control over my typically healthy eating habits, and revisited the *Fresh Donut* stand two more times.

In between eating baked goods and sugarcoated donuts still warm from the deep fryer, I helped Teri weigh out vegetables and take money from the customers.

Wall Walla onions were the hot seller at our table. Old women stopped by and pointed at the basket of softball-sized onions. "Give me three Walla Walla sweets," one woman said. "Can you find me a one-pounder?" an old man asked me.

Nearly every customer exchanged smiles with us or paused

to chat with Teri, even if they weren't buying anything. Teri was well known at the farmers market, both for her high quality organic vegetables and her easygoing personality.

The sugar snaps and snow peas sold fairly well, but the purple peas pretty much went untouched. They served more as a curiosity. Several people stopped and stared at the strangely colored peas, but nobody wanted to buy them, especially with the description Teri and I started off with: "They're not as sweet as the sugar snaps. You can use them the same way as snow peas, but they're not as crisp." That was the truth. The purple peas weren't nearly as tasty as the green peas, but Teri and I knew if we wanted to unload any of them, we'd have to change our marketing strategy.

As people continued inquiring about the purple peas, I developed a new sales pitch that started bringing in a few dollars. The pitch went like this: "These are a Dutch Purple heirloom, a relative of the snow pea. They have a mild, slightly earthy flavor, and they're great for salads and stir-fries, since they hold their color."

Everything I said was completely true, but even Sassy wouldn't have bought that nonsense. She would've said, "Give me my sugar snaps!" or just "Hee-haw!"

By the time the closing bell rang at 1:30p.m., I'd polished off close to a dozen donuts, a strawberry rhubarb turnover, and a stack of oatmeal raisin cookies. I didn't touch one sugar snap pea that day. They lost their appeal in the midst of a truly hardcore junk food binge.

Within an hour after the closing bell rang, everybody's vans and trucks were loaded up with equipment and unsold produce. As quickly as the village of food sprouted, it evaporated back into an empty parking lot. Regulars of the famers market would have to wait another week for an opportunity to buy fresh donuts, Walla Walla sweets, and purple peas.

*Runnymede Farm*

## People of the Farm

My favorite part of going to the farmers market was spending the day with Terri. She was one of the nicest and most relaxed people I'd ever worked for, always walking around with a warm smile on her face, never irritable or over talkative. I understood why all the old customers hung around Runnymede's booth.

As for my fellow wwoofers, I worked in the company of some eccentric individuals. Ryan, a recent college graduate, had ridden his bicycle along the entire Mexico-US border, consuming Spaghetti-Os and energy bars as his primary pedaling fuel. He planned to write a book on his experience. Ryan was a history buff and sometimes delivered long and detailed lectures on Mexican-American history while we planted sweet potatoes or picked peas.

Taylor and his girlfriend, the full-season interns, were Art and Teri's most reliable workers. They worked 40 hours a week in exchange for room, board, and a weekly stipend of a hundred dollars. I chose to forgo the stipend in exchange for a more leisurely schedule of 25 hours per week.

For the most part, I'd say the Spaghetti-Os guy and the full-season interns had their lives together. They were mentally stable and had clear plans for their college degrees and Fulbright scholarship. Jeremy, the wwoofer in the tent next to mine, was a different story. Jeremy was a loose cannon.

## Does Anyone do Meth?

Jeremy smoked a lot of weed, and I'm not talking about the chamomile that grew wild on Runnymede Farm. He repeatedly tried to get me high. At first, I told him "No thanks," but he didn't get the message, so I had to state clearly, "Sorry Jeremy, I don't smoke."

In response, he said, "You don't even have to hit it, just take the pipe and pass it back." I think he wanted community and bonding more than he wanted to get high.

I enjoyed Jeremy's company. He was an intelligent and

friendly guy, yet he made consistently bad decisions and then puzzled over why things didn't work out his way.

For example, Teri and Art offered an unlimited buffet of organic vegetables, raw milk, and fresh eggs, yet Jeremy opted to live on Mike's Hard Lemonade, whiskey and coke, and jellybeans. After a morning of heavy drinking, he complained of dehydration as we transplanted lettuce. He seemed to have no idea why he felt so crummy, so I enlightened him. I explained the dynamics of alcohol and working in the hot sun, but he didn't seem interested. He lit up a cigarette and nodded. I don't think he wanted to believe his own decisions led him to where he was.

Jeremy had a rough history, and he wasn't shy about sharing it with us. During his first night on the farm, as we all sat around an outdoor picnic table and had dinner with Art and Teri, Jeremy said, "Does anyone do coke?" An awkward silence fell over the table before Jeremy pulled a can of Coca Cola from under his t-shirt.

Then he said, "Does anyone do meth?" I waited for the joke, but none came.

There was no punch line to that question. Jeremy was serious. I think he actually meant to say, "Do you want to know about my meth-experience?"

With everyone's undivided attention, he told us he'd been a user for several years and was fresh out of prison after being arrested for possession. He went on to tell us about his traumatic childhood, including how his parents died in a meth-lab explosion when he was six.

He might've been unraveling a tall tale in order to get sympathy, but I think that part of his story was true. His decayed teeth, manic behavior, and the rapid pace at which he smoked and drank seemed to be vestiges of an old meth-life. He also lacked almost all inhibitions.

During another dinner table faux pas, Jeremy blurted out that he'd slept with twenty-two women. Teri told him, "Too much information, Jeremy!"

Runnymede Farm

Art and Jeremy had an especially unique relationship. Art couldn't have been more different from Jeremy. He was a hardworking punctual man who took his farm seriously. He didn't have patience for laziness or frivolous talk.

Outside the barn one day, I overhead Jeremy talking to Art about the evolution of mushrooms. Jeremy told Art in an authoritative voice, "Don't you know? Mushrooms are from Mars."

Art didn't find any humor in this absurd comment. He lost his patience and responded in a loud voice, "You don't know mushrooms are from Mars!" I think Art was more upset that Jeremy was standing by idly, not doing any work.

For a number of reasons, Jeremy was politely asked to leave the farm. No one spoke badly of him. In fact, he became a minor legend. His wacky comments were the topic of many dinner conversations and much laughter. Although Jeremy had come from a dark past, he filled our lives with light. I just hoped he could do the same for his own life someday.

## Mushroom Hunting

My only trip off the farm involved hunting for morels. Teri's son Bobby had stumbled upon a choice mushroom spot during his time fighting forest fires in southern Oregon. Mushroom hunting grounds are a tightly guarded secret, so I jumped on the opportunity when Bobby invited me, Taylor, and the Spaghetti-Os guy to hunt for morels in the mountains north of Ashland.

Morels are prized by chefs for their earthy, meaty, nutty flavor when sautéed in butter. Unlike shitake and portabella mushrooms, which can be found year around in the grocery store, morels are elusive. They're only available for a short period of time in the spring forest. Plus, you have to know *where* to look. Luckily, Bobby knew the general direction.

The four of us packed into Bobby's Volkswagen convertible and drove to a high altitude forest of pine trees and Douglas fir. Bobby eased off the gas pedal when he recognized the spot

*Runnymede Farm*

where he'd found morels the previous year. He parked his car along the shoulder of the road and we all set off in different directions with our plastic bags.

Things started off slow for me. I looked piercingly into the leaf litter, around the trunks of fallen trees, and in recently burned clearings, as Bobby recommended, but I didn't see anything. I imagined the shape of a morel, a wrinkled honeycomb cap on a white stem. Forty minutes went by, and then I finally spotted one. I pinched the cap from its stem and the slimy mushroom fell apart between my fingers. *Bummer*, I thought, tossing it back on the leaves. I'd found a bad one, but I caught the thrill of the hunt.

For the next few hours, I became absorbed in the hunt. I obsessed over the dark swirly pinecone shape hiding in plain sight on the forest floor. People driving by probably thought I looked crazy. Imagine driving along a remote forest road and coming upon a man walking with his head to the ground and a plastic grocery bag tied to his wrist.

I barely heard the cars, I was so focused. When I found a morel, I got a rush of adrenaline, probably similar to what a prospector feels when uncovering a hunk of gold. Each mushroom generated a feeling of *Eureka!* My heartbeat quickened, pupils dilated, and after the euphoria of finding one morel wore off, I craved another. I was addicted.

Mushrooms are unlike anything in the forest. With something like a flower, the colorful petals practically shout at you, "Look at me! Check me out!" Flowers are nature's billboards, advertising their nectar and sweet scents. They want to be visited.

Mushrooms are reclusive. They have no welcome sign for the birds and the bees. The only time mushrooms put on bright colors is to say, "I'm dangerous! Don't come anywhere near me." Mushrooms are the anti-social beings of the forest.

This may be why morels take on such a dark earthy color and are shaped like the many pinecones scattered around. Even when I looked directly at one, the morel appeared slightly out of focus.

Often times, after I found one mushroom, I stood in the same spot for another five or ten minutes, knowing mushroom buddies might be nearby. After feeling satisfied I'd scanned the ground thoroughly, just before I set off to a new spot, I noticed two darkly colored mushroom caps inches from my foot. I felt like I'd cracked the code on a magic eye optical illusion.

Over the course of the hunt, I found a total of 19 morels. One of them was so big it completely filled the palm of my hand. None of us hit the jackpot in our half-day mushroom hunt, but I turned into a mushroom hunting junkie in the process, especially after tasting the rewards.

When we got back to the farm, we soaked the morels in a bowl of salt water to evacuate any creepy crawlers that might be living in the mushroom cap. Next, we sautéed them in a pool of butter. They needed no further ingredients. Each morel packed an amazingly earthy flavor. I felt like I'd just bitten into the succulent, buttery flesh of Mother Nature herself.

For dinner, Teri sautéed some morels and added them to a soup stock with a generous helping of Daisy's cream. I ate the morel and cream of Daisy soup with gusto, enjoying the choicest treats the spring forest produces.

## This is Where You Belong

Sammy the Bull left the farm the day before I did. He'd visited Art and Teri's farm for the sole purpose of impregnating the dairy cows, a task he may or may not have succeeded in. One thing was clear though. Sammy had grown attached to the good-looking cows of Runnymede Farm. He didn't want to leave Daisy behind. Or to put it another way, Sammy did not want to leave Daisy's behind.

The farmer who loaned Sammy to Art and Teri showed up with a cattle trailer to haul Sammy back to his original home, a farm down the road. Getting Sammy onto the trailer was quite a spectacle.

First, Sammy's original owner, a man dressed in denim

> Runnymede Farm

overalls with a red baseball cap, tried to lure Sammy up the trailer ramp with a bowl of sweet grains. When that didn't work, the farmer shifted to brute force. He rammed his shoulder against Sammy's behind and tried to push him onto the trailer. In the middle of trying to move his bull, the farmer said things like, "Git!" and "This is where you belong." Finally, completely out of breath, the man succeeded in getting Sammy to follow a bowl of sweet grains into the back of the trailer. Daisy and Hayden seemed oblivious to the fact that their short-term boyfriend was being carted off.

My exit from the farm was less dramatic. Nobody had to lure me into my car with a bowl of sweet grains or tell me to "Git!" I left of my own accord. A month on Runnymede had passed. I collected eggs from the chicken coop one last time, and said goodbye to Sassy with a handful of sugar snaps.

Teri and Art gave me my best all-around farm experience. I worked with farm animals, crops, customers, and farmhands. I enjoyed raw milk and fresh eggs, produce harvested fifty feet from the kitchen, and delectable mushrooms taken from the surrounding forests.

I enjoyed the country life, the balance between work and relaxing in a wide-open space. Looking back on my time at Runnymede, I remember one particular moment that made me think "*This* is what I left teaching for."

The morning after I cleaned out the chicken coop, I walked across the road to Evans Creek for a swim. I wanted to wash off the sweat and fecal dust and get as far away from the squawking hens as possible. I waded in from the bank and dunked my head in the cool water. The chicken filth washed downstream.

The creek was deep enough that I could swim without kicking up sand and gravel. I put my goggles on and waded out to the center, paddling upstream to keep the current from carrying me over the shallow rocky areas. When I put my head in the water, I saw crawfish scurrying around on the creek bottom. Schools of steelhead fry swam around my feet. When

## Runnymede Farm

I floated motionless for a few seconds, the minnow-sized fish became curious and started nibbling at my toes.

The newly hatched steelhead trout were in the process of fattening up for their voyage out to sea. Once they reached a certain size, they'd follow Evans Creek to Rogue River, where they'd swim downstream until they reached the Pacific Ocean. Several years down the road, the fish would return to Evans Creek as fully mature trout. They'd spawn a whole new generation of steelhead to hatch from eggs and nibble on the toes of future wwoofers.

In that moment of relaxation, after cleaning the chicken coop, I knew my life was much easier than those steelhead fry. After swimming in the creek, I sat on the grassy bank and watched the water form small whirlpools on the downstream side of rocks. The reflection of puffy cumulus clouds shimmered and danced on the water's surface. Best of all, I didn't hear a peep from the chickens. Evans Creek produced a soft sound, like a small waterfall pouring into a pond.

I basked in the sun and felt the warm summer breeze dry my hair. I knew I'd found a true slice of the country life.

# Chapter 12
## *Going Home*

Volunteering on organic farms brought the rewards of incredibly fresh food, sunshine on my face, and no paperwork in my life. I felt closer to the earth and healthier for it, but I also knew I wasn't destined to be a farmer.

I looked forward to a cleaner life – one where I didn't have to pick dirt from underneath my fingernails and knock cakes of dried manure off my boots. I desired a bed free of earwigs and spiders, and a kitchen where I didn't have to hide my clean dishes from wwoofers with dishwashing-phobia.

I longed for a stationary life, one where I didn't have to unzip my tent and sleeping bag every day, and then zip it right back up.

After a year of travel, I still didn't know where to settle down. Ohio seemed a distant memory. With my future unresolved, I decided to travel northward and see the cities and mountains of the Pacific Northwest. Perhaps the great outdoors of Oregon and Washington would lure me in.

### Bob Wisdom

Coinciding with my departure from Runnymede Farm, Teri's son Bobby and Ryan, the Spaghetti O's guy, decided to sit a ten day meditation course. The center was situated only eight miles from the farm, so I signed up as a server. While

## Going Home

Bobby and Ryan sharpened their minds and dissolved mental impurities, I performed the much easier task of preparing meals and washing dishes.

Bob, a wiry old man from Arkansas, served as assistant teacher for the course. While the meditators observed noble silence, Bob chatted with me and the other servers in a thick southern drawl, sharing pieces of his life story.

As I scrubbed dishes and measured out oatmeal, Bob discussed his restless years traveling the planet, drinking, and chasing women. "I was actively seeking enlightenment," he told me. "Of course, neither booze nor women did the trick."

"I found Vipassana in the seventies while looking for a guru in India. It's taken a long time since then, but my morality is finally strong." Then he added, "But I talk too much."

As I chopped onions one day, Bob leaned over the counter eating a cookie, and said, "Life is going well, now that I've realized my wife isn't responsible for my happiness."

Another time, in reference to his own death, he said in an upbeat tone, "My rate of deterioration is right on schedule."

With such words, Bob shared the simple truths learned during his life. The simple truths were these: Everyone is responsible for their own happiness. And death is not something to fear. It's on everyone's schedule. That was Bob's wisdom.

## Portland

Fifty miles north of Rogue River on the way to Portland, the gas pedal went floppy and my car stalled. The timing couldn't have been better. I'd finished eleven months of farming and had nowhere to be. I stood on the side of the road, basking in the sun, and waited for a tow-truck that would take me to Eugene.

After a mechanic fixed my car, I drove to Portland and pitched my tent in the backyard of a middle-aged woman I met through couchsurfing. The woman, a bus driver for the city transit system, let me sleep in her backyard for the entire

## Going Home

week, and when she returned home from her twilight bus route, she gave me a free bus pass for the day.

With my unlimited bus rides, I rode to a farmers market nearly every day of the week. I hiked up Mt. Tabor, a small but live volcano in the middle of the city. I wandered through Portland's world famous rose garden and witnessed a teenage girl collapse to her knees in hysterical laughter. Apparently, she couldn't handle all the roses. A security guard had to escort the laughing girl out of the garden.

New cities always have a peculiar effect on me. With no set routine, I felt an obligation to eat my way around the city with no concern for my dietary health. My first bout of heavy snacking occurred when I found a Portland bakery called Dave's Killer Bread. I sampled an organic cinnamon roll, gooey with molasses and rolled in sunflower seeds. This so-called Sin Dawg bread became my staff of life while I rode the bus around Portland.

I complemented the Sin Dawg diet with fruit from the farmers market. The July farm booths overflowed with blueberries, cherries, and raspberries. I ate yellow-skinned Rainer cherries with a delicately sweet flesh, plus several pints of the more traditional Bing and Lambert cherries, which held a hint of tartness in their deep red flesh.

I bought a pint of blueberries for my host, the bus driver, and she fixed blueberry pancakes for the two of us on my last morning in Portland. The buttery hotcakes, drizzled with maple syrup, accompanied a side of cinnamon roll bread.

After a week of pushing my pancreas to new limits, my sister and her family flew into Portland to visit me. Seeing familiar faces felt wonderful after living like a gypsy for months, with relationships reduced to a series of introductions and farewells. People zipped in and out of my life as quickly as I zipped up my gear and moved on to the next place. With most couchsurfers and wwoofers, I went straight from "Hello, how're you doing?" to "Take care and have a nice life."

Jack, Andrea, and my two-year-old niece Annabelle put me

at ease. I could sit back, relax, and let someone else do the driving for awhile. Minutes after I greeted my sister with a hug, she let me know how far I'd come from the clean and polished schoolteacher I'd once been. Andrea said, "Brian, I can wash that shirt for you if you want."

I'd gone almost a year without wearing deodorant. The wwoofers and farm animals didn't mind. Waking up in the morning and not putting on deodorant became as habitual as waking up and not putting on my dress shoes and collared shirt.

## Crown-Shaped Nuggets

The best part of my family's visit was spending time with my monkey-sized niece, Annabelle. Andrea, Jack, and I went on a five mile hike through the redwood forests, on a trail called Damnation Creek, and every now and then we put Annabelle on her own two feet and watched as she half-ran, half-staggered over the exposed redwood roots. She ran at full speed, keeping just ahead of our slow walking pace. As she pattered against the ground, she caressed every fern and pointed at insects, birds, and trees, trying to articulate what she saw. "Ball?" she asked, looking up to her mom for reassurance. "Tree? Hello? Ball?"

At the end of the trail, we reached the ocean and Annabelle pointed at the choppy waters and said, "Pool?"

I had such love for little Annabelle, and for that reason I had a difficult time with what my sister fed her. On one occasion, after she pulled through the Burger King drive-thru, Andrea popped a chicken nugget into Annabelle's mouth, turned around to me, and asked, "Does it make you sad that I'm feeding Annabelle all this stuff?"

I thought about exactly what my sister was feeding her. Hydrogenated soybean oil, genetically modified corn, factory-farmed chicken, preservatives, food coloring, and artificial flavors. The crown-shaped chicken nugget was yet another Franken Food that found its way into the standard American diet. I watched Annabelle reach out her tiny hand for more.

"Yes, it does make me sad," I said.

Although I'd gone on a Sin Dawg binge the previous week, I didn't want to see my precious niece pollute her body with artificial food. Nonetheless, I recognized my sister had every right to feed her daughter whatever she deemed fit, affordable, and convenient.

I didn't protest or evangelize. Instead, I fed Annabelle bananas and organic blueberries and strawberries. She ate the fresh fruit with even more enthusiasm than she ate the crown-shaped nuggets. She reached out her little monkey hand and demanded, "More B!" in reference to the blueberries and bananas. More B, indeed. She knew what was good for her.

## Mt. Rainer

After hugging my family goodbye, I traveled farther north into a higher elevation. I only needed one look at the Washington map to know which mountain I wanted to camp on: Glacier-covered Mt. Rainier, 14,411-foot behemoth east of Olympia would be my home for a week.

I'd gazed at many mountains during my cross-country driving, but none of them were as dramatic as Mt. Rainer. I rounded a bend in the highway, and suddenly the snow-capped mountain slid into view. Mesmerized by its sheer size and solitude, I had to force my attention back to the road to keep from swerving onto the shoulder. Mt. Rainier peered down on Olympia, Seattle, and the Pacific Coast like a god made of rock and snow.

After driving a mile up the mountain, I set up my tent and ate a bag of cherries from Olympia's farmers market. My campsite was beside Mowich Lake, a pristine blue lake that reflected the image of tall pine trees on its glassy surface. On clear days the lake reflected Mt. Rainer's snowy summit.

The first trail I hiked meandered along a small stretch of the Wonderland Trail, a 93-mile hiking track circling the entire mountain. A spur trail led me to an emerald green body of

## Going Home

water called Eunice Lake, which took the prize for the most gorgeous lake I'd ever seen. I sat on a rocky precipice covered with lichens and admired the peaceful waters. No waves rolled across Eunice Lake; only gentle ripples from the ever-present wind. Sitting above the tree line, with only the sound of birds and a soft whistling wind, I felt I'd reached the top of the world.

On my way back to camp I followed the Wonderland Trail as it dipped into green valleys filled with wildflowers. Snowpack remained unmelted on the north side of large rocks, while grasses and small plants sprang from the meager soil on the south side, anxious to capture the short window of summer warmth and sunshine.

As I hiked, I thought about the fact that Mt. Rainer sat directly over a crack in the Earth's mantle. I walked on the outer skin of a live volcano, finding it hard to believe that directly below my feet, magma hot enough to melt my car had accumulated in pressurized lakes of liquid fire. One day the calm surface of Eunice and Mowich Lakes would ripple with tectonic vibrations. Mt. Rainer would split open and pour forth lava.

With all of the pressure and magma out of sight, I usually forgot about the activity that brewed beneath my feet. The Mt. Rainer I experienced was a gentle one, bursting with widlife and breathtaking views. Every day I packed my pen, notebook, fresh fruit, water, and several bars of chocolate, then walked two-miles through alpine forest to a place called Eagle Lookout Point.

I never saw an eagle from the lookout point, but I fell in love with the place from the moment I stepped onto its rocky ledge and saw Mt. Rainier's icy peak staring back at me through fast-moving clouds. On the far side of an immense ravine, waterfalls poured over the cliff, delivering snow melt to the forests below. The waterfalls were so distant, they appeared to pour in slow motion.

During my hours on Eagle Lookout Point, I observed

many hikers who wanted to step onto the ledge for a photo. I established such a presence on the lookout point, with my scattering of fruit rinds, boots, windbreaker, and notebooks that they acted as if they'd intruded on my campsite. One mother said to her boisterous son, "Shhhh. Quiet, he's writing."

I served as photographer for couples and families. I learned about the glaciers and volcanic activity from Boy Scouts. On two separate occasions, middle-aged men asked me if I'd accepted Jesus as my Savior. The most memorable encounter was when a family of six from Georgia emerged on Eagle Lookout Point for a forced family photo.

Three of the four children knew the drill and obediently took their places where Mom told them to stand. The youngest boy, Aden, wanted to play on the rocks and stir a stick around in the dirt.

Aden's dad yelled at him, "Stop with the dirt. Stop with the dirt already!"

Then Aden's mom joined in and said, "This is not the land of do what you want. Turn around and look where we are. Look where we are! Do you realize where we are? Most people don't get to leave their backyards!"

After the yelling proved ineffective, Aden's father walked over to his son in a threatening manner. I sat motionless five feet away, watching all this unfold.

Aden started crying and raised his arm in defense. He obviously knew what was coming. Aden's father picked him up by his collar and carried him with his feet dangling two feet above the ground. Dad positioned his son in front of the camera, straightened his collar and told him in a stern voice, "Now, stay put!"

Tears streamed down Aden's cheeks, yet he managed to put on a smile while his mom snapped the photo. The entire snowy summit was exposed at that moment, a rarity in the usually cloudy vista, but no one in the family acknowledged it.

I don't know if Aden learned any lessons from that event: perhaps to obey his parents unquestioningly until he turned

# Going Home

eighteen. For me at least, Aden's mom demonstrated an important point. She made it abundantly clear that a sense of privilege can't be forced on someone.

Aden only wanted to stir a stick around the dirt and revel in his own imagination. His parents wanted to document the moment. I can't say whether Aden or his parents were more justified in their actions, but from my quiet observation post I sided with Aden. I've never been a fan of posing for cameras either.

## Huckleberry Pie

I descended Mt. Rainier, feeling rejuvenated from seven days of mountain air and leisurely hikes through the forest. At the same time, I also felt homeless. Those seven days of mountain air didn't include a shower or shave, and when I checked my phone I discovered my couchsurfing host in Seattle had bailed out.

To top it off, I unknowingly contracted giardia, a nasty intestinal parasite. In the week following my vacation on Mt. Rainer, the protozoan hitchhiker lay dormant in my gut like a ticking time bomb.

In the calm before the storm, so to speak, it appeared as though things had turned in my favor. I connected with a young couple on couchsurfing who agreed to host me for my entire week in Seattle. Plus, on my way through Enumclaw, Washington, a small town just ten miles from the base of Mt. Rainer, I spotted a roadside pie stand.

An elderly woman sat at a card table with three pies in front of her and a sign reading: "Wild Huckleberry Pie: $2/slice." I slammed on my brakes and pulled off the road.

Feeling starved for baked goods after a week on the mountain, I ordered two slices. The woman opened up a folding chair for me and served up the pie on a paper plate with a plastic fork.

"Do you want cream on that?" she asked. For a moment I thought she was going to pull out freshly whipped cream from her own cows, but instead she produced a can of Reddi-Wip.

After I ate the first round of wild-picked huckleberry pie, topped with a giant mound of whipped cream, I ordered a third slice. At that price, I knew I'd never find such a good deal. I reached my hand into my wallet for two more dollar bills, but the woman refused payment. She said, "No, that's all right. This one's on me."

Sensing I was in good company, I ate my third slice slowly and listened to the woman share her memories of Mt. Rainer. She recounted the emerald green beauty of Eunice Lake and her hikes across the glaciers, wearing spiked shoes. She told me about her time picking huckleberries, blueberries, and wild mushrooms on the mountain. "I haven't been up there in twenty years," she said. "Now, the mountain's just a wonderful piece of scenery in my backyard."

## One Sockeye!

I arrived in Seattle with a full huckleberry pie for my couchsurfing hosts, Johnny and Trisha. The two of them basically adopted me as their roommate. They gave me my own bedroom and key to the house, and encouraged me to forage for blackberries from their backyard. They took me to the farmers market and out to their favorite German pub and sushi bar.

While Johnny went off to work and Trisha to midwifery school, I explored the city on my own. I spent most of my time wandering around Pike Place Market, browsing the food stalls, snacking on fresh cherries, smoked salmon, and superb clam chowder from a place called Pike Place Chowder.

During my three visits to Pike Place Market, I always made a point to watch the fishmongers. The outdoor fish market looked like an ordinary seafood shop – crab, lobster, fish and bivalves on ice – but the fishmongers turned it into theatre with the way they tossed the fish around and communicated in call and response style. Large crowds of camera-toting tourists gathered to watch the action.

## Going Home

When a customer stepped up to place an order, say a whole salmon, a grizzly looking man with orange rubber overalls relayed the order by shouting, "One sockeye!" When the rest of the fishmongers heard the call, they stopped what they were doing, filleting a fish or packing ice around the crab and oysters, and yelled back in unison, at the top of their lungs, "One sockeye!"

After the call back, people in the crowd positioned their cameras for the fish-toss. A fishmonger picked up the sockeye salmon, 20-30 pounds in size, and sent it flying through the air. A guy behind the counter caught the fish in a sheet of newspaper, and all the spectators clapped and nudged their neighbors, "Did you see that?"

Anytime a fish or crab went airborne, people raised their cameras or cell phones to capture the moment. Families and couples lined up to get their photo taken with the fish-tosser, and it wasn't uncommon to see a grimy-looking fishmonger signing autographs.

By the time my week in Seattle ended, I had my fill of seafood. I also had my first wave of intense stomachaches. Still unaware of the hitchhiker in my gut, I thought I'd overdone it with clam chowder and smoked salmon. I didn't realize the full extent of my condition for another few days, after I met up with my parents who'd flown out from Ohio, this time to visit the San Juan Islands with me.

### San Juan Islands

My car died the day I picked my parents up from the Seattle airport. Through twenty states, the old Taurus had endured frost heaves in Maine, dust storms in Texas, and near vertical roads along California's northern coast. Two blocks from the ferry crossing to the San Juan Islands, the car made a grinding noise and called it quits.

After my parents and I made it to Orcas Island, mechanical problems turned into health problems. My dad, a strong man of unwavering good health, suffered a bout of vertigo. While

> Going Home

my mom and I shopped for lamb sausage, heirloom tomatoes, and purple carrots at the San Juan Island farmers market, my dad stayed in the rental car. When we returned with the food, he confessed, "I felt like I just had a small stroke."

We took him to the local hospital, and the island doctor recommended a rather unique treatment. He prescribed pills to suppress the nausea, and then told my dad, "Have a beer and relax."

The day after my Dad's vertigo attack, my mom was visited by a series of migraine headaches. Although the headaches felt like a vice clamping down on her temples, Mom was no stranger to the unpleasant sensation. She continued eating cinnamon rolls and blueberry pancakes, unfazed by the pain.

I usually don't play games of one-upmanship, but I had both of my parents beat. Two days into our stay on Orcas Island, my protozoan hitchhiker made itself known.

The pain began with sharp shooting sensations in my stomach. I thought I'd eaten too much ice cream. Next, the pain elevated to something akin to a steak knife traveling through my stomach and small intestine. I began sleeping on the bathroom floor, so I could be within a few seconds of the toilet.

I felt as though I was going into labor, though I wasn't anatomically built for such a feat. One moment I writhed on the floor with the most extreme intestinal cramps I'd ever known, and then the pain gradually subsided for a moment of relief. For several days, I went through these horrendous cycles of contracted pain and relief, with no baby to show for it, only a foul cream of wheat looking diarrhea. I gave birth to thousands of microscopic giardia, all identical twins, and then flushed them right down the toilet.

Occasionally, I tried to enjoy the natural beauty surrounding me. From the deck of the vacation house my parents rented, I watched pods of orca whales swim by just a few hundred feet offshore. Through my dad's binoculars, I watched as one of the sleek 30-foot-long mammals emerged from the water, its massive black and white body glistening in the sun for a second before landing with an incredible splash.

My dad spotted foxes, bald eagles, and sea otters, but I had entered such an all-consuming misery that the outside world became an insignificant blur.

I suspected food poisoning from the lamb sausage. Dad suggested, "Maybe all of that healthy organic food isn't settling right." If I'd gone to the island doctor, I bet he would've advised me to, "Have a beer and relax."

In the middle of lying on the bathroom floor one night, with my head rested on the rim of the toilet seat, I had an epiphany. I replayed the evening on Mt. Rainer when I'd casually dipped my soup pot into the stream to rinse off vegetable soup residue. That was it! The next morning when I brewed up some tea, the cyst must have survived the partial boil.

Giardia, that flagella-propelled parasite, had hatched from its indestructible cyst and latched onto the walls of my intestines. For two weeks, it graciously accepted my offerings of cherries, blackberries, fish, ice cream, and clam chowder while I nurtured a new generation of giardia. A doctor in Seattle confirmed my suspicion.

## Going Home

My compassionate parents offered to cancel their flight home and drive me back to Ohio. I knew that was the best plan. I purchased a used mini-van in Burlington, Washington and we set off on an unexpected cross-country trip.

In a marathon driving session, we traversed the country in three days. For most of the trip I remained curled up in the fetal position in the back of the van. I nibbled on flakes of Special K cereal, the only food I could stomach, and caught glimpses of the changing landscape.

Through the tinted windows of the mini-van's sliding door, I watched the mountains and rivers of Montana turn into the dry rounded hills of the Badlands. We drove through Sturgis, South Dakota in the middle of an Aerosmith concert, and motorcycles outnumbered cars on the highway ten to one. They sent tremors through the mini-van like a swarm of gigantic bees. After South Dakota, the land flattened into Minnesota and Wisconsin. Cornfields returned to the landscape.

Twelve high-powered antibiotics, a half-box of Special K, and two bottles of Sprite after leaving Seattle, we arrived in my hometown of Findlay, Ohio. I felt a little less organic than I had during the previous year.

Dad pulled off the highway, and I saw the familiar sights of home. Cooper Tire and the faint smell of rubber greeted me, then Dairy Queen, Behnke's Funeral Home, and a residential area, each property with a neatly manicured front lawn, a two-car garage, and a front porch attached to a large wooden house. This was the kind of place where people in the slums of third-world countries dreamed of living.

I watched the neighborhood of my childhood pass by: the house of my first best friend, the front lawns where I played soccer and football, and the tree-lined streets where I rode my bicycle until I reached the immense cornfields surrounding Findlay. I knew I'd arrived home, but I also knew this was a place of the past for me.

Over the course of the next month I overcame the intestinal parasite, reunited with friends and family, and then packed my gear into the mini-van and drove back across the country. A new home awaited me in the Pacific Northwest.

## Friendly Area

Before experiencing the rose gardens, cherries, unlimited bus rides, and gooey cinnamon roll bread in Portland, I'd pit-stopped in Eugene, Oregon while a mechanic fixed my car.

I couchsurfed with a sweet couple in their sixties. Denis and Camille were avid globe trekkers, and during the two nights I camped in their backyard beside a row of lavender bushes abuzz with honeybees, Denis mapped out the details of their next trip – a six month jaunt through India and Thailand.

The three of us established an easy rapport, sharing stories

## Going Home

from our travels. They evidently trusted me, because over dinner, Camille asked if I wanted to housesit for them while they were gone.

As I neared the end of my journey around the country, Camille and Denis literally opened a new door for me. Initially, I saw Eugene as a passing city on my way to Portland, but after being stranded in the city for three days, I discovered I'd been towed to the very place I wanted to live. Eugene had a thriving farmers market, a good population of musicians and artists, and ranked as one of the most bike-friendly cities in the country. Easy access to mountains, rugged coastline, and natural hot springs made the place even more desirable. I accepted Camille's offer.

Denis and Camille's neighborhood was a treasure. Called the Friendly Area, a large population of urban gardeners inhabited this neighborhood, along with backyard chicken keepers, beekeepers, and folks interested in making their community sustainable.

I parked my mini-van in Denis and Camille's driveway and moved into the Friendly Area. The day I arrived, I set off on a walk around my new neighborhood.

Instead of neatly mowed lawns, many of my new neighbors planted native ferns, flowering perennials, rosemary, lavender, blueberries, bamboo, and vegetable beds. Two blocks from my new house, I passed an alleyway with a bountiful garden of nearly fifteen tomato plants, cucumbers, squash, beans, kale, and corn. Everything was ripe for the picking, and to my astonishment a hand-written placard encouraged me to take whatever I wanted.

The sign read, "Edible Alleyway: We planted this garden for the neighbors. Please harvest anything you like." The note was signed by Anne and Chris, a couple who lived adjacent to the alleyway and planted the garden. I pulled a cucumber and three tomatoes off the vine and returned home to sample the complimentary fruit of the Friendly Area.

*Going Home*

## Common Ground Garden

A week after I moved to Eugene, the notorious rain season began. Natives of the Pacific Northwest refer to it as "entering the tunnel." For the next eight months the ocean sent an armada of rain clouds to shower the farms, vineyards, urban gardens, and blackberries of the Willamette Valley.

One night in late September, I bundled up in my new rain jacket and Gortex pants and pedaled my bike down the street to harvest green beans from the Edible Alleyway. As I rolled up to Anne and Chris' neighborhood garden, I looked across the street and saw an energetic woman and her ten-year-old son shoveling manure onto an open lot. The woman appeared to be running on an endless supply of energy, but her pickup truck was filled to the brim with manure, so I walked across the street and offered to help.

"Hi. Can I give you a hand with that?" I asked.

The woman didn't act the least bit surprised that a complete stranger offered to help her shovel manure. "Sure!" she said enthusiastically. "There's an extra pitchfork right here."

"I'm Anne," she said.

As Anne's son Caleb and I spread a fresh layer of manure over the half-dead crabgrass, Anne discussed her plans for the site. She and a group of local gardeners, known as the Friendly Neighborhood Farmers, planned to convert the vacant lot into a neighborhood garden. The Friendly Farmers got approval from the city and devised a clear plan for the garden, which would become an open food source for everyone in the neighborhood, much like the Edible Alleyway. A name for the new garden had already been conceived: Common Ground Garden.

Over the course of my six-month house sitting post, I joined forces with the Friendly Farmers. We removed concrete rubble, beer bottles, and other urban trash from the site and spread liberal amounts of cow and horse manure over the compacted clay. We hired a tractor to drive into the city and till the land into more workable soil.

## Going Home

As fall progressed, Anne arranged for the city's fleet of leaf-collectors to drop off mountains of leaves in front of the Common Ground Garden. We spread a foot-deep layer of leaf mulch over the entire area. As the winter rains persisted, the leaves decomposed into nitrogen and carbon-rich organic matter. By the time spring rolled around, we stepped onto the spongy garden and turned the newly amended soil with our shovels, rakes, and pitchforks.

We scratched a garden out of the once abandoned land. In it, we planted garlic, potatoes, peas, kale, salad greens, onions, carrots, beets, tomatoes, beans, peppers, squash, and culinary herbs.

By the time I found my own place the following summer, the Common Ground Garden had blossomed into a monument of local food and community. Residents of the Friendly Area walked their dogs past the garden and stopped to admire the progression of vegetables. Neighbors who didn't know the first thing about gardening showed up for work parties and helped pull weeds from the garlic beds, plant tomatoes, and build wire cages for the peas.

Everybody enjoyed the harvest. Most of all, everyone shared smiles in this common pursuit. A good and loving spirit hung in the air during work parties. Honeybees buzzed around the marigolds and ducks landed in puddles that accumulated in the street. Everybody who visited the Common Ground Garden left with a feeling of accomplishment, no matter how simple their contribution or harvest. I had truly found myself in the company of friendly farmers.

### Be the Change You Wish to See in the World

I knew I'd made the best decision of my life by leaving behind the financial stability of my teaching career and setting off on a tour of the countryside. Without this trip, I might never have found the Friendly Farmers of Eugene or the gem of Vipassana Meditation. I surely wouldn't have tasted Jane the Goat's milk or learned how to make kefir from an Eskimo.

## Going Home

The stunning sunset from Lion Rock would've been forever lost to my eyes.

Now I feel blessed to have a comfortable bed, a clean kitchen, and a part-time job that doesn't involve cleaning out a chicken coop. I had the good fortune of landing a job in a plant nursery at a hip gardening store called Down to Earth.

On weekends, I drive into the country and pick up my gallon of raw milk. I watch the small herd of Jersey cows graze on the green pastures while escaped hens peck around in the cow pies, looking for grubs. I get to experience the farm as a guest. I reach clean hands into my wallet and put $10 in a glass jar. I fill my milk bottle, then stroll around the farm, watching the piglets drink skim-milk left over from the butter operation, and the ducks waddle along the horse path searching for slugs.

For the first time of my life I have my own garden, and I couldn't be in better company. Most of my neighbors and co-workers have been gardening since I crawled out of the womb, so when I have a problem, the answer is never far away. When slugs devoured my cabbage and peas, I asked a friend at Down to Earth, "What should I do?"

"Sprinkle Sluggo around your garden," he advised. "Or rent a duck."

When the local deer found a way through my fence and ate my tomato plants and carrots down the ground, I about gave up on the garden.

"You need a ten-foot tall fence," a co-worker suggested. "If you don't want to do that, then at least soak some sticks in your own urine and stake those all around your backyard. Cougar urine is even better." I took his advice with the urine-soaked sticks and so far the deer haven't nibbled a leaf from my garden.

After a year of living on farms and discovering how therapeutic it is to have my hands in the soil and the sun on my face, I knew I needed to retain at least part of that lifestyle. My own backyard and the Common Ground Garden are places where I stay in touch with the earth and enjoy fresh,

## Going Home

local, organic food.

My first bite of the Common Ground Garden came with the spring leaves of kale and chard. As the winter rains gradually tapered off in June, the sugar snap peas came into full harvest.

One sunny day, in the height of the pea season, I pedaled my bike over to the garden for a snack. As I walked on the spongy garden path, which felt like a trampoline underfoot, I thought of Sassy the Donkey and how she would've devoured every pea on the vines.

I thought about Hugo from Lucy's Farm and how he constantly asked me, "Are you happy, Brian?"

As I plucked a pea from the vine, I knew the answer to Hugo's question. I thought about the incredible spectrum of people I met on my trip; the brilliant orange, red, and yellow leaves that showered me as I farmed down the east coast, and the spring wildflowers that carpeted my path as I farmed up the west coast.

I looked around at the Common Ground Garden, at the big leaves of kale and chard ready to be harvested. I admired the beets and carrots, which would be ready in a week or two. I assessed the tomato plants we'd planted the previous weekend. They looked stunted from the cool late rain, but I knew even those slow-growing tomatoes would take off and bear fruit someday.

I looked at the plump sugar snap pea in my own hand, ready to eat at that very moment. I crunched into the pod and tasted the sweet juice, a combination of winter rain and sunshine. I knew I could answer Hugo's question with a sincere, "Yes, I'm happy. I'm growing. I'm dying. I'm always learning. And forever changing."

## About the Author

Brian J. Bender earned degrees from Ohio University and the University of Findlay, but he found a more meaningful education after he left his teaching career and traveled around the country as a volunteer farmer and student of Vipassana meditation. Brian now lives and works in Eugene, Oregon.

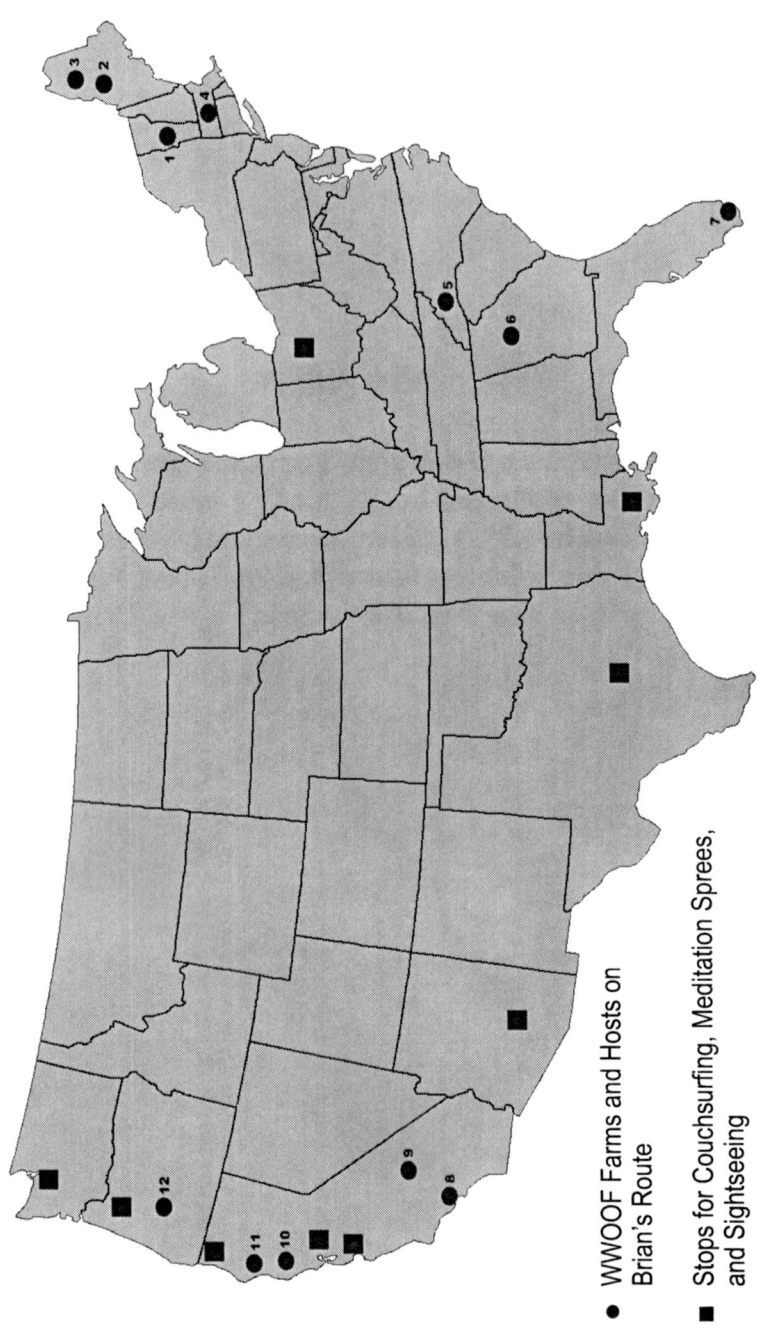

● **WWOOF Farms and Hosts on Brian's Route** ●

1. Manchester, Vermont: Hector's Farm
2. Rangley, Maine: Applesauce Hill
   Joanne Dunlap
   Applesauce Hill Icelandics
   P.O. Box 946
   Rangeley, ME 04970
   207 864-9949
   jfmccd@gwi.net
3. Madrid, Maine: Peace and Plenty Farm
4. Shelburne Falls, Massachusetts: Woodsong Farm
5. Burnsville, North Carolina: Clear Creek Homestead
6. Milledgeville, Georgia: Salamander Springs
7. Miami, Florida: Lucy's Farm
8. Santa Barbara, California: Henry's Farm and Hostel
9. Three Rivers, California: Farm in the Canyon
10. Chestnut Hill: Ukiah, California
11. Willits, California: Rock n' Ridge Ranch
12. Rogue River, Oregon: Runnymede Farm
    Arthur and Teri White
    Runnymede Farm
    1831 West Evans Creek Road
    Rogue River, OR 97537
    541-582-6193

■ **Stops for Couchsurfing, Meditation Sprees, and Sightseeing** ■

New Orleans, Louisiana
Austin, Texas
Tucson, Arizona
Monterey, California
San Francisco, California
North Fork, California
Humboldt State Redwoods
Lost Coast
Portland, Oregon,
Mt. Rainer, Washington
Seattle, Washington,
Findlay, Ohio
Final stop: Eugene, Oregon

# Available from NorlightsPress and fine booksellers everywhere

**Toll free:** 888-558-4354     **Online:** www.norlightspress.com

**Shipping Info:** Add $2.95 for first item and $1.00 for each additional item

Name _____

Address _____

Daytime Phone _____

E-mail _____

| No. Copies | Title | Price (each) | Total Cost |
|---|---|---|---|
|  |  |  |  |
|  |  |  |  |
|  |  |  |  |
|  |  |  |  |
|  |  |  |  |
|  |  |  |  |
|  |  |  |  |

|  | Subtotal |  |
|---|---|---|
|  | Shipping |  |
|  | Total |  |

Payment by (circle one):

   Check     Visa     Mastercard     Discover     Am Express

Card number _____ 3 digit code _____

Exp.date _____ Signature _____

## Mailing Address:
2721 Tulip Tree Rd.
Nashville, IN 47448

### Sign up to receive our catalogue at www.norlightspress.com

CPSIA information can be obtained at www.ICGtesting.com
Printed in the USA
244649LV00001B/38/P